Archaeological constructs
An aspect of theoretical archaeology

This book is published as part of the joint publishing agreement established in 1977 between the Fondation de la Maison des Sciences de l'Homme and the Press Syndicate of the University of Cambridge. Titles published under this arrangement may appear in any European language or, in the case of volumes of collected essays, in several languages.

New books will appear either as individual titles or in one of the series which the Maison des Sciences de l'Homme and the Cambridge University Press have jointly agreed to publish. All books published jointly by the Maison des Sciences de l'Homme and the Cambridge University Press will be distributed by the Press throughout the world.

Archaeological constructs

*AN ASPECT OF THEORETICAL
ARCHAEOLOGY*

JEAN-CLAUDE GARDIN

*Centre National de la Recherche Scientifique and
Ecole des Hautes Etudes en Sciences Sociales, Paris*

CAMBRIDGE UNIVERSITY PRESS
Cambridge
London New York New Rochelle Melbourne Sydney
& EDITIONS DE LA MAISON DES
SCIENCES DE L'HOMME
Paris

CAMBRIDGE UNIVERSITY PRESS
Cambridge, New York, Melbourne, Madrid, Cape Town, Singapore, São Paulo, Delhi

Cambridge University Press
The Edinburgh Building, Cambridge CB2 8RU, UK

With Editions de la Maison des Sciences de l'Homme
54 Boulevard Raspail, 75270 Paris Cedex 06, France

Published in the United States of America by Cambridge University Press, New York

www.cambridge.org
Information on this title: www.cambridge.org/9780521109383

First published 1980
This digitally printed version 2009

A catalogue record for this publication is available from the British Library

Library of Congress Cataloguing in Publication data
Gardin, Jean Claude.
Archaeological constructs.

Bibliography: p.
Includes index.
1. Archaeology – Philosophy. I. Title.
CC72.G37   930′.1′01   79–14624

ISBN 978-0-521-22080-4 hardback
ISBN 978-0-521-10938-3 paperback

'The critical scrutiny of patterns of archaeological reasoning immediately exposes the basic importance of archaeological logic within archaeological philosophy and theory. Archaeological logic should outline for us the theory of correct reasoning within our discipline, without making any unwarranted assumptions that the principles of logic and explanation are simple universals which may be transferred from one discipline and level to another . . . It raises the problem of the nature of the logical relationships between archaeological conclusions and the ground for those conclusions.' (Clarke 1973: 15)

'There is a gorilla in your closet whenever no one is looking for him.' (Miller & Johnson-Laird 1976: 164)

'An anarchist is like an undercover agent who plays the game of reason in order to undercut the authority of reason.' (Feyerabend 1978: 433)

Contents

Preface

This book is an analysis of intellectual processes in archaeology, as we may observe them through the writings which form the literature of this discipline: excavation reports, catalogues, monographs, etc. The reasons which led me to take an interest in this subject were twofold. The original one was the ineradicable feeling of monotony which came upon me from the day I first had to read this literature, despite the variety of its topics and my taste for many of them; at the risk of raising doubts about my own intellectual processes, I confess that I spent no less than twenty years trying to understand the causes of this contradiction. The second reason was that in doing so, I came to a schematization of archaeological reasonings which not only 'explained' monotony, but somehow excused it, provided that we were ready to draw a few lessons from the exercise.

My purpose is to present this schematization as well as certain aspects of the lessons to be drawn from it as I see them, regarding for instance the scientific status of archaeological constructions, the opposition, real or forced between traditional archaeology and the so-called new archaeology, the virtues and limitations of formal procedures derived from mathematics, computer science, and systems analysis, in handling archaeological data, the need for reform of publication patterns in archaeology, etc. The apparent diversity of these questions should not be misunderstood: I am not proposing a new handbook on archaeological theory, from which students can learn the techniques of observation and interpretation now current in our trade; a number of substantial books of recent date already meet that purpose (see p. 1). My goal is only to present a personal appreciation of *one* aspect of archaeological science that logically precedes the study of specific methods or techniques, namely an analysis of the mental operations carried out in archaeological constructions of all sorts, from the collecting of data to the writing of an article or book in published form.

Dealing with abstract operations, this book may be found less easy to read than publications concerning the material entities with which archaeology is concerned (objects, sites, monuments, remains of the past in general), their physical handling, or the historical speculations which they bring forth. I have tried nevertheless to remain as close as possible to the actual modes of archaeological thinking by providing examples from the literature in support of my argument. The reader may, however, regret that many of these examples are cited in reference to earlier publications which are not all easily accessible, rather than fully developed in this book. In adopting this course, I have been moved by the desire to devote all the space available to a presentation of what may be regarded as a synthesis of these earlier works, without having to do more than cite or summarize them in their due place.

This book was originally announced under another title, 'Formal Methods in Archaeology'; and such indeed was the heading which I had myself given to a short outline submitted many years ago to the late David Clarke, after he had kindly invited me to present my views on this topic. Then, while I was preparing the book, I realized that formal methods were only one part of the subject, since I was led to give as much consideration to the non-formal ones, in so far as they often manage to produce empirically valid conclusions, despite their formal weaknesses. Faced on the one hand with concepts verified by observations, but without any explicit mathematical or logical foundations, and on the other hand with theories obtained through a formal calculus, but poorly correlated with empirical data. I decided to include both categories of constructions in the scope of the book, as I became convinced that they each had something to teach us with respect to the requirements of a Theoretical archaeology.

The substance of this book was first presented as a course which I was invited to give at the University of Geneva in 1975/6: without the incentive received from my friends in the Department of Anthropology and in the museums of that city, the patience of the Cambridge University Press would have been tried for a few more years.

I am grateful to Micheline Sourigues for her pains in typing the original manuscript; to Gerard Paul for the drawings from which the printed figures have been made; to Joan Bernard and Francis Brooke for their efforts in bringing my text closer to standard English. The whole has benefited from the suggestions of George L. Cowgill, who kindly agreed to referee an earlier version of the book.

August 1978   J.-C.G.

I
The analysis of archaeological constructions

'An analysis of intellectual processes in archaeology': this introductory sentence in the Preface summarizes my purpose, on condition that we agree on the exact meaning of each word: what is the scope of *archaeology*, as compared with other disciplines such as history, the ethnology of past societies, or palaeogeography? Which *processes* should we examine, under a heading which may well seem redundant (are not all research processes *intellectual* by definition)? And to what form of *analysis* shall we submit them, of all those methods which might be so termed? Let me first answer these three questions.

1.1 *The scope of archaeology*

I shall not undertake to define again the specific nature of archaeology, considered as a discipline in its own right: definitions of this sort are to be found in all handbooks of archaeology, as well as in the various method-ological treatises that have appeared in several languages and countries during the last ten years (Chang 1967a, Deetz 1967, Clarke 1968, Moberg 1969, Binford 1972, Redman 1973, Malina 1975, Kamenetskij *et al.* 1975, Schiffer 1976, South 1977, etc.). What I need for the purpose of the ensuing discussion is rather to considerably broaden the semantic field of the word, so that we may be allowed to consider as Archaeology a wide variety of works which differ in their areas, their goals and naturally in the kind of objects studied.

1.1.1 *Areas*

A broad vision of archaeology with respect first to the areas of obser-vation: I refer here not only to the space and time coordinates of a given investigation, but also to the kind of human entities to which the material remains are attributed – e.g. an ethnocultural group of varying specificity (Hopi Indians, Byzantian blacksmiths), an organized society, again observed at varying levels (ice-age hunters of the Ukraine, the kingdom of Pergamon), an individual or a specific community (the Greek painter Sophilos, Assyrian merchants in Cappadocia), etc. The diversity of the more or less established fields of archaeological research is the product of conventional divisions on one or the other of these three planes: the local (L) and temporal (T) domains, and the human entities (H) under study – for example:

– Archaeology of South America, Oriental archaeology (division according to L)
– Prehistory, Industrial archaeology (division according to T)
– Medieval archaeology, classical archaeology (division according to L and T combined).
– Islamic archaeology, Archaeology of the Eskimos (division according to H)
– Archaeology of Celtic Ireland, Palaeochristian archaeology (divisions according to combination LH and TH respectively).

A number of these distinctions result from the strength of usage or tradition rather than strict reason; yet many archaeologists still believe in the specificity of certain branches, such as prehistory *vs*. the archaeology of literate civilizations, or again classical archaeology *vs*. all the others, etc. Opinions may well differ on this matter; I wish only to stress that *for the purpose of the ensuing discussion,* classifications of this sort are irrelevant, in the same way as judgments of value between the more or less esteemed sectors of archaeological research, are irrelevant. We shall here regard as pertaining to archaeology all research works or publications bearing on the material products of an activity carried out by men of the past (H), in a given geo-historical setting (LT), without any restrictions on the possible values of H, L, or T.

1.1.2 *Goals*

I shall take the same broad view with respect to the diversity of goals which may be envisaged in archaeology. Besides the so-called scientific publications which are meant to present the material remains and the ideas held about them by specialists, there are others which are not considered worthy of the same consideration because they are written by amateurs (travellers, collectors, etc.), or intended for a wider audience. It is difficult however to find criteria upon which this distinction could be based. To some, the difference lies in the essentially descriptive character of amateur publications, as opposed to the strong interpretative trend of scholarly works. Examples are numerous, however, in which the professional archaeologist stops at descriptions which do not call for a wider knowledge than is available to enlightened collectors, whereas conversely the amateur shows a gift for historical constructions which professional archaeologists do not all possess. We are therefore under no obligation to follow those prejudices and I shall tend towards a broad definition of archaeology, in which the depth or strength of the proposed constructions is of more import than the academic status of the author, or the nature of the public to which they are addressed.

The diversity of goals is also manifest when the study of material remains is the basis of inferences of all kinds on the nature of the activity which produced them, the circumstances in which it took place, the system of social relations which made it possible or necessary, the role of natural forces in its genesis or evolution, etc. Let us take for instance the case of a survey of traces of ancient settlement in a given area; if they are abundant enough, some insight can be gained into many subjects, such as historical demography, architectural techniques, patterns of soil use, social functions and technical activities at different periods, the nature and distribution of political power, etc. (e.g. Willey 1953, Nelken-Terner & MacNeish 1971). Shall we then declare that we have left archaeology proper, and entered the fields of history, sociology, geography, technology, ecology, with a prefix 'palaeo' where needed . . . Opinions here again differ; but we have no more reason than above to become involved in such debates. Given the purpose of this book, we must clearly be concerned with the whole reasoning process, from the initial description of the materials to the final interpretative propositions, whatever discipline may be chosen to account for it: history, sociology, geography, etc. The most convenient stand then is to accept that all such constructions be assumed under the title archaeology, because of their common material basis, without bothering too much about the various secondary labels that might reflect the diversity of the end products.

1.1.3 *Objects*

Let us finally consider the variety of objects that are often comprised under the heading 'material culture': chipped stones, post holes, beads, slags, temples, potsherds, wall-paintings. It is taken for granted that archaeology can deal with all the paraphernalia of ancient man, without limitations. Yet, some restrictions are still common, if only implicit. One of them is a result of a current opposition between objects and monuments proper, of any category, and the inscriptions which are to be found on some of them; or more generally, an opposition between inscribed materials and ancient texts on the one hand, to be studied by epigraphists or historians, and material objects on the other hand, left to the competence of archaeologists or prehistorians. We shall once more dodge the issue, which is largely a matter of convention: the discovery of inscriptions or literary sources pertaining to ancient societies hitherto known through material data alone is obviously of interest to the archaeologist immersed in a study of those societies; and it is of little avail to discuss whether he deserves a new name, or a compound one, when he erects his constructions both on the analysis of inscribed materials and on the study of material objects. I shall therefore adhere to the same broad viewpoint as above: for my present purpose, archaeology is the universe of intellectual constructions based on the study of objects of all sorts, with or without inscriptions, as well as on the study of inscriptions themselves, or for that matter any other written sources which may enlarge the knowledge drawn from the analysis of monuments.

Another current opposition concerns two broad categories of material remains: those which are considered as works of art, according to any criteria (the creator's intentions, the function of the monument in its original context, the traditions and taste of the modern commentator, etc.), and a residual group which can best be defined as the complement of the former, viz. the set of material remains that are *not* considered as works of art. This distinction is so unstable through time and space that I shall eschew it also: the archaeology of works of art will not be differentiated from the archaeology of other monuments, and we shall not attempt to decide whether a study of the most ancient churches in Italy must be considered Palaeochristian archaeology, subheading Architecture, or History of Western Art, subheading Religious monuments . . . The only point of interest to us is the nature of the reasoning followed by the commentator in order to proceed from the initial perception of a set of objects to whatever he has to say about them on a higher conceptual level, including the level of aesthetic judgments when that is relevant.

Let us finally recall that the material objects which archaeologists have to be concerned with are not only the so-called artifacts, from chipped stones to cathedrals. Especially in prehistory, but also in the archaeology of historical periods, the study of natural remains is just as important for the reconstitution of past events and behavioural patterns: human and animal bones, ancient soils, fossils, pollens, sediments, in brief any material which may throw some light on the natural *milieu* in which ancient men conducted their activities, and on the ways in which they exploited it for their own needs and pleasures, in a given time and at a given place. A new word has been proposed to designate this category of data: 'ecofacts' of nature, modified or not by human action, as opposed to the 'artifacts' of material culture, produced by men. The wide range of objects or remains to which we shall refer should hence be quite clear: ecofacts are part of it, whenever they are instrumental in an archaeological construction.

1.1.4 *Definition*

Speaking of the manifold variety of objects which archaeology may embrace, we have reached the same broad position as above à propos of the diversity of research goals: sociological, economic, aesthetic, etc. . . . . An objection immediately springs up: in asserting that any construction based on the study of material remains is related to archaeology, do we not run the risk of obscuring the more specific processes of that discipline, intellectually speaking, to the benefit of a much wider inquiry into the constructions of anthropological or behavioral sciences in general? Nothing could be truer, but in the following sense: the schematization of archaeological reasonings to which we shall be led will indeed prove fairly unspecific, and I hope to bring out the case for extending it to constructions of many other kinds in the sciences of man, in order to satisfy the same epistemological requirements (see § 7.2). But we first have a long way to go; let us for the moment summarize the results reached in this section, in the form of a deliberately broad definition: archaeology, for the purpose of the present book, is *the sum of studies bearing on material objects which may throw some light, in conjunction with other data, on the history and ways of life of ancient peoples (specific events, daily activities, institutions, beliefs, etc.).*

1.2 *Intellectual processes in archaeology*

The intellectual processes at work in such studies may be divided into two categories. A number of them are related to the acquisition and manipulation of material objects, in the broad sense indicated above (§ 1.1.3): excavation practices, survey methods, sampling techniques, conservation methods *in situ* or in the laboratory, etc. Then come the mental operations by which the archaeologist moves from the perception of the collected data to the formulation of verbal statements concerning them, on various levels: chronological or geographical attributions, reconstitution of historical events, inferences about social organization, about the economy, religious behaviour, technology, etc. (§ 1.1.2). Figure 1 indicates the relative position of these two categories of intellectual activities in a simplified linear chain of information processing, (*a*) beginning with 'acquisition' processes, that lead to the constitution of a material corpus (objects, monuments, sites, physical samples, etc., with contextual indications attached, in terms of various locational

Figure 1   The chain of information processing in archaeology: from the *acquisition* or collecting of *materials* (objects, monuments, physical remains of all sorts, etc.) to their *comment* in terms of discursive *propositions*.

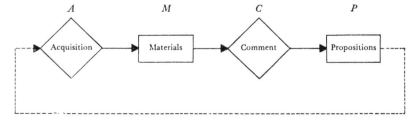

units), and (*b*) finishing with 'comment' in a broad sense, i.e. the formulation of verbal statements as above. At first sight, the intellectual processes which are of concern to us are manifest in those comments alone, but with two reservations. First, it goes without saying that acquisition processes are not confined to material operations; they are the province or product of reasoned considerations bearing on the techniques of data acquisition, as with all observation procedures in the sciences of man or nature. In addition, there is an obvious interaction between the two categories of activities, which is not apparent in the linear representation: acquisition procedures, in libraries or museums as well as in the field, are or should always be subordinated to more or less explicit strategies of observation, based on states of knowledge and

Figure 2   Another presentation of fig. 1 showing the parts of the cycle studied in this book: first and foremost, the transition from *M* to *P*, i.e. the production of archaeological writings, and subserviently from *P* to *A*, i.e. the design of observation strategies. The actual acquisition processes, *A–M*, are not included in this investigation.

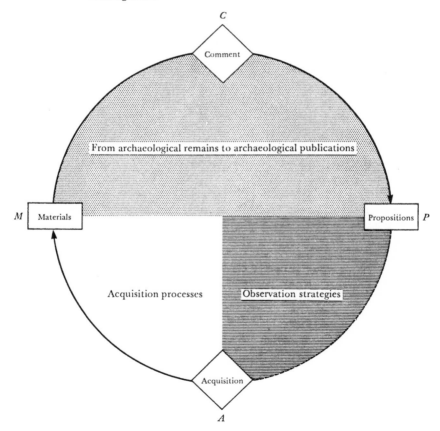

selections of research goals that are in turn the product of reasoned comments, past or present. We must therefore add a feedback arrow to our diagram, viz. a loop from right to left (dotted line on fig. 1), and include the strategies in question among the intellectual processes under study.

Segment *A–M* in this diagram covers the various observation procedures, considered from a technical or tactical viewpoint (e.g. sifting practices, degree of stratigraphical differentiations, scope and nature of conservation steps *in situ*, number of geophysical measurements to be taken in a given survey, etc.): nothing will be said about them in this book, nor of the underlying rationales, technical or tactical. But we shall have to include loop *P–A* within our compass, because of the essential part which observation strategies are going to play in the following discussion.

Figure 2 brings out the parts of the cycle considered in this book. The upper half indicates our primary concern: by which intellectual processes do we move from the apprehension of a set of archaeological materials, *M*, to the formulation of verbal statements, *P*? The lower half of the diagram is divided into two segments. The first one, *P–A*, recalls that the process of data acquisition is, or should be, determined by some kind of consideration for the relevant *P* statements, namely propositions expressing the state of knowledge in the domain under study, as well as the hypotheses or goals of the research project undertaken in that domain. We shall have to give some thought to the relation between these observation strategies *P–A* and the antecedent or subsequent phases *M–P* of the cycle. The second segment, *A–M*, corresponds to the actual application of the acquisition processes or techniques in order to collect the required bodies of data; it is not part of our present investigation.

1.3 *'Analysis' under the terms of logicism*
The kind of analysis to which the above processes will be submitted, and the goal of the exercise beyond the cursory indications given in the introduction, remain to be clarified. I shall first make sure that figure 2 is well understood, through examples intended to demonstrate its general applicability, as well as the relative *monotony* of the theoretical problems that are met whenever one goes through a complete cycle of reasoning leading to a set of *P* statements.

1.3.1 *Example 1: cataloguing* (fig. 3, line *a*)
The more simple propositions, at first sight, are those which we formulate when describing archaeological objects, with no other goal, it would seem, than to reveal the existence and nature of the latter before or while

they are submitted to investigations of a higher order. The publications which are supposed to serve that goal are of several kinds: excavation reports, archaeological inventories, museum catalogues, national or international corpora, etc. What they have in common is the room given to lists of descriptions that concern sets of objects or monuments selected on the basis of similar characteristics, such as the place of discovery (e.g. excavation report), their physical nature or function (catalogue of sculptures, tools, etc.), the place of conservation (museum catalogues). Let us for the moment ignore the diversity of such publications, and group them under a simple heading, for instance 'catalogues' in a broad sense; and let us now go back to figure 2.

The *P* statements are here the descriptions: descriptions of sherds in the chapter 'Pottery' of an excavation report, descriptions of coins in the numismatic catalogue of a museum, descriptions of painted representations in the *Corpus Vasorum Antiquorum*, etc. Clearly, the nature of these descriptions reflects the knowledge which cataloguers have of the materials under consideration; but it should also bear the mark of the kind of usage for which the catalogue is intended – which is, curiously enough, far less clear. The same head of Athena may legitimately be described in different ways, depending on the function of the catalogue: museum inventory, auction, scientific corpus, etc.; but no one would dare to assert that we have a clear idea of the relations that should exist between the various formulations.

Our problem will therefore be, in this context, the rationality of decisions taken with respect to the representation of a given object in terms of any descriptive system or language: are there arguments that can justify the differences observed from one catalogue to another, when both the objects and the objectives are comparable if not wholly identical? Or, conversely, can one think of any procedure such that different observers could produce the same descriptions when confronted with the same objects, assuming that they were all agreed upon the purpose of these descriptions?

Seen from this angle, the process of cataloguing in archaeology is clearly an instance of the situation illustrated in figure 2: the comment stage comes down to the problem of finding an adequate representation, in the above sense, while the propositions are to be identified with the descriptions themselves (fig. 3, line *a*). The process may seem quite elementary: its rationalization, however, is not, as we shall discover in the chapter devoted to this major category of archaeological constructions (chapter 3).

1.3.2 *Example 2: classification* (fig. 3, line *b*)
The representation of archaeological remains, as understood above, is generally regarded as an intermediate operation between the initial

Figure 3   Four examples of transfer from physical materials to discursive propositions, according to the basic process shown in figs. 1 and 2. Examples *a, b, c, d* are discussed in § 1.3.1 to 1.3.4 respectively.

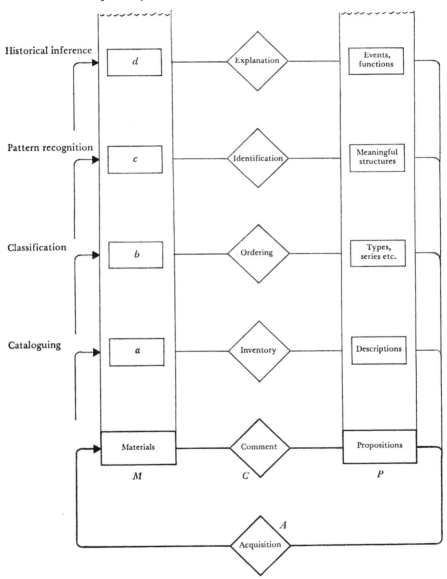

perception of material objects and the formulation of propositions of a more sophisticated nature than the mere description of every one of them, taken separately. Classifications are a good example of theoretical constructs of a higher order, even though they do not constitute the ultimate goal of archaeological research. We all know that the grouping of physical remains into 'bundles' of various sorts – classes, types, modes, schools, styles, workshops, cultures, etc. – is a common exercise among archaeologists, and quite a legitimate one, as in any science where the multitude of individual entities (plants, chemical bodies, fossils, etc.) makes it necessary to organize them into a smaller number of groups, each characterized by a set of attributes shared by all members of the group. The classification thus formed may in turn exhibit distinctive features of its own, from a structural viewpoint, to which various technical names are given: hierarchies, trees, polythetic classifications, etc. The diversity of those possible classifications need not detain us at this stage, except in so far as it reflects the variety of ways in which perceptive or descriptive data can be arranged, in a given field of observation, according to the goal of the classification. For example, a classification of coins based on the time and place of issue may provide for convenient retrieval, in the same way as the organization of stamps in philately; but it is likely to conceal subtle affinities between, for instance, the motifs or inscriptions engraved on those coins, which transcend distinctions of cities and dates. Conversely, a classification based on such affinities may provide the basis for distinguishing a number of 'styles', each assigned to a particular slice of time and space; but the proposed groups may be so questionable that the classification will be considered as inadequate for documentation purposes. Both forms of organization are thus admissible, and more generally *all* consistent forms of organization, provided that every one of them meets with equal success the different requirements of the users for which it is intended. The only question which may then be raised, from our standpoint, is again that of the rationality of the operations that underlie each classification: are there well defined procedures, applicable to any kind of material objects, that generate 'successful' organizations in the above sense? Or, to put it in the terms of figure 2, what are the intellectual processes involved in moving from the observation of unordered 'materials' to the formulation of 'propositions' that define the various groups in each of the suggested classifications? Figure 3, line *b*, shows the formal analogy between this problem and that of description, in the preceding example; we shall examine in chapter 4 a number of possible answers to that basic question.

1.3.3. *Example 3: pattern recognition* (fig. 3, line *c*)

In the two preceding cases, we have assumed that the perception of the

materials raised no special difficulties: we could hesitate between different ways of describing or classifying sites or monuments, but not in the
actual apprehension of each one of them, prior to this operation. A
number of archaeological publications are, however, devoted to problems of perception, or should we say 'understanding', as a result of the
cryptographic nature of our materials: understanding epigraphic documents, for instance, when the goal of our comments is to establish the
text of ambiguous inscriptions; understanding iconographical data,
when we are striving to identify meaningful forms in figures which have
no straightforward signification, or to reconstruct the missing parts of a
fresco, relief, etc. In all such cases, experience and reason conspire to
show that it is difficult to separate a formal phase of the construction, in
which we would merely reconstitute material 'signs' such as the form
of letters, the contour of motives, without trying to understand them,
from a semantic phase directed at the discovery of the 'meaning' of
those signs. These two phases are more often than not interdependent, so
that the reconstitution of the identity or integrity of a monument tends to
be identical with the formulation of hypotheses pertaining to its structure
and function. It is not necessary to call upon the refinements of *Gestalt-
theorie* in order to give support to this trivial fact; anyone can find
thousands of examples of archaeological constructs where the description
of an object is subordinated to a vision – conditioned or reasoned – of
its 'nature', which should always be regarded as open to discussion, as a
matter of principle.

Phenomena of this sort can occur within all categories of archaeological
remains, from the simpler kinds of artifacts – for instance a potsherd,
which we shall describe differently depending on whether we 'recognize'
it as a wide-mouthed cup or, turned upside down, a lid – to the most
complex monuments, e.g. an ancient city, the map of which will be read
in different ways according to the distinctions postulated between
courtyards and public squares, corridors and streets, etc. In all such
situations, the object of our comments is to assign a particular structure
to forms which can be perceived or interpreted in several fashions.
Supposing however that we understand the words 'form' and 'structure'
in a very broad sense, covering not only physical objects, but also abstract
constructs, then the above analysis does not apply to perception or
pattern recognition problems alone; it can be extended to all kinds of
archaeological comments in so far as they involve the discovery of
meaningful structures.

The synecdoche is not new: it is not uncommon to designate in the
same way under the heading 'pattern recognition' the study of all kinds
of intellectual processes (see for instance Chen 1976: 128 *et seq.*, 172);
and there is indeed much to be said in favour of this usage, from a formal viewpoint. We shall avoid it, however, for the sake of clarity, and
restrict our third example of archaeological constructions to the identi-

fication of individual monuments that can be perceived in different ways, owing to some indeterminacy regarding their function or meaning.

A vivid example of this situation is to be found in the analysis of iconographical data when the purport of the motives or scenes is not clear. We shall examine one such case in detail further on (§ 4.4.2); let us summarize it right now, in order to illustrate the present point. Suppose an author wishes to comment upon the meaning of a bas-relief showing: (*a*) 'two persons facing each other, wearing the same long cloaks; one seated, holding a bird on his right fist, gloved; the other standing, with the left hand tucked into his belt, the right hand resting on the belt of the seated figure (fig. 21, p. 109). After a few pages discussion, our author concludes that the meaning of the scene is as follows: (*b*) 'a ceremony of investiture related to hunting'. The question which will detain us will be the following: by which operations do we go from sentences such as *a* to sentences such as *b*? Or again, in the terms of figure 2, how does our author generate the second 'proposition' on the basis of the words contained in the first one, considered as providing the 'materials' of the construction?

A naïve response would probably be that anyone interested in this process should read the article in which the author describes it . . . adding that iconographical analysis is precisely to be commended for the explicit formulation of the reasons that sustain its end products, as opposed to what happens in the case of a 'simple' description or a 'straightforward' classification. The argument, unfortunately, does not hold: first because the rationalizations provided by iconologists usually fall short of our requirements, as we shall show later (§ 4.4); and also because, notwithstanding current beliefs to the contrary, the rationalization of descriptions or classifications that are taken to be simple, i.e. 'that go without saying', raises problems of the same nature as the rationalization of the more subtle iconographical interpretations (as indicated by figure 3, line *c*), except that they are probably *more* difficult to solve in the former case than in the latter.

1.3.4 *Example* 4: *historical inference* (fig. 3, line *d*)

The transition from the description of a given scene to its interpretation, in the above sense, already provides an example of historical inference: starting from distinctive elements or motives considered one by one or *n* by *n*, the commentator infers propositions (for instance, from the *bird – held on – a gloved fist* to the reading of a *hawk* trained for *hunting*), which in turn enter into combination with historical data, so as to give birth to propositions of a more and more specific nature, until the final interpretation is reached (example in § 4.4.2). All archaeological constructions of any intellectual ambition follow this same path. For instance, having established that the types laid down in a given classification of artifacts are distributed differently over space and time, the archaeologist infers propositions relating to the circumstances which may account for such differences. Or again, observing correlations between architectural structures and associated objects, he may infer hypotheses on the functions of either category of finds, or both, in different perspectives (practical use, social differentiations, etc.). Elsewhere, recording the modifications undergone through time by a large city, and matching them with information from written sources, he might be led to historical 'explanations' of the observed changes. One can produce endless examples of constructions of that nature in archaeology, 'traditional' or modern, old or 'new'; and I shall not be proclaiming an epistemological revolution when demonstrating that the intellectual process is roughly the same in all of them, and formally comparable to the kind of reasoning observed above in constructions which we take to be simpler only because we do not seek to elucidate their underlying mechanisms: catalogues, classifications, iconographical analysis, etc.

1.3.5 *The approach of logicism*

The preceding examples, and the manner in which I have chosen to present them, illustrate the way in which I propose to examine the intellectual processes of archaeology, at any level of complexity. The current archaeological publications will be the place where I shall observe them, without regard for distinctions of schools or styles: the term *construction*, which I have already used abundantly without defining it, will henceforward designate *any written text presented as a distinct unit in the archaeological literature – article, book, lecture, etc., with the appended illustrations – for the purpose of presenting the results of a survey or excavation, the contents of a collection, the interpretation of a monument or group of monuments, or the lessons that may be drawn from any such data with respect to the history and ways of life of ancient men*, in accordance with our definition (§ 1.1.4). I shall use the symbol C, borrowed from another book of a wider purport (Gardin 1974a: 21 *et seq.*), as an abridged form of the word 'constructions' in the above sense. The pattern of analysis will be the same for all kinds of constructions: essentially, our problem will consist in isolating the three major constituents indicated in figure 3:

(*a*) the initial set of objects selected by the author, in accordance with his objectives (§ 1.1.2), as the raw materials, M, of the construction;

(*b*) the terminal propositions, P, i.e. the assertions of all sorts (descriptions, classifications, historical statements, etc.) that express or summarize the end product of the construction;

(*c*) the intermediate data and operations involved in the transition from M to P, when they can be elucidated, i.e. the explicit elements of the commentary, *C*, plus implicit ones if necessary, which are needed to account for this transformation.

An additional remark is in order, concerning this last item. The intermediate data and operations just mentioned may be defined either by the author himself, heedful of the obligation to state explicitly the building bricks of his construction, or by the analyst when this obligation is not fully met. In the latter case, *the resulting rationalization may have little in common with the author's own account of the process.* The former situation being rather rare, I shall be more concerned with the latter, in order to demonstrate later that the sentence in italics does not impair the theoretical value of the exercise (§ 4.4.3).

An analysis conducted in this way inevitably calls to mind a mode of reasoning widely used in formal disciplines such as cybernetics, systems analysis, computer science, where the goal is to express the nature of various processes in the form of sequences of logical operations to be carried out by an automaton. The traditional diagram in this case is that of the 'black box': how are we to represent what is going on in a machine (a robot, a human brain, a computer) responsible for the transformation of materials M into products P, in the physical or abstract sense of both terms? Or again, by which set of programmable operations can one go from a given state S_i of matter or knowledge, however defined, to another state S_j selected as the goal of the process?

Going back to the examples of figure 3, we can see what S_i and S_j represent in our field. S_i corresponds to our more or less immediate apprehension of material objects as we have been accustomed or trained to see them, through diffuse learning or systematic teaching, with or without the assistance of instruments other than our senses. To those primitive data related to archaeological objects proper may be added, in S_i, *available* information regarding the men who made, used or destroyed those objects, the events with which they were associated, or their modes of life and forms of social organization. As for S_j, it corresponds to the *additional* knowledge of men and monuments which we gain at the end of a 'construction' in which the archaeologist has followed one or several of the courses illustrated on figure 3: (*a*) the representation of material objects in terms of a given descriptive system; (*b*) the ordering of objects in classes or series produced by carrying out more or less systematic operations on the descriptive symbols; (*c*) the identification of physical forms, in the broadest sense (pictures, inscriptions, etc.), i.e. their translation or conversion in terms of meaningful structures; (*d*) the explanation of material facts that have already been submitted to one of the above operations, e.g. the study of their relationships to data drawn from other sources (texts, other objects, physical environment, etc.) for the purpose of drawing inferences of various sorts – historical, sociological or whatever.

The 'black box', then, is to be understood as a sequence of such operations, producing the transformation $M \to P$. In the applied perspective of computer science, the analysis of these operations should be pushed to the point where programs can be written that will carry out the proposed transformation through electronic means; indeed, there exist already quite a number of well-known programs of that kind, at each of the various levels illustrated in figure 3: pattern recognition (cases a, c), automatic classification (case b), simulation of archaeological reasoning (cases c, d), etc. Our goal here is less ambitious: we certainly do want to analyse the same processes $M \to P$, as they appear in the archaeological literature, but without going to the pains of producing programs, let alone algorithms, capable of repeating the same transformations on a computer. The basic constituents of the reasoning process in this book will be intellectual operations similar to those which we carry out in the mental acts of daily life, rather than the atomized and minute operations which must be used in a program, or in an algorithm worthy of the name.

Our analysis cannot therefore pretend to be a logical one, in the technical sense of the word, nor a formal one, except in a metaphorical sense. Since my goal is none the less to reformulate archaeological constructions in order to come closer to the requirements of logical thinking, I have looked for a term that might convey this. The word 'logicism' is my suggestion, with the understanding that it should not in turn be taken in a specialized sense[1]: the meaning of the root is clear enough, and yet somewhat debased, as it should be, by a suffix which indicates the metaphorical nature of the reference to logic, or indeed the part of fancy in a game that will be conducted 'after the manner of' logical analysis, but with no relation whatsoever to any propositional calculus.

The following chapters will illustrate, I hope, the nature and value of logicism, as a method of reasoning that stands half way between the usual freedom of archaeological discourse and the narrow constraints of formal thinking. Let us for the moment be satisfied with the following rough definition: *the goal of logicist analysis is to express in the form of chains of*

---

1 The specialized sense to which I am referring is that of the logicians themselves, when they wish to consider mathematical constructions as the products of the rules and theorems of logic, or at least *a* particular logic which they have to specify (e.g. Frege, cited in Gochet 1978: 162–3). An interesting attempt of logicism in this sense is the analysis of grammatical structures found in mathematical discourse (e.g. Hiż 1967); our use of the same term for the analysis of *all* kinds of scientific discourse – here archaeological, but others will be mentioned in a later chapter (§ 7.2) – obviously leads to empty the reference to logic of any technical content. Unless one accepts the idea, or hope, that some technical content may one day be given to the concept of 'natural logic', as proposed by a number of specialists of language or discourse analysis in the last ten years (see § 4.4.3): even then, the relation is rather remote from the formal logic of mathematicians.

explicitly defined operations the reasonings that underlie the constructions of archaeology.

The borrowing or creation of any new word in 'ism' is, I admit, usually questionable. The value of this one is that it may serve to designate a movement of ideas that is apparent among other sciences of man, but which has not yet been recognized, nor therefore named, in an adequate way. I shall present, further on, a number of facts in support of this thesis, so as to reset the subject of the present book in its proper framework, beyond the present concentration on the particular case of archaeology (§ 7.2).

This is not to say that I count myself among the apostles of one of the 'revolutions' so often proclaimed in the sciences of man in general, and in the 'new' archaeology more specifically, during the last ten or fifteen years. Nor should the movement to which I am referring under the name of logicism be confused with the noisy declarations that are now to be heard so often in favour of any particular method regarded as indispensable for the growth or birth of a truly scientific archaeology: quantitative analysis, the hypothetico-deductive method, the process approach, systems analysis, the formulation of laws, or, worse, computation techniques in the mathematical or data-processing sense of the expression, when they are presented as a pre-requisite of well-formed constructions. Needless to say, none of those paths is here rejected; but conversely, I refuse to consider that any of them is essential to our purpose, for two reasons. First, the methodological issues that are at stake in this book are of a much more general order, and in many respects more trivial than those which come up under any of the aforesaid banners. Secondly, contrary to modern crusades in favour of science, the logicist trend as I see it aims at revealing not only the merits but also the limits of well-formed scientific constructions for the understanding of empirical facts, at least in the present state of our sensory and intellectual faculties. The acknowledgement of those limits is at least as important as the grounding of archaeological constructions on a firmer basis. The few pages devoted to this question, at the end of the book (§ 7.3), are intended as a reminder of the need to preserve some balance between different ways of reconstructing the history of man – the logicist way being only one of them.

2
Compilations and explanations

The definition given of archaeological constructions (§ 1.3.5) allows us to consider as such any proposition or sequence of propositions relating to material objects which are regarded as providing information on ancient peoples. We have just observed the wide variety of works that could be covered by such a broad definition: catalogues, classifications, commentaries of all kinds, etc. (§ 1.3); the object of the present chapter is to show first that this diversity is more apparent than real, and that a single dialectical movement can be observed throughout all archaeological writings, from a more or less immediate *perception* of objects to a more or less sophisticated *conception* of their cognitive value, which necessarily interact with each other, though in a sense and to a degree which vary according to the kind of constructions under examination (§ 2.1).

It will however prove convenient, as a second stage, to divide archaeological constructions between two broad classes (§ 2.2), depending on whether they deal more closely with the material objects (§ 2.3) or with the historical inferences that may be drawn from them (§ 2.4). This distinction will remind us of a number of similar dichotomies proposed not long ago by other theoreticians; I shall conclude by stating the reasons which have led me to prefer my formulation to others in the present case (§ 2.5).

2.1 *The relative uniformity of archaeological constructions*

Let us begin with a simple case. Suppose we discover in an excavation or in a museum an object which we regard as singular, for any number of possible reasons: the form is strange, the function is unknown, the material is exceptional, the origin is doubtful, etc. The archaeologist is trained to attract public attention to objects of this sort by publishing notes (articles, conference papers), always organized roughly on the same lines: circumstances and description of the find, obscurities in the understanding of the object (origin, date, function, etc.), explanatory hypotheses suggested by the author.

This last part, however, may be missing, if the obscure or strange points remain unexplained. The publication is none the less a 'construction' even in this case, according both to the letter and to the spirit of our definition. Literally speaking, the description alone is enough to form a sequence of propositions relating to a monument which is supposed to be of potential value for the knowledge of ancient men, failing which the publication would have no object. As for the spirit of the definition, it is preserved in the fact that the confession of an obscurity proves that the author has at least attempted to provide an historical explanation, which goes beyond the neutral task of description.

We shall therefore readily admit that the most elementary descriptive or explanatory publications referring to any sort of object are all constructions in their own right, in so far as they are the product of some reflection on the nature, origin, function or meaning of these objects. The examples of figure 4 are intended to suggest, through their very heterogeneity, the varying and often sizeable distance which may separate the immediate perception of the object and the written statements found in its description or interpretation, at different levels of sophistication.

Let us now imagine that, for any of the objects illustrated in figure 4, the archaeologist feels it necessary to present not the particular piece, but a series of objects which he takes to be more or less similar in function, origin, manufacture, etc. Most archaeological constructions are founded on the study of such series; and it is standard practice to publish serial

Figure 4   The heterogeneity of the archaeological record, as a reminder of the wide variations that must be expected between the immediate perception of materials M and the formulation of descriptive or interpretative statements P, depending on whether we are dealing with relatively simple artifacts (a, a nail) or complex architectural structures (h, a fortification of the Bronze age, island of Syros, Greece; i, a Scythian tomb in Pazyryk, Siberia); with crude figurines (d, a paleolithic mammoth from Andreevo, Ukraine), abstract ornament (b, a clay seal, from neolithic layers of Çatal Hüyük, Anatolia), or highly conventionalized representations (c, a feathered serpent from the earlier murals at Teotihuacán, Mexico, ca. 400 AD); with organic remains of macroscopic size (e, a cob of domesticated corn from Tehuacán, Mexico, ca. 3000 BC; g, a skull from Keilor, Australia, ca. 18,000 years old), or microscopic (f, a grain of corn pollen, Mexico City, estimated 80,000 years old), etc. Note that the simple 'artifact', a, may be described in terms of highly sophisticated laboratory measurements, while the 'crude' figurines, d, may move historians of art or religion to wild appreciations.
Drawings reproduced (except a) from Fagan, B. (ed.) 1975, pp. 149 (b, J. Mellaart), 231 (c, R. Millon), 75 (d, R. Klein), 174 (e, R. MacNeish), 175 (f, id.), 82 (g, D. Mulvaney), 241 (h, C. Renfrew), 251 (i, M. Artamonov).

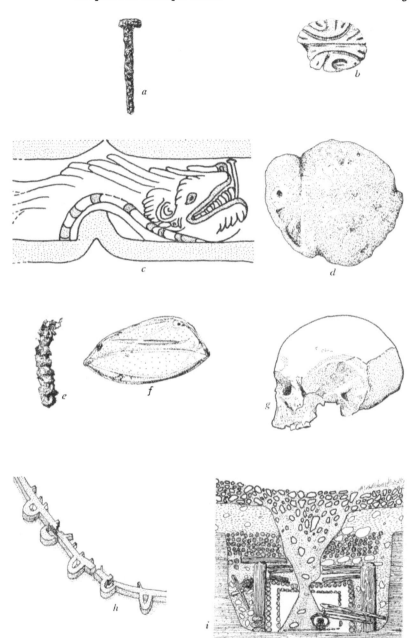

catalogues of all kinds, as the basic documentation tool of archaeology. Going back to the examples of figure 4, for instance, titles of existing or potential catalogues immediately come to mind, according to different selection criteria: according to sites (e.g. catalogue of nails found in the excavations at Olynthus, Greece), themes (e.g. catalogue of fantastic representations in Maya art), type of materials (e.g. catalogue of pollens from Eurasia), function (e.g. catalogue of fortified settlements in neolithic times), the usual boundaries in time and space being specified in each case. Publications of this sort are quite current in archaeology; their common characteristic is that, because of their serial basis, they are usually presented in the form of tables or classifications, the structure and substance of which are the outcome of reasoned considerations that make up the essence of the construction, intellectually speaking.

Let us take for instance the case of a catalogue of coins; the material can be presented in any number of ways. One may choose to classify coins according to dates (chronological catalogue), or mints (geographical catalogue), or a combination of both criteria (dates, then mints; or mints, then dates). One may also adopt a classification based on the nature of motifs or inscriptions that have been struck on the coins (iconographical catalogue, epigraphical catalogue), taking them into consideration either before or after the preceding geo-chronological distinctions; such will be the case of a catalogue intended to give support to a historical interpretation, at the same time that it is used for retrieval purposes. One may even dispense with classification altogether, and present coins in the more or less accidental order of their discovery or accession in a collection, adding then to the catalogue a number of indexes and analytical tables so designed as to make retrospective searches easier: index of mints, index of themes and motifs, index of the words or sentences found in the legends, etc. Some museum catalogues are conceived in this fashion, and likewise many of the catalogues found in excavation reports, except that the analytical tables and indexes are then usually lacking. Another possibility, lastly, opened up by the progress of computers in archaeology, consists in doing without both classifications and indexes, and describing the coins in a specialized analytical language or 'code', all terms of which can be used as search criteria or access points in an electronic file (Le Rider, 1975).

The choice between these different arrangements obviously depends on the goals of the publication; let us only observe at this stage that the formation of series, in the above sense, is again a case of two-sided constructions, in which the course taken for *describing* each class necessarily rests upon more or less learned and explicit considerations regarding the present or potential utility of those classes for *explaining* the variability of the archaeological record.

This interaction between the order of description and that of explanation is clearer still when the proposed classifications or series are directly related to a theoretical interpretation. The most common example is that of 'typologies', in the narrower sense (see p. 70, n. 5), where the differences between types, whatever the material under study (potsherds, houses, jewels, etc.) are held to reflect meaningful distinctions from the historian's viewpoint: separate origins, distinct time periods, different utilitarian or social functions, etc. But we may generalize further. The definition of a 'type' always proceeds from the observation of resemblance or dissimilarity between the objects under study: for instance, on figure 5, the analogies between the plans and roofs of houses M1, M2, M3 are sufficiently strong to justify the hypothesis that we are here dealing with several manifestations of a simple 'type' (geographical, chronological, functional), whereas houses M4, M5, M6 are set apart because of their different structure, with or without reference to one or several corresponding types. Now, this game of establishing points of similarity or 'parallels' between material objects is by no means restricted to typological constructions: whenever

Figure 5 The plurality of possible classifications based on *selected* analogies and differences in the archaeological records – e.g. disposition of rooms in M1, 6, and possibly M5 *vs.* M2, 3 *vs.* M4; roofing in M1–4 *vs.* M5, 6; disposition of rooms *and* roofing in M1, 2 and possibly M3 *vs.* M4 *vs.* M5, 6, etc.

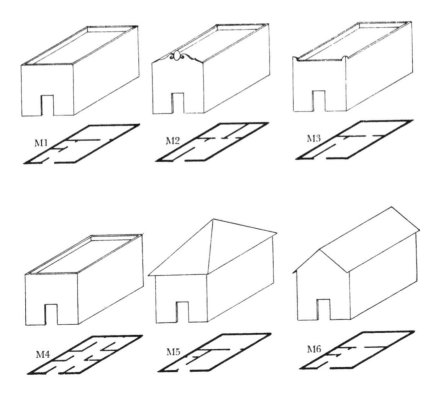

the formula '*x* resembles *y*' is stated or implied, under any of its countless paraphrases in archaeological discourse, a class is formed, namely class $\{x, y\}$, which is formally comparable to a type even if the nature and interpretation of the parallel do not always justify the use of the term. Thus, going back to the houses of figure 5, one may draw a parallel between the mud roof on $M4$ and the same feature on $M1$, $M2$, $M3$, without thereby implying that the group $\{M1, \ldots, M4\}$ constitutes a single type, in any historical or functional sense of the word; but a class has nevertheless been formed in the process, characterized by a trait which all the members of the class share in common, namely the mud roof. If moreover the group $\{M1, M2, M3\}$ is a homogeneous one in terms of time and space, or function, the tendency will be to 'explain' the parallel between $M4$ and this group – in other words, to explain class $\{M1, \ldots, M4\}$ – with the help of the usual concepts: diffusion, influences, evolution, technical determinants, etc. The class $\{M1, \ldots, M4\}$ will then appear for what it really is, namely not a 'natural' group forcing itself upon our senses or mind, but a highly artificial one, selected among many other possible groups in order to provide a basis for a given historical construction, and which has no scientific reality other than by virtue of this construction.

To sum up, we are clearly unable to perceive and describe archaeological objects otherwise than through predetermined filters, reflecting past usage. Any scientific description is thus at the same time the fruit of past constructions, and – so we hope – the source of present and future constructions designed to enrich the former, or to replace them. Seen from this angle, archaeological publications are all somewhat alike; no one can describe an object without referring implicitly to a state of knowledge and to research objectives that should determine, given a sound methodology, the substance and form of descriptions. It follows that a catalogue is a theoretical construct for the same reason if not to the same degree as a historical essay.

There remains this difference of degree: I shall now proceed from it, in order to show that it is convenient to separate the constructions of archaeology into two broad classes, for the needs of our presentation, on the basis of a polarity that does not coincide exactly with the contrast between descriptions and interpretations of archaeological data, as just discussed.

2.2 *Two poles of construction: compilation and explanation*

Notwithstanding their diversity in form and substance, archaeological writings may readily be divided into two broad categories: one of them comprises works of compilation, in which the primary goal is to disclose materials hitherto unpublished, or not easily accessible, while the other group is made up of more speculative texts meant to diffuse new ideas on various aspects of life in ancient times (technology, symbolic functions, social organization, etc.), grounded in the study of material remains. The same publication may naturally combine the two. This is what happens for instance in excavation reports, where the author begins with a presentation of his finds, to no other end, it would seem, than to describe with precision their stratigraphical origin and immediate properties (material, form, decoration etc.); but he seldom stops at this point, normally adding historical comments inferred from a preliminary study of the finds. Even then, however, it is usually easy to separate in a given archaeological construction the segments which belong to each of the two lines. Under the heading of Compilation, for instance, we shall subsume most catalogues, in the broad sense indicated above (§ 1.3.1), or at least those which are so organized as to make way for retrieval operations rather than historical conclusions. The part of reflection will be deemed larger, on the other hand, in classifications designed to bring to light meaningful groups (types, schools, styles, etc.: see § 1.3.2); it will emerge as the dominant component in the avowedly interpretative studies, where the author describes and classes archaeological data in so far as it enables him to establish a number of historical theses. I have given earlier a few examples of the latter sort (§ 1.3.3 and 1.3.4), and have shown in particular that the use of the comparative method, so common in archaeology, implies by definition a speculative orientation of this kind (§ 2.1). It therefore seems possible to order archaeological constructions on a continuum, going from the less to the more ambitious, intellectually speaking, or, say, from the more neutral to the more biased, depending on whether compilation is the main goal, or on the contrary only a means towards the establishment of historical propositions born of more subtle mental processes.

The merit of this systematization is that it underlines the essentially relative nature of the opposition between the two categories: reflection plays a part even in the most succinct catalogues, while conversely there is no historical construction that does not imply some compilation. More than a dichotomy, the picture is rather that of a 'polarity', i.e. an oscillation between two poles such that intermediate cases are likely to be most common. We shall indeed meet some when discussing for instance a class of taxonomic constructions that are thought to have more historical meaning than the ordinary catalogues, though they are generated much in the same manner as plain compilations (§ 4.2.1).

Let us now turn to a more precise definition of the two categories.

2.3 *Compilations,* C_c

I shall use the same term 'Compilation(s)' to designate both the intellectual process which characterizes our first category, and the products of that process. By 'Compilations' in the plural, I therefore mean the publications resulting from the activity indicated by the same word in the singular. Since symbol C represents the total set of archaeological constructions (§ 1.3.5), I shall use C_c for the subset of Compilations.

We have not hitherto attempted to circumscribe this category other than through a number of examples: regional inventories of historical monuments, museum catalogues, excavation reports, etc. Let us now try to reach a definition. Looking at the most patent properties which are shared by publications of these various sorts, one cannot fail to observe the conspicuous role of descriptions: descriptions of objects or classes of objects, descriptions of the circumstances of their discovery and present situation, descriptions of the environment associated with finds or sites, etc. Shall we say therefore that Compilations are defined by this common property, and that they are contrasted with more elaborate constructions in the same way as description is contrasted with interpretation? Some archaeologists would agree to this, on the basis of a stubborn faith in the existence and virtues of what they call an 'objective description' of the data, prior to historical research proper: to them, inventories and catalogues should provide us with the raw material of subsequent archaeological speculations, but in a neutral way, shielded from the variations of 'subjectivity' which necessarily imprints the latter, etc.

The inverted commas, as well as the 'etc.', suggest that I do not share those views. Positions of this sort are indeed anachronistic: they betray a persistent failure to recognize that the course of scientific thought goes exactly in the opposite direction: from the relative arbitrariness of immediate observations, subjective *in this sense*, to the reasoned order of verifiable theories, objective *in this sense*.[1] A quick glance at the descriptions found in archaeological compilations will indeed immediately reveal that they are anything but stable from one observer to another, and, further, that they all bear the stamp – entirely legitimate – of the knowledge and goals peculiar to each compiler. Are proofs necessary? Let anyone examine for instance the descriptions of Greek vase paintings found in the many volumes of the *Corpus Vasorum Antiquorum* edited by the International Academic Union; or the list of themes and motifs registered in the monumental *Index of Christian Art*, at the University of Princeton; or again the succinct indications given for the thousands of more common artifacts reproduced in Mariën's *Inventaria Archaeologica* (tools, pots, beads, etc.): in all such cases, the information that is provided in writing (as opposed to the illustrations) clearly does not represent the so-called 'objective' part that all archaeologists perceive or recognize in the objects, but rather a selection of a few distinctive

1 What I mean is this: the classification of chemical bodies by Mendeleiev is the product of experiments and reasonings that make it a more 'objective' construction, *in the perspective of science,* than any other classification based on more immediate observations, such as could be proposed by enlightened collectors of former or present times.

traits, picked from among thousands of others, of which the least that can be said is that it is always a largely subjective selection, even when an attempt is made to control it through the formulation of standard rules.

I shall later come back to this point, which is still the subject of much confusion (§ 3.3); meanwhile, we may agree that one should not seek to characterize compilation only through this reference to supposedly neutral, non-interpretative descriptions. Other common properties however come to mind: one of them is the tabular form of presentation, as opposed to the linear exposition of historical constructions. It seems at first sight true that, whereas the latter are always written in the form of a continuous discourse, the catalogues and inventories with which we are presently concerned are usually fragmented into as many different parts as there are entities, groups, or categories of materials to be described. In other words, a compilation often takes the form of a classification: classification of finds by functional categories in an excavation report (Architecture, Pottery, Tools, etc.); classification of objects by periods or cultural areas in a museum catalogue (Prehistory, Classical antiquity, Oriental civilizations, etc.); classification of objects by regions in a national inventory (Swiss cantons, French departments, American states, etc.). Those various courses are well known, as well as the practice which consists in adding indexes of all kinds to such classifications, so that the user may easily retrieve data scattered in different classes (materials, origins, decorative elements, etc.). Is this classificatory, or more generally tabular structure the criterion by which we may separate compilations from other constructions?

Here again, the answer cannot be clear-cut. There are many examples of published works that are presented in the fashion indicated, but in which the proposed structure is there to testify to higher intellectual ambitions than mere compilation. Such is the case of the innumerable monographs dealing with specific categories of objects (e.g. Mycenaean pottery, Oriental tools of the bronze age, archaic Greek sculpture), in which the author acts both as a compiler and as a historian. Or better, if he acts as a compiler while building up the ordered catalogue of objects pertaining to the category under study, it is only because he hopes to reach in this way historical conclusions of which that order is supposed to be both the reflection and the source. The classification structure is not therefore a sufficient criterion by which one may decide whether an archaeological publication is a compilation, and nothing more than that.

There remains a third possible characteristic, suggested by the counter-example just discussed. If a typological classification cannot be assimilated with a catalogue (even assuming that the range and ordering of the inventory are entirely identical in both constructions), is it not simply because the purpose of each is different? In a typology, the classification of materials is directed toward the presentation of historical views suggested or supported by that very organization; in a catalogue, on the contrary, the author's goal is to present archaeological data in a form which will enable others to retrieve them without too much effort, in connection with comparative or historical investigations which the compiler can neither anticipate, nor confine to his own interests. It is to this latter kind of work alone that I shall henceforward reserve the term 'compilation', without however concealing the perplexity that may be met in a number of borderline cases (discussed in § 4.1.2).

If we accept that our dichotomy rests on the *purpose* of constructions, rather than on their substance or structure, it becomes perfectly clear that the same objects are amenable simultaneously to constructions of both sorts: 'compilations', intended to provide access to what is known of these objects at any given time, and studies of a more synthetic kind, intended to propose new insights about the place or meaning of any one of them in the history of a particular human group.

We are now in a position to offer a definition of Compilation that will circumscribe the place which it occupies among archaeological constructions in general: *a compilation (symbol C_c) is a set of propositions, interrelated in various ways, describing material remains that have been brought together in a systematic whole so as to facilitate the study of ancient peoples.* The theoretical problems related to this first category of constructions will be examined in the next chapter.

2.4 *Explanations, C_e*

I exposed in § 2.2 the movement which leads archaeologists to derive from compilations the substance of more ambitious constructions, relating not only to the objects left by ancient peoples but also to those peoples themselves, to the events which marked their history, or to the way they lived, both in a physical and in a social sense. Such is the function of constructions which I shall call 'explanatory' – or in abridged form 'Explanations', symbol C_e – in contrast with the former: the material remains are here the means by which knowledge may be gained not only of the products of human industry as such, in a given slice of time and space, but also, through them, of the unique or recurrent forms of activity which the peoples 'behind the remains' probably went through. Manufacturing material objects is obviously one such form of activity: we attempt to grasp, on the basis of physical observations, the techniques used for the extraction or transformation of matter in manufacturing processes. In the same way, the study of 'ecofacts' tells us something about the natural environment in which ancient men lived, and the ways in which they drew their sustenance from it, either directly (agriculture, husbandry, etc.) or indirectly (industry, commerce, etc.). Further, the explanatory constructions of archaeology are not restricted to physical activities: starting from the same concrete data, one may draw inferences that bear on all kinds of abstract phenomena, such as mental representations, religious beliefs (based on the examination of iconographical documents), social stratification and political organization (from the analysis of settlement patterns), economic institutions and trade circuits (through the study of the circulation of goods or coins), etc. In all such constructions, the intellectual process is approximately the same: the starting point is the formulation of propositions expressing selected attributes of material *objects*, this selection being more or less explicitly based on the goal or guiding hypothesis of the construction. Then, through logical or mathematical operations which we shall soon explore in detail (chapter 4), and in which both induction and deduction usually come into play (§ 5.3), the author reaches statements concerning the *peoples* (persons or groups) who had something to do with those objects in any way. This shift in the system of reference, from objects to peoples, is the clearest manifestation of the difference between Compilations and Explanations, respectively, in our systematization. It should therefore be reflected in our definition of the latter, as follows: *an archaeological explanation is an ordered set of propositions meant to offer a reconstitution of past events or ways of life related to particular individuals or groups, on the basis of the properties exhibited by a given body of material remains, together with other possible information.*[2]

The selection of those remains, as well as of their distinctive properties, may well be inspired by previous compilations, or even completely determined by them: it is for instance conceivable that a catalogue of coins first produced as a documentation tool, with no historical goal in view, may some day provide the substance of an explanatory construction based on the observation of correlations between fineness of metal, date of coinage, iconographical motifs, or any other category of attributes recorded in the catalogue. The explanation, in this case, can be regarded as a direct product of the compilation; and it is all too easy to find or imagine any number of similar derivations, for all kinds of objects – architecture, vessels, tools, etc. It does not follow, however, that compilation is a necessary step towards the production of explanations. In other words, the succession of those two categories in time is not by any means a methodological requirement: one could easily find innumerable examples of archaeological constructions where the compilatory prologue, i.e. the initial *description* of the data, is in fact determined, both in

2 It might be objected that the reconstitution of past events or ways of life is not an explanation of the latter: I agree with this, and only wish to emphasize that the present study is restricted to explanations *of the archaeological record* as the product of 'past events or ways of life'. As for explanations of the latter through alleged laws or determinants of human behaviour, it is not, to me, the subject of archaeology *per se*, even if archaeologists are of course entitled to present their personal views on the matter.

scope and substance, by the explanatory peroration in which the author presents his *conclusions*.

This fusion or confusion of the two courses may seem inevitable; it is nevertheless rejected by most archaeologists of the so-called 'traditional' brand, as well as by a number of those whom we shall call 'modern' for the sake of symmetry. I shall therefore return to it on several occasions throughout this book. Meanwhile, let us admit provisionally that the stream which leads to the Explanations of archaeological science sometimes passes through those reservoirs of knowledge called Compilations, while at other times it draws directly from the sources, namely the physical remains themselves, as if the two categories of processes could not then be dissociated (fig. 6).

2.5   *Other formulations of the distinction* C_c/C_e

The alternative just mentioned is related to a problem of strategy which is of some importance in present day archaeology: considering that 'data banks' are an advanced form of compilation, should we encourage their multiplication on the assumption that they will eventually serve the progress of scientific explanations, as in path $a - c$ of figure 6? Ot is it not wiser to explore first the reasons for the preference often given to the direct path, b, even in sectors where the existence of data banks (or for that matter compilations of any sort) would seem to hint at its inefficiency? We shall be better able to answer such questions after we have examined more closely the structure and function of both categories of constructions (chapter 6). Meanwhile, the reader should bear in mind that the proposed duality is not new: it is not very different,

Figure 6   The two complementary ways in which Explanations C_e may be derived from the study of archaeological materials: through the use of existing Compilations C_c (path c), or by direct examination of the materials (path b). Compilations C_c are here considered as drawing their substance directly from the archaeological materials (path a); their relation to C_e will be discussed further on (§ 3.3.4 and fig. 11).

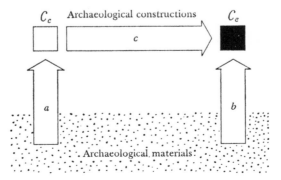

for instance, from the distinction suggested a few years ago by Irving Rouse, in the USA, between analytic archaeology, which deals with material remains as such (Rouse, 1973: 23), and synthetic archaeology, more interested in the peoples who made or used them (*ibid.*, pp. 25–6). The danger of this phraseology, however, is that it may lead some to think that there exist two distinct branches of archaeology, between which a choice is possible according to one's tastes or goals. It is clear on the contrary that analytic archaeology in that sense can only be understood as a phase or as a tool of archaeology at large, without further qualification, for the simple reason that studies of remains would soon become a bore to all of us if they did not end up with portrayals of 'the history and ways of life of ancient people', beyond the stone and mud.[3]

The same qualifications hold for other formulations of a similar dichotomy, for instance by C.-A. Moberg, in Sweden, who contrasts 'archaeography', defined as the systematic study of material remains, with archaeology proper, which is the study of men through their remains (Moberg, 1969: 41–3; rephrased as an opposition between 'find structures' and 'live structures' in Moberg, 1976).

Granted that compilation is thus only a *moment* of archaeological research, on the way to historical explanations and syntheses, a different and on the whole more fruitful analogy comes to mind, applicable to all sciences of man, if not to scientific reasoning in general, irrespective of the objects concerned: it is the well-known distinction developed by the American linguist Kenneth Pike between two ways of analysing human behaviour (Pike, 1967). The first one consists in recording more or less blindly a large number of features pertaining to the event or phenomenon under study. Supposing this event were an unknown religious ceremony, the observer could set down a multitude of details about the participants (age, sex, clothes, etc.), their attitudes and gestures at different moments of the ceremony, the setting of the scene, the objects that seem to form part of it, etc. But this description, however minute, will not necessarily reveal the meaning of the phenomenon, nor its inner structure; and it may even be misleading in two ways: either because the recorded data

---

3 It would be ridiculous, besides, to imagine that Irving Rouse himself could think differently: the long debate which opposed him to K. C. Chang on this point (see Chang 1968: 1–30) is but an example among others of those constrained misunderstandings which help to maintain the fiction that there is a deep gulf between today and yesterday, in the small world of archaeological thinking (same words of caution by Gordon Willey ten years ago, in Chang 1968: 209). More generally, I do not see that the archaeologists of yesterday were ever reluctant to behave as sociologists, economists, or indeed historians when they had enough data to do so: counter-examples are so many that such a charge can only be based on ignorance or blindness. That is why I am unwilling to admit that the abundant literature published in the last fifteen years in praise of 'archaeology as anthropology' (e.g. Binford 1962, Longacre 1970, Meggers 1968, etc.) marks a turning point in the intellectual history of our discipline.

play no part in the system of behaviour (e.g. the exact number of strokes on the bell before and after the celebration of a Catholic mass), or conversely because features that are relevant to the system are not part of the inventory (as would happen for instance if the observer failed to record some 'responses' of the congregation to the 'stimuli' of the officiant). The search for structure and meaning thus demands another form of analysis, in which description becomes a reasoned process aiming at the discovery of the truly 'distinctive' data, in the technical sense of that term: distinctiveness, here, is not a quality that immediately strikes our senses, as in the first approach, but a concept bound to reasoning procedures of a more complex nature.

Such is the alternative on which Pike has built up the opposition now common in various branches of cultural anthropology between the so-called 'etic' descriptions, derived from an immediate apprehension of the outer world, and 'emic' descriptions that are the product of reasoned operations – the former being acceptable in science only in so far as they may help to develop the latter.[4] We shall have to explore further the importance of this distinction for our purpose, and especially the still debatable nature of the genetic relationship that is supposed to hold between the two forms of observation, as we may see it in archaeology (§ 3.3.3). Suffice it to say that the 'etic/emic' contrast coincides to a large extent with our polarity C_c/C_e: *with some fundamental reservations regarding the interdependence and relativity of the two orders*, we may consider that Compilations operate at the 'etic' level of observation, whereas Explanations seek to discover 'emic' elements that can be used in the building-up of theoretical constructs.[5]

4 Besides Pike's fundamental work (1967), the reader interested in the applications of this distinction in several fields may consult the following works, listed in chronological order: Gardin (1958b), Dundes (1962), Scott (1965), Goodenough (1970: 104–30), Brend (1972), Roulet (1974), Waterhouse (1974), Harris (1976).

5 Another possible reservation, suggested to me by George Cowgill, might be that the 'emic' approach aims at discovering the categories and concepts that the people under study have in mind – a goal which is usually out of reach in archaeology, except in the rare cases where textual evidence is both available and reliable for that purpose. My answer to this would be, to make it short, that most native speakers of English do *not* have in their mind the 'emic' categories of English phonemics – which is of little concern to the phonologist; on this matter, namely the ethnocultural value of analytic units devised by anthropologists, see the discussion initiated by Burling (1964).

3
The analysis of compilations

Let us go back to the set of archaeological constructions grouped under the heading of Compilations, C_c: it includes works of different forms, but which all aim towards the same goal, namely to provide 'descriptions of material remains that have been brought together in a systematic whole so as to facilitate the study of ancient peoples' (§ 2.3). Our first task will be to show that this common goal has more weight than circumstantial differences from one compilation to another, however striking these may seem superficially, and that we can therefore reduce to a single model the chain of operations that underlie *all* compilations.

3.1 *The structure and function of Compilations*

The diversity of the set is due for one thing to the variety of forms which the compiler may use to present the material entities under study. The writing of descriptions is only one such form: archaeologists attach at least as much value to graphical presentations (plans, photographs, drawings), which serve to mitigate the uncertainties of their prose. Furthermore, this iconic part of description may grow to the point where it becomes a physical substitute for the artifact (castings, models, copies), such that written discourse would appear more and more unnecessary, if only we could distribute the surrogates just as we distribute books.

This is not all: once the form of presentation has been selected, there remains a wide range of possible variations with regard to content. For there are dozens of acceptable renderings of any of the 'structures' in figure 4 – to take but one concrete example – hundreds of acceptable compromises between the relative importance of text and illustrations in their presentation, and an infinity of sentences that may be used to describe them in the strict sense, viz. with words rather than images. Moreover, the course adopted for the recording of architectural remains will have to be redefined for chipped stones, pots, bones, etc.: one does not describe a Maya temple according to the same conventions as a scraper, nor a potsherd on the same basis as a Greek sculpture. Are we not therefore in a rather desperate position when trying to reduce all problems of compilation to a single formulation, in the unifying but perhaps oversimplifying perspective of logicism?

My reasons for optimism lie in a *truism* and in a *postulate* which I find encouraging for our purpose. The *truism*, first, has to do with the part which written discourse is bound to play in compilations, with all due deference to the champions of other channels of communication. It is not enough to photograph, nor even to gather in the same museum, mouldings of 'all the Greek coins found on Iranian sites' (a mere supposition, for the sake of the argument): the resulting collection of plates or casts does not constitute an inventory or catalogue of those objects. The reason is that this mute mass of documents lacks several categories of informations that are not observable in the collection, even though they certainly should be present in all forms of archaeological compilations; let me mention some of them. (*a*) The extrinsic data are the most obviously wanting, namely data that are not observable on the objects or their reproductions and that must therefore be 'worded' in some way: origin, archaeological context (stratigraphy, associated finds, etc.), environment, etc.; (*b*) then come certain intrinsic data which are not conveyed by reproductions, such as the metal in which the money is made, its weight, etc.; (*c*) lastly, we have data of both kinds that are the products of more sophisticated analyses than either *a* or *b*, in a physical sense (e.g. identification of chemical constituents), or in a symbolic sense (e.g. reading of inscriptions, iconographical interpretation), and which the compiler certainly has to mention, if available, in order to provide a full description of the collection.

What is true of the compilation of our Greek coins from Iran is true for any other compilation which we may think of, concerning for instance potsherds found in an excavation, inscriptions included in a corpus, sculptures held by a museum, the architectural remains observed in the course of a survey, etc. In all such cases, the compiler's task does not stop at the taking of casts or photographs, and it is a mistake to contend that the advance in iconic records in general (e.g. mouldings, photogrammetry) are an answer to our all too familiar 'problems of description', as some archaeologists would still have it.[1]

Let me now state the *postulate*: the part of verbal data in archaeological compilations is not only inevitable, as a complement to iconic data, but also desirable to the point where the former should eventually oust the latter. This postulate rests on two rather simple arguments. The first one

---

[1] I am here referring to recommendations heard many times in learned assemblies when problems of description were being examined, in favour of 'solving' them through illustrations. Strangely enough, the advocates of pictorial documentation do not seem to realize how paradoxical these proposals are, not to say more, in a context of *science* (see for instance the discussions in Vallet 1977: 282–8). The argument which follows is intended to ward off such aberrations.

consists only in recalling that the function of compilations, in the context of *science*, is to further the advancement of knowledge in ways that are not identical to those of a collector, however enlightened. I shall not insult the reader by such an obvious fact, which is perfectly summarized by the following aphorism enunciated some two centuries ago, by Condorcet I believe: 'La science est une langue bien faite.' The idea of shunning the difficulties of verbal or symbolic representation, *à propos* of certain facts, amounts to no less than closing the door to a 'science' of those facts. It can certainly be argued that the evil is not great if the need for science is slight (see § 7.3.3). But assuming that the references to science which keep coming up in archaeology are to be taken seriously, one has to consider just as seriously Condorcet's aphorism, as well as its immediate consequences with respect to the discursive, or more generally symbolic form that should be given to the representation of archaeological remains, even at the stage of compilation (for further developments on this point, see Gardin 1975).

The second argument, similarly, is related to the increasing part which those verbal or symbolic representations are to play in data retrieval operations. Bringing together thousands of artifacts is one thing; providing access to the information required by archaeologists in the course of research is quite another. There was a time, not far back, when leading scholars were plainly opposed to the idea that others should be helped in mastering large sets of documents which they had themselves spent many years in gathering and recording for their own benefit. The publication of a corpus was felt by the more insular to be a sufficient concession; why should anyone be so naïve as to call in addition for a large-scale production of computer indexes that would enable just about anybody to collect in no time the references or data relevant to any research topic, without having first gone to the trouble of gaining an intimate knowledge of the remains? This attitude has not really gone; it has rather given way to a kind of acquiescence in the inevitable, namely an obligation to forsake documentation practices that have become properly absurd with the passage of time, and which no one dares defend anymore.

Here again, I shall not linger over a demonstration of the need for reform as I presented it more than twenty years ago (Gardin 1955, 1958a, b). The information crisis experienced in all sectors of science during this period has awoken archaeologists of the younger generations to a consciousness of the required changes, abundantly discussed elsewhere (Chenhall 1968, 1971, 1975; Gardin 1968, 1974b, 1975; Scholtz and Chenhall 1976, etc.). One point should however be borne in mind, in connection with the present discussion: namely, the fact that the methods and techniques that are intended to improve our control of the archaeological data all imply that solutions must be found to the problem of representing material remains in terms better suited than

those of natural language to the requirements of information retrieval.

We are thus led by two different paths to the same conclusion:
although Compilations are often conceived without much further
thought as mere compendia of scattered materials, they are in fact
essentially *symbolic constructions*, in so far as a system or language of
representation must necessarily be resorted to, in order to satisfy both
the theoretical requisites of science and the practical demands of
documentation. The observed differences in the form and content of
current compilations then lose much of their weight, as compared with
this common function; this is why I think they can be disregarded as one
tries to bring out the basic principle of all such constructions, viewed as
symbolic systems of communication between the materials of archaeology
and the research workers who study them.

Figure 7   The chain of operations in the design and use of
Compilations C_c. The selected materials M are recorded in
appropriate symbolic forms (or representations R_m), amenable
to searches or queries Q formulated according to the same
conventions, R_q. In designing the representation system or
language, tentative R_m and R_q are successively considered until
the required links are established between M and Q, as seen by
the compiler (upper dotted line). The use of C_c consists in
matching R_m and R_q through a collating device of some sort
(visual, mechanical, electronic), in order to obtain answers P to
given queries Q. The efficiency of the process is evaluated by
comparing P with standard lists of M established for the same
queries by the user (lower dotted line).

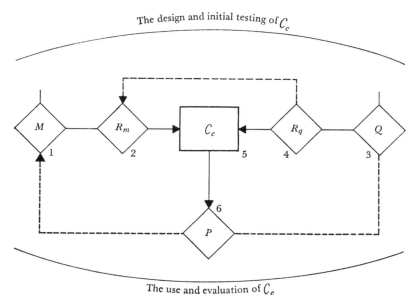

The design and initial testing of C_c

The use and evaluation of C_c

Figure 7 illustrates the functioning of such a system, and the way in which it gradually takes shape. (*A*) The objective, first, is to present a set of materials M, selected among many others (box 1), under a form (representation R_m, box 2) such that the resulting compilation, C_c, will provide answers to certain queries Q again selected among others (box 3) and expressed in the same form (R_q, box 4). (*B*) The function of C_c comes out clearly: it is used as a retrieval 'machine', in which data and queries are matched according to more or less stringent rules (box 5), leading to products P which are supposed to meet the specifications of the search. (*C*) The efficiency of the system is evaluated through a comparison of products P with those which should have been derived from set M for each of the proposed queries Q (box 6), according to the questioner or to competent 'judges'; the result is a list of adjustments to be introduced into the procedure, at any stage, in order to make it more efficient (feedback loop on fig. 7).

This diagram is nothing but a standard representation of information systems in general, when the central machine is a computer;[2] this, however, is only one of several possibilities, and the principle remains the same when the matching process $M \leftrightarrow Q$ is carried out by 'machines' of a simpler sort: printed indexes and catalogues, card files, punched cards, indexes, etc.[3] In understanding Compilations in this broad way, we can single out three major theoretical problems:

(*a*) Through which procedures and by which criteria does one select the materials that form the substance of Compilations (box 1)?

(*b*) For which reasons does one stop at a given representation language? In particular, does this choice reflect a clear view of the kind of queries which the Compilation should help to handle (boxes 2, 3, 4)?

(*c*) Through which operations does one make sure that the Compilation answers its purpose, and what are the provisions for modifying its substance or its form when shortcomings are detected (boxes 5, 6)?

2 Beginners in these matters would derive benefit from reading one of the many standard books published on automatic documentation, or more generally on the methods of information science: in English, Vickery (1973), Meadow (1973), etc.; in French, Alouche *et al.* (1967), etc.; in both languages (and also in Spanish, Russian, etc.), the widely circulated study sponsored by the International Council of Scientific Unions and Unesco in 1970 on the feasibility of a world science information system, which contains an overall presentation of information processes that may be found useful for our present concern (Gardin 1971: 25–61).

3 This unified view of information systems has sometimes been challenged, on the basis of a conviction that the power of the computer was such as to eliminate the need to consider the theoretical problems related to the matching process $M \leftrightarrow Q$. The fault in this argument should be kept in mind (see below, § 3.3.2), as well as the resulting error in the prophecy: all the major computerized information systems that are now in operation rely on analytical or representational methods that are not in essence different from the methods used in non-mechanical systems (Gardin 1973: 141 and 160, n. 2).

The following sections are devoted to these three questions, taken in the same order.

3.2 *The selection of materials*

I have stressed in the very first pages of this book the reasoning which leads us to consider the selection of the set of materials in any archaeological construction as part of our field of investigation (§ 1.2, figs. 1 and 2). We must therefore probe the rationality of the choices made at this early stage in Compilations: on which arguments does the archaeologist base his initial delineation of the field, and his decisions to include a given object in the set of materials, or to reject it?

The selection criteria can be divided into two groups, which may be used separately or jointly: (*a*) on the one hand, the origin or location of material remains, irrespective of their nature (e.g. excavation archives, museum catalogues, national or regional inventories, etc.); (*b*) conversely, the nature of material remains, irrespective of their origin or present location, as in the case of the major international corpora (*Corpus Vasorum Antiquorum, Corpus Inscriptionum Graecorum*), or of serial inventories conducted within stated time and space limits (Ornament, Funereal monuments, etc., in region *x*, period *y*, etc.). In fact, the two criteria are seldom used separately: compilations of the first kind are nearly always classified by categories of objects (e.g. Pottery, Sculpture, Coins, etc.), and those of the second group by location, i.e. place of origin or conservation (e.g. Ornament: Egypt, Near East, Iran etc; Greek Vases: British Museum, Hermitage, Louvre etc.). The two approaches thus tend to merge: the catalogues of the British Museum on Greek vases should have something in common with those of the *Corpus Vasorum Antiquorum* on the holdings of the British Museum . . . The distinction is nevertheless useful, because it indicates where and how problems of selection are met in the genesis of Compilations, as we shall now verify.

The handling of the first criteria, to begin with, would not seem to raise much difficulty: marking the boundaries of a site, a country or a collection for which an archaeological inventory is to be carried out does not leave much leeway for subjective waverings. But we are still faced with a problem of choice, relating to the principle of this strategy: what is the rationale behind the decision to base the boundaries of Compilations on spatial criteria of this kind? The answer is self-evident: whether the compiler has thought about it or not, the rationale here is that of a *producer*, rather than a user. Let me amplify this: if we keep in mind that the goal of Compilations is 'to facilitate the study of ancient people' through systematic collection of their remains, we must ask ourselves if this goal is indeed reached when the systematic component consists in organizing the records on the basis of such contingent facts as the location of Parthian sites in the Soviet Union, or the appropriation

of an Etruscan jewel by a private collector in Peru . . . The only justification for such a strange course is that it simplifies the compilation
process itself, and in particular the division of labour between the
countries, organizations and persons that *produce* compilations; but no
one would dare to say that it is consequently the most rational course,
from the standpoint of those who are to *use* compilations.

Criticism is so easy on this point that we need not linger over it much
further. It is less easy, however, to think of an alternative strategy, such
that the boundaries of Compilations might coincide with standard
frontiers between fields or themes of research in archaeology. The
introduction of the second criterion, according to the above dichotomy,
is a step in this direction: a segmentation based on categories of archaeological materials is more relevant, from a user's viewpoint, than a geo-
political or museological one, especially if these categories are defined
not only by the function or nature of the materials (e.g. Architecture,
Fossils, etc.), but also by geo-chronological or 'cultural' specifications
which are hopefully understood in the same sense by everyone (e.g.
Pharaonic Egypt, Upper Palaeolithic, etc.). However a difficulty arises
from the overlapping of these fields: a compilation of *funeral monuments*
in Egypt cannot be unrelated to an inventory of *artifacts* from the Nile
Valley, to the extent that objects of daily life are abundant in tombs.
On the other hand, funeral architecture should not be dissociated from
architecture in general, if the compilation is to be suitable for the study
of building techniques in ancient Egypt . . . But then, should we merge
all those compilations into one, encompassing Pharaonic habitations,
tombs, artifacts, etc., at the risk of burdening information searches that
are currently conducted in one sector *or* another, rather than all of them
at the same time? Furthermore, what shall we do with Egyptian objects
found at sites in Phoenicia, Cyprus, Anatolia, etc.? Should they not be
recorded in compilations concerned with the history of those lands
rather than with the history of Egypt? Or again, turning to limits in
time, when shall we decide that objects found in Egypt cease to be
Egyptian in a Pharaonic sense, and that they should rather be recorded
in compilations dealing with Graeco-Egyptian monuments of hellenistic
times?

Endless questions of this kind could be raised *à propos* of any archaeological compilation, real or imaginary, in order to show the drawbacks
and ambiguities that are associated with the principle of an ordering of
materials by functional and geo-chronological categories. Does it follow
that we have to renounce rationality in the definition of our compilatory
fields? I do not think so, provided that the problem be reformulated in
the following way. Let us first agree, on the basis of the foregoing
observations, that all the courses which one might think of in this area are
objectionable, for one reason or another, and that there is therefore no
point in continuing to look for a universal allocation scheme that would

meet everyone's requirements (the organizational structure needed in order to enforce such a scheme, if it were accepted, is at least as problematical: see Gardin, 1974b: 24–6 and 1975: 820–3). It is therefore wiser to consider present and future compilations as so many local contributions to the information apparatus of archaeology, without much planned interdependence between them, but such that their sum might form a rationalized whole, *a posteriori*, if a number of steps were taken in order to facilitate the progressive integration of all the various parts. By 'integration', I mean on the one hand the elicitation of limits that have hitherto received little attention between compilations conducted independently, even though they present areas of overlap with respect to materials, space and time; on the other hand, the adoption of principles of representation and organization common to all parties, which should never lead to standards or norms, inadvisable in this context, but only to a more efficient use of the whole apparatus.

The first step is essentially an organizational one: it calls for agreements between the sponsors of archaeological research with a view to the gradual setting-up of an information network of international scope, the unique function of which would be to give individual workers access to scattered compilations relevant to their needs, in any number of ways, from the mailbox to teleprocessing or other means of remote access.[4] The second step, on the other hand, is of a more technical purport, and probably not so readily feasible: it requires careful studies of possible compromises between the right of compilers to draw up and arrange descriptions of their own free way, and the no less legitimate right of users to a certain rationality in the make-up of the documentation tools that are offered to them (Le Maître 1978). It is to this rationality that we shall address ourselves in the following pages.

3.3 *The representation problem*

Let me first recall the postulate on which the discussion in the present chapter is based: what distinguishes a scientific compilation from the prose of a collector is that it resorts to a representational language that is supposed to have higher merits, both theoretically, for the accumulation of scientific knowledge, and practically, for the handling of information. A correlate of this assumption is that, as we have emphasized earlier, a mere collection of objects or reproductions (photographs, drawings, casts) does not constitute a scientific compilation. I would like to demonstrate now that the same reservation holds for a particular kind

4 Networks of this nature have been in existence for many years in several sectors of the physical as well as behavioural sciences, under a variety of names: referral networks, data networks, switching systems of information transfer, etc. On their overall philosophy, see Gardin, 1971: 19–20, 68–9, 112–13, 120–1; on their applications in the social sciences in particular, see the state-of-the-art report by David Nasatir (1973).

of pseudo-compilation also based on the collecting of images, in which a number of persons believe that they have found the solution to the representation problems that harass archaeology: I am referring to the automatic analysis of shapes with a computer. The principle is well known, and I shall only illustrate it through a simple diagram (fig. 8). Using various sensors, or a camera connected to a computer, one converts a given object (here, restricted to two dimensions, e.g. pottery profiles, plans of buildings, etc.) into a series of numbers indicating the position which it occupies on a standard grid. Knowing this numerical expression, one can conversely reconstruct the shape of the object, to a degree of precision that varies with the definition of the grid. At this point, it is easy to jump to the conclusion that one has found a way to produce 'objective' descriptions of shapes:[5] the shortcomings of conventional designations seem to be by-passed (multiplicity of languages, terminological fluctuations, variations in the scale of observation, etc.), whereas the joint use of machines and numbers is expected to remedy the weakness of human faculties. This strategy has only one defect: it grossly ignores the purposes which symbolic representations of form are intended to serve in archaeology,[6] or for that matter in any science. Their primary function in Compilations is to make way for the *retrieval* and *comparison* of morphological data pertaining to objects the shape of which is held to be meaningful: anyone can realize how difficult it would be to carry out either operation through numerical expressions alone, as derived from

Figure 8   The simplistic view of automatic pattern recognition in archaeology: two-dimensional shapes recorded as a sequence of $\{x, y\}$ coordinates indicating the squares 'sensed' on a grid of varying definition.

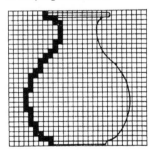

5 A step candidly taken by some archaeologists, on the advice of over-enthusiastic computer experts: see for instance Ankel (1969) and Gundlach (1969). The critical remarks that follow are not levelled at the use of computers for the preparation of plans or maps (Doran & Hodson 1975: 81–6), but only at the thesis according to which computer-initiated graphical products constitute an acceptable representation of objects or monuments, for the purpose of scientific thinking.

6 Not to mention a more obvious limitation, namely the fact that the description of archaeological materials is not confined to the analysis of form alone.

figure 8.[7] Another function of representations is to supply the symbolic elements that go into the *formulation of theories*, at a higher level of reasoning: the least we can say is that the $\{x, y\}$ coordinates which make up those expressions are not very promising in this respect.

We therefore have to fall back upon *ad hoc* representation systems, or codes, which may certainly call upon the language of numbers if needed, but in which qualitative elements are usually required for the two reasons just mentioned. The so-called 'natural' language, that is the language we use in most of our verbal communications, is clearly one such system. Indeed, of all systems of signs, or semiological systems, in the terminology of Ferdinand de Saussure, natural language is the most common; and archaeologists are prone to admit that, unlike biologists or physicists, they need not innovate much in the vocabulary and grammar of their mother tongue in order to discuss the objects and phenomena which are of concern to them. Except when they deal with ancient texts, the archaeological publications are usually intelligible to specialists of the natural sciences; the converse has not been true for the past two or three centuries. We shall therefore have to consider natural language as one of the categories of symbolic systems used for the representation of material entities, in archaeological compilations, bearing in mind however that this category includes many different systems (Chinese, English, Arabic, etc.), each of which imposes its own grids for the segmentation and designation of the world in general, and the archaeological world in particular.[8] I shall henceforward use the abbreviation NL to designate either natural language in general, considered as a class of symbolic systems among others, or any particular language taken as a member of that class.

We must, however, qualify what has just been said in one respect. However untechnical it may be, the language of archaeology tends to grow richer in specialized words or expressions sometimes borrowed from other fields of study (e.g. architecture, geology), sometimes forged by the archaeologist himself in order to designate with precision and concision a number of facts that would otherwise have to be described

7 If a demonstration is needed, the reader will find it in Borillo *et al.* (1973), *à propos* of an experiment which again concerns the automatic analysis of pottery shapes, as in the Ankel and Gundlach project.

8 This influence of the mother tongue on the way we apprehend and name the objects around us has long been the subject of reflection by philosophers and linguists alike (Von Humboldt, Sapir, etc.) until it became a field of research in its own right, following Whorf's well-known work in ethnolinguistics (1956): see for instance Conklin (1955, 1972), Hymes (1964), Tyler (1969), etc. The language spoken by an archaeologist clearly has a similar effect on his patterns of description: this can be verified by comparing the terminologies borrowed from different natural languages for the classification of, say, pottery types (e.g. Mugs, Tankards, Jugs, etc.), and observing how difficult it is to translate one into another. On the value of ethnolinguistic methods for the study of those phenomena in archaeology, see Gardin (1965b).

through lengthy and somewhat obscure propositions in the layman's language. Those innovations may even take a more or less systematic turn, as they become the subject of discussions and decisions bearing on archaeological terminology, until we finally end up with 'special languages', as linguists of the school of Meillet and Vendryes used to call them, entirely dependent on natural language as far as grammar is concerned, but endowed with some measure of lexical autonomy. Archaeology is no doubt a field of special languages in this sense, even if their relationship with natural language is still a very close one; we shall therefore admit that a second category of symbolic systems is at work in the representation of archaeological remains, more or less akin to natural language, but which is destined to depart from it more and more, in the same way as the language of science has progressively parted company with natural language in other disciplines in the course of recent centuries. Special language, scholarly language, scientific language, I shall accept all these expressions, notwithstanding a number of reservations which will be brought in at a later stage (§ 3.3.3); and I shall use the abbreviation SL to designate the whole class, as well as any of its members.

Finally, systems of signs of yet a third kind have come to light in the last twenty years, as both NL and SL have come under fire from information scientists: namely, 'information languages', or 'documentary languages', designed to alleviate the difficulties of data handling and retrieval in archaeology, for all sorts of objects.[9] The major trait of these

9 For an early criticism of information handling methods in archaeology, see Gardin (1955) (further developed in Gardin 1963 and 1968); for prototypes of information languages concerning artifacts (tools, pottery), iconographical representations (coins, seals, ornament), and written records (clay tablets), see Gardin (1958a, b). These languages, to which I gave the somewhat misleading name of 'codes' (see below, § 3.3.1), have had different fates. Some of them have been used in their original form for building up compilations that have been made public, if not published, in a variety of ways: hand-sorted punched card indexes (Deshayes & Gardin 1956); peek-a-boo card indexes (Christophe & Deshayes 1964); electronic files (Digard *et al.* 1975). Others have led to a number of adaptations in different geohistorical fields (Gardin 1976: 9). Others still have had no other outcome than their long-deferred publication, twenty years after they had been devised and tested on experimental files (Le Rider 1975, Gardin 1978a, Salomé 1978, 1979); while in the same time other codes were being developed for other categories of material (essentially, architecture: Lagrange 1975, Nivelle 1975), in connection with an ambitious data bank project covering all historical monuments located in France (Gardin 1972a). Similar efforts have not been lacking elsewhere – the foregoing codes all being the product of a single group, the Centre d'Analyse Documentaire pour l'Archéologie (1955–72) – but with some differences: the proposed descriptive languages usually reflect a more synthetic vision of things (e.g. Ericson and Stickel 1973), if not a frankly typological one (especially in the case of lithic analysis: see for example Bordes (1961), Brézillon (1968), Laming-Emperaire (1969), etc.), which is at variance with the principles of analyticity and neutrality of the

systems is that they break away from the standard order of traditional discourse in its natural (NL) or scholarly form (SL), in order to make way for analytical expressions the elements of which are combined according to rules of morphology or syntax that have nothing to do with the way words or phrases are formed in literary language (or rather in texts: by literary language, I do not mean the language of belles-lettres, but more generally the language of printed publications, irrespective of stylistic quality). The reason for this break is a technical one: the very growth of archaeological compilations, both in size and number, is likely sooner or later to require the use of powerful retrieval tools, in the form of indexes of increasing sophistication, the structure and function of which will tend to coincide with the structure and function of indexing systems in general as understood in library and information science.[10] The analogy need not be pushed very far to reveal that the content of archaeological compilations can easily be represented by means of such systems, provided that the lexical and syntactical resources of the latter be developed to the point where literary descriptions can be dispensed with altogether. The index then becomes the central piece in the construction, instead of an optional complement; and the indexing language takes the place of natural language for the purpose of data analysis and retrieval (for concrete manifestations of both substitutes, see Allard *et al.*, 1963; Christophe & Deshayes, 1964; Digard *et al.*, 1975).

I shall henceforth use the symbol IL to indicate the whole range of information or indexing languages in the above sense, or any individual system of signs especially designed for the handling of archaeological documents in a broad sense (viz. not only the monuments but also the publications relating to them), according to a logic which differs from the way NL or SL is used for the same purpose.

The representational problem in constructions C_c can thus be set forth as a problem of choice between languages which may belong to any of the three classes just defined: NL, SL, or IL. We shall begin with the least familiar, IL (§ 3.3.1), and examine its relation first with NL (§ 3.3.2), then with SL (§ 3.3.3), so as to gain a better view of the part that falls to each in Compilations (§ 3.3.4).

3.3.1 *Representations in an information language (IL)*

Contrary to widely-held opinion, the idea of resorting to *ad hoc* codes for

preceding codes; or else, they are merely used as tools for the construction of 'data matrices', with statistical investigations in mind, rather than information retrieval proper (bibliography and discussion in Doran & Hodson 1975: 99–114).

10 It was on the strength of this convergence that I was led to explore the semiological aspects of information processing in general, with a particular emphasis on the behavioural sciences: Gardin (1962a, 1964a,b, 1969).

the analysis and retrieval of scientific data is neither historically nor logically related to the development of punched cards and computers. As I have just stressed, the classification of a library or the organization of a card index by subjects (disciplines, fields, topics, etc.) already hints at the existence of such a code, namely the standard list of terms or symbols by which the selected subjects have been designated. The set of these terms, however they may be referred to (subject headings, descriptors, index entries, keywords, etc.), constitutes the *lexicon* of the representation language; and the rules which lay out the permissible combinations of these terms into compound expressions (e.g. 'Welding by Laser, in the Aeronautical industry') form the *syntax* of that language. Clearly, we are dealing in both respects with an autonomous system rather than with a simplified or standardized form of natural language, even if the elements and relations which make up the system are usually designated in the terms of a given NL, for the sake of convenience.[11] This is why I have recommended elsewhere that semiological systems of that sort be considered as 'metalanguages' in relation to NL (Gardin 1969; 1973: 144 et seq.): the same term, for instance 'Foundation', is not used in the same way, nor does it necessarily have the same meaning(s), depending on whether it belongs to the 'natural' lexicon of English or to the 'artificial' lexicon of an information (meta)language which carries its own definitions.

In assimilating our archaeological codes to the metalanguages of library and information science, however, we may give rise to an objection: how can one compare systems of description that refer to material objects in the first instance, with written documents in the second? And is it not likely that the problems of representation will be radically different in the two cases? My answer to this last question is unhesitatingly no: rather than an abstract demonstration, however, which would take too much time here, let me give a practical illustration of the identity of the two structures. Suppose we have to describe a monument such as the bas-relief of fig. 21 (p. 109) for inclusion in a compilation on Islamic sculpture or iconography; and let us assume that

11 Should the reader be unconvinced, let him consider the case of a classification or of an indexing system presented in several languages: the Japanese, Russian, or Spanish editions of the Universal Decimal Classification, for instance, are in fact NL translations of a unique metalinguistic system, which is composed of the symbols used in the Universal Decimal Classification, together with the definitions attached to them in Japanese, Russian, or Spanish. Consequently, the nature of those symbols is of little import, except for the convenience of notation: a coded designation is not more precise than a natural denomination, definitions alone matter, in one case as in the other. Our use of the word 'codes' when speaking of information languages in archaeology may therefore be misleading: the virtue of a code does not lie in the substitution of alphanumerical symbols to plain language, as some naïvely believe, but only in the quality of the definitions and conceptual organization that are associated with it.

we agree with an interpretation given by one of the commentators of this monument, according to whom it represents 'the solemn transfer of hunting rights by the king to his son'. In what terms shall we choose to formulate the IL description in C_c? Should we stop at an indication of this theme, without going to the pains of enumerating the 'objective' elements which make up the scene (the two men, their respective attitudes, attributes, etc.)? But in this case, are we right in rejecting other interpretations given by different commentators, e.g. 'a conversation of a spiritual master with a disciple', or 'an episode in the training of the hawk', etc.? Further, if we decide to mention also the individual elements, should we restrict ourselves to those features which give support to the proposed interpretation(s), or on the contrary broaden the description so that it will include all features which we regard as distinctive, on any ground (semantic, technical, stylistic, etc.)? Whatever course we may take, it stands to reason that our IL representation will be related not only to an image of the bas-relief as a physical *object*, but also to a 'reading' of the latter through the various *texts* that have been devoted to the description and interpretation of this particular object, or others that have something in common with it. In other words, the IL representation can be regarded indifferently as the representation of an image, or as the representation of a discourse associated with the image: its 'legend', so to speak, in the etymological sense of the word. This ambivalence, especially conspicuous in the case of iconographical materials, is no less present in other categories of objects: the representation of a tool, a house, a piece of jewellery, etc., in any information language, is meant to convey what has been or what could be *said* of each object in one or several natural languages, so that we may regard it as a metalinguistic formulation of either the object or its possible descriptions and interpretations. The opposition between material data and textual data thus loses some of the prominence which we would tend to give it, on practical grounds alone;[12] and it is certainly not such as to debar us from embracing in the same vision the codes needed for the compilation of archaeological materials and the metalanguages of a more general scope that are used in libraries and information centres for the compilation of scientific texts – including the texts of archaeology.

The advantage in this proposal is that it allows us to draw on the findings of research conducted in the last fifteen or twenty years on the structure and function of information languages in general, for any

12 Though not necessarily in theory: it can be argued that the semiological constructions of any science refer indifferently (or rather, simultaneously) to physical phenomena or (and) to the symbolic representations that have already been given of the latter, in the course of compilations or explanations. Whether the language used in these representations is a simple derivation of natural language, as in archaeology, or a fully-grown autonomous language, as in the harder sciences, has no bearing on the principle of this two-fold reference.

field or level of application, and to abridge accordingly our discussion of the same topic in archaeology. As propounded in a number of text-books on the subject (Gardin 1964a, 1966, 1973; Coyaud 1966; Hutchins 1975, etc.), the essential features of information languages can be summarized in the following way. (*A*) The basic component is a specialized *lexicon*, that is the set of terms used for designating the entities that one has decided to individualize, and therefore to name, in a given field of research. Let us stress once more that these terms do not belong to natural language, even when their form is that of NL words: they are conventional symbols accompanied each by an explicit or implicit definition that holds only within the limits of the information language, and which does not necessarily coincide with the definition of the corresponding NL word if it exists (fig. 9). (*B*) Another important feature is the *lexical structure*, i.e. the set of relations established *a priori* between IL terms, through a variety of means: grouping of terms into classes, hierarchical or other arrangements of those classes, codification of terms expressing recurrent semantic components as in the morphology of NL words, etc. These relations can be shown to be of two main kinds:

Figure 9 The non-natural status of natural language terms used in information languages, illustrated by an extract from the code used in Digard (1975) for the analysis of oriental cylinder seals (vol. 2, pp. 225–7, chapter on Seats). (*a*) The French word 'tabouret' as used in this code, or its English translation 'stool', does not have the same meaning as in NL: it appears only in compound terms, 'tabouret *a*', 'stool *b*'. (*b*) 'Chaise' or 'chair' has a narrower field than the corresponding NL words in French or English, which would probably include some of the seats described as 'tabouret *b*', or 'stool *b*'. (*c*) The term 'ixe' is not a French word anyway, nor is its possible equivalent 'iks', a standard phonetic transcription of the letter 'X' in French. (*d*) All the seemingly NL words are in fact literal equivalents of the numerical symbols '769' . . . '773', of which they share the conventional meaning in IL: they therefore belong to IL, notwithstanding their NL form.

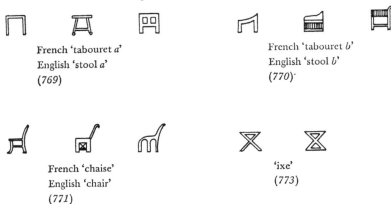

French 'tabouret *a*'
English 'stool *a*'
(769)

French 'tabouret *b*'
English 'stool *b*'
(770)

French 'chaise'
English 'chair'
(771)

'ixe'
(773)

some of them indicate semantic links that hold good in any context (for instance, the link between the generic term 'seat' and the specific term 'chair', in the example of fig. 9), while others express logical relations that obtain only in a particular context (for instance, the relation between human beings as 'subjects' or a given action or scene – e.g. attacking, taking care of, worshipping, etc. – and animals as 'objects' of the same action), and that can be expressed by functional or 'role' indicators attached to the IL terms, e.g. Human beings / Subject, Animals / Object. (*C*) In the latter case, the morphology of the IL lexicon in fact performs a syntactical function; and we could just as well separate the two kinds of relations, semantic and logical, in order to consider under *B*, above, only the semantic component of IL, while regrouping under a distinct title all its syntactical constituents, i.e. the different means by which logical relations can be expressed between IL terms, such as functional affixes or classes, as above, or compound terms, parentheses, relational symbols, etc.[13]

All the existing representational languages can be described in terms of this general model (Gardin 1973), and in particular the information languages or codes devised for archaeology. This can be verified by observing how easy it is to isolate in any such language the three constituents in question: (*a*) the lexical base, i.e. the minimal units of designation, their definition, and the symbols (natural or artificial) used to name them; (*b*) the semantic relationships that are established *a priori* between some or all of these units, in an explicit way, and the ways in which they are expressed; (*c*) lastly, the provision made for indicating syntactical relations between some or all of the same units within specific representations, viz. *a posteriori* relations in this sense, in contrast with the former.

The characterization of ILs thus raises no difficulties; this is not true, however, of the formulation of rules which might account for the genesis of every single IL. The most critical step is the constitution of the lexical base: given a set of archaeological materials, which minimal distinctive features should one use in describing them so as to meet the requirements of potential users of C_c, in accordance with figure 7? This reference to the purpose of Compilations is fundamental: it is only by using a given C_c that one can evaluate the adequacy of the construction, which means, essentially, the adequacy of the information language that determines its content; and it is quite vain to persist in dealing with problems of description and cataloguing in an absolute manner, as if

13 This trilogy – the lexicon, its semantic or 'paradigmatic' organization, and the rules of syntactical or 'syntagmatic' composition – has been presented in detail in Gardin (1964a) (also Cros, Gardin & Lévy 1964, Gardin 1965a, etc.), as well as in a few recent handbooks on information languages (e.g. Hutchins 1975: 29 et seq.). For more specific studies on lexical organization see Gardin (1966); on the syntactical function of certain lexical features, Gardin (1962b, 1965c).

there existed in each case an ideal solution, independent of the use to which the construction is to be put. I shall therefore make a point of *not* answering the question raised above until we have examined the mechanisms through which the merits of a Compilation may be gauged (§ 3.5).

The tactical aspect of the question can, however, be dealt with right now: once the level of observation has been set, how are we to achieve some degree of uniformity in the representation of the same objects by different compilers? I have proposed elsewhere a systematization of the kind of rules that are necessary to that end, in the following way: (*a*) *orientation* rules, which lay down a standard position of the object in relation to the observer; (*b*) *segmentation* rules, which account for the conventional division of an object or monument into separate parts (for instance, for pottery shapes, the body, the neck, the base, etc.; for iconographic materials, the central subject or scene, the subordinate or secondary elements, the decorative motifs, etc.), this partition being usually reflected in the structure of the information language; (*c*) lastly, *differentiation* rules, which determine the scope and nature of the distinctions which are to be recorded for each part, through the proposed language. The procedure is the same for all categories of archaeological remains, from nails or pins to mosaics and cathedrals; for an overall presentation, see Gardin 1967a, as well as the various codes listed above (note 9), all born from a more or less systematic application of those principles to different categories of objects.

3.3.2 *Data processing in natural language (NL)*

To many archaeologists, the somewhat abstract bent of our discussion is a reason to regard it with suspicion: do we need to be concerned with so many theoretical issues in building up straightforward catalogues? Furthermore, are we not to be blamed for giving up so quickly the virtues of literary prose for the benefit of analytical expressions that are utterly unreadable, to say the least? We need not spend much time in refuting such objections: the first is ill-advised, since it is precisely the analysis of the function of catalogues that leads us to question the suitability of their literary form; as for the second, it is based on a doubly false presupposition, namely, that catalogues are meant to be read, and that they are indeed readable in their traditional form . . . We should not either be detained by the contention that the learning and handling of information languages are unduly complex matters, as opposed to the easy control of natural language: while the observation is at first sight correct, it only makes sense under an implicit restriction such as 'other things being equal'. What I mean here is that if it is true that information languages may often seem unwieldy for analysis and retrieval operations, it remains to be shown that natural languages constitute a better tool, *for the same purpose and at the same level of efficiency* (precision, rapidity, flexibility, etc.). The least we can say is that the spectacular progress of information languages in all fields of science during the last twenty years does not corroborate this belief.

A number of experts have nevertheless continued to argue in favour of the use of natural language as the most convenient vehicle for scientific information in general, on the understanding that its more obvious

Figure 10   The true nature of the contrast between standard retrieval procedures in an information or indexing language IL (case I), and the more advanced procedures designated as 'searching in natural language' (case II). The allegation that no IL is needed in the latter case is unfounded: the difference lies only in the respective position or role of IL in the processing system described in fig. 7. In case I, IL is used for *reducing* different NL formulations of the same object to a standard representation (R_m), while in case II, IL is used for *amplifying* the original formulation of a query into the various forms which may represent it (R_q) in the NL store. It stands to reason that the same kind of semantic tool is needed in both cases, namely a 'thesaurus' indicating the more or less equivalent terms by which different authors or inquirers may refer to the same entities, in one or several natural languages, the appreciation of 'sameness' depending on the products (P) expected from C_c. All such thesauri are ILs under another name, whether they are used as shown in case I or as in case II.

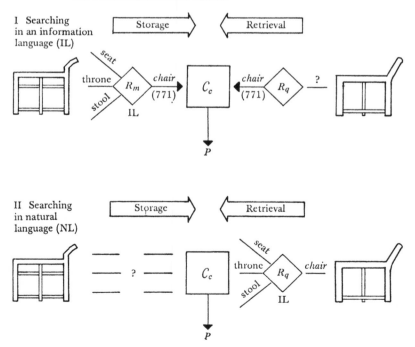

I   Searching in an information language (IL)

II   Searching in natural language (NL)

drawbacks (ambiguities, synonymies, redundancy, etc.) could be corrected or compensated by the sheer power of computers, presented as the retrieval tool of the future. The first champion of this strategy was Swanson (1960); his reasons had nothing to do with humanistic traditions, but rather with measures of relative efficiency of a highly technical nature. Unfortunately – for there were superb benefits to be reaped, had Swanson been right – the measures were correct, but not the conclusions drawn from them. A careful analysis of the procedures advocated showed that in fact they implied the same kind of linguistic transformations *in the wording of queries* as those which we were invited to dispense with, in the wording of documents or data (demonstration in Cros, Gardin & Lévy 1964: 26–31). The myth of documentation in natural language has, however, persisted to this day – archaeology included (Ginouvès 1971) – so that it may be worth while to recall the error or misunderstanding which underlies it. The error, first, consists in believing that 'searching in natural language' does away with information languages altogether, as the expression would seem to imply; figure 10 shows that this is not the case, and that the role of ILs in such procedures is only displaced rather than deleted.[14] The misunderstanding, second, comes from the fact that the natural language which champions of NL searching procedures have in mind is the language in which *queries* are formulated, rather than the language in which the information is to be recorded; what is then at stake is the development of conversational procedures in a more or less standardized or 'basic' form of natural language, the use of which in no way implies that the contents of the files are expressed in the same language.

In fact, and by way of conclusion, there are few if any examples of scientific information systems in operation where natural language is the standard medium for expressing data and queries, without any kind of constraint on the accepted terminology or phraseology.[15] The opposite, indeed, would be surprising: it is time for us to go back to the function of Compilations, which may have been forgotten during this digression, and recall that it implies in a quasi-tautological way an inexorable

14 Strangely enough, it took a long time before this truism was generally acknowledged in information science: see the demonstration by Montgomery (1972), in the USA, which repeats the one by Cros, Gardin & Lévy in 1964 (as shown in Gardin 1973: 141, and 160, n. 2).
15 The only apparent exceptions would be cases in which the literal form of written documents constitutes the very subject matter of research (e.g. philological studies on ancient texts, archives, etc.), and where one should therefore be satisfied in principle with procedures carried out on untransformed NL symbols, for the purpose of producing tables (indexes, concordances) or statistical counts. But the reality is again different: it is well-known that applications of this kind in fact require preliminary annotations of the text (pre-edition), or table look-up procedures for assigning grammatical or semantic categories to NL words or groups of words, which amounts in both cases to using an indexing or information language, even if a primitive one.

divergence between the language used in publications of this sort and natural language. If the endeavours reported in this section have any value, it is in confirming through their very limitations that such a movement is indeed unavoidable, and that the good use of computers emphasizes more than it reduces the role of information languages in Compilations. We now have to show that the logical outcome of this movement is, conversely, a growing subordination of Compilations to the language of science (SL), which goes against the kind of linguistic freedom that some had hoped to preserve.

3.3.3 *Information language and scientific language (SL)*

Our objections to the NL strategy would seem to fall if what was meant under NL was not the language of daily life, but the language of science itself, only subject to the same grammatical rules as natural language. There would be no need then to be concerned with terminological laxities, since they should have been already eliminated at the source, by the scientists themselves; as for phraseological variations, we could hope to control them through a proper formalization of NL grammars. Proposals of this sort are not *a priori* absurd, and a number of information scientists have been prone to support them.[16] Their major defect is that they are applicable only within the limits of *one* natural language at a time: I can think of no field where scientific terminologies have evolved into a true lingua franca used by research workers of all nations instead of their own vocabulary (the case of mathematics and chemistry, though often mentioned in this context, is by no means one of unilingual publications), so that we would still have to face then the problem of correspondences between one natural language and another. The solution is well known: construction of multilingual thesauri, and adoption of standard symbols for the designation of each list of terminological equivalents . . . which means creeping back furtively to a metalexicon, which is not a lexicon of English even if the standard symbols in question have been chosen for the sake of convenience among words of the English language. Furthermore, turning from lexical to syntactical control, the multiplicity of natural languages which would still be accepted – hopefully – in scientific literature would compel us accordingly to build up as many syntactical analysers or formal grammars as there were natural languages in use, and then to establish rules of equivalence or correspondence from one grammar to another in order finally to regroup the different ways of expressing the same logical

16 At least when their own mother tongue was such as to warrant the practicality of the idea: it is no wonder that proposals for equating information languages with the language of science should always come from specialists for whom English seems to be the only conceivable language of scientific publications, rather than Chinese or Greek.

configurations in each of the accepted languages.[17] In addition to the fact that we find ourselves once again confronted with a metalanguage in the form of a standard grammar, natural or other, considered as the most convenient conversion tool, the major obstacle is here a practical one: notwithstanding the amount of work devoted to the formal analysis and translation of natural languages in the last twenty years, no one would dare assert that we are today in a position to uphold this strategy, even at the most primitive level (Gardin 1973: 151 *et seq.*).

But this is not all. Even assuming that we had to deal with documents written in a unique scientific language and that we had at our command all the linguistic tools needed for reducing lexical and syntactical irregularities, it does not follow that we would not still feel the need for an artificial language of representation in the sense defined above (§ 3.3.1). The reason is simple. First, it is wrong to imagine that a scientific or scholarly language is by definition a unified language: divergences are still present, which are not all the consequence of dialectal idiosyncrasies, but rather the reflection of different but equally acceptable views about the way in which empirical facts should be apprehended and named. The coexistence of several systems of designation in the language of science, far from being a source of trouble, is to be regarded as a necessary condition of survival; and only ignorance or blindness can lead us to dream of a state of language where such phenomena would have no part, on the sheer strength of standardizing decrees, and which yet would still deserve a scientific qualification. True, it is the compiler's duty to bring out cases of synonymies or overlap in competing terminologies, to the point where he may find it convenient to propose his own system of designation, in order to make conversions easier from one terminology to another; but he is not authorized, as a compiler, to *choose* between those terminologies, at least when they reflect different theoretical visions rather than being merely the consequence of tradition or want of thought. The need for a metalinguistic tool thus emerges once more, even when the languages to which it refers are as 'scholarly' as they can be.

A second, independent reason is that scientific language as used in publications follows the same rhetorical rules as natural language, which as we all know does not make retrieval operations easy: the use of synonymous words or expressions is not only authorized but recommended, synthetical designations are allowed in order to summarize elements

17 I am here assuming first that information retrieval processes cannot develop successfully unless some at least of the logical relations between NL words be taken into consideration, and secondly that this logical analysis can be formulated in terms of rules that may be executed by a computer. The first assumption, though it was sometimes challenged fifteen or twenty years ago, today needs no justification; as for the second one, I only mention it in order to leave no excuse for underestimating the requirements of an information metalanguage in the strict sense.

of meaning that are named or implied elsewhere by other terms, many different syntactical structures have the same meaning with respect to the logical relations holding between pairs of entities x, y – e.g. x influences y, effects of x on y, variations of y according to x, correlations between x and y, presence of x features in y, etc. All these properties of NL, which were virtues in a certain rhetorical tradition, here become vices which have to be corrected in one way or another. The addition of indexes to scholarly publications is one such way: it stands to reason that the role of subject indexes is not just to list the various occurrences of selected words or expressions, in a given text, but rather to indicate under each index 'entry' the different sections of the text where the same entity or topic is being dealt with *under any linguistic form*. The metalinguistic status of such entries is therefore indisputable; and we have stressed earlier that indexes were to be considered for that reason as a prefiguration of the more elaborate information languages developed in the last twenty years under the banner of the newly-born information science (§ 3.3.1). Considering that publications written in a scientific language as disciplined as the language of physics or chemistry is taken to be are still the subject of printed indexes and retrieval-oriented IL compilations on an industrial scale, it is unwise to prophesy that the publications of archaeology will soon benefit from such an advanced scholarly language that reformulations in the terms of information languages will become unnecessary.

The conclusion is self-evident: even in the naïve perspective of an impending powerfully specialized and systematized language (SL) in archaeology, there would still be a call for the parallel development of information languages (IL), acting as a metalanguage with respect to the former. One may even note ironically the strength of a converse movement, in which it is often through the discussion of descriptive codes that archaeologists discover or rediscover the need to improve the scientific language.[18] This situation has its own dangers: the inversion of the proper order may be transformed into a rule, with the result that the codes in question will be advocated as a better approximation of the language of science when archaeologists suddenly discover that their respective dialects are unacceptable as such. Nothing could be more absurd: let us again emphasize that the language of science and the language of information do not aim at the same goals, and that it is a rash act of faith to believe that the former can simply be derived from the latter, even if a few happy accidents can be mentioned in support of this strange belief.[19]

18 Many conferences on the use of computers in archaeology, for retrieval or other purposes, thus lead to ill-advised claims for a 'standardization' of terminologies, candidly presented as the solution of the semiological problems raised by Compilations.

19 The happy accidents which I have in mind are for instance a number of constructions based on mathematical methods of classification or

3.3.4 *Conclusion: IL, the language of Compilations*

It is time to sum up our discussion. We have established that the function of Compilations is such as to impose the use of *ad hoc* symbolic systems of representation, to which we have given the generic name of information languages (IL), necessarily different from natural language (NL) even in disciplines where the latter tends to be replaced by a highly specialized, scientific language (SL), as for instance in physics or chemistry. Archaeology, *a fortiori*, cannot, by an ill-placed confidence in the virtues of standardized terminologies, escape this obligation. Conversely, should information languages develop satisfactorily in archaeology, we should not expect that they will bring about a revolution in the theoretical constructions of the discipline: the sole purpose of these languages is to help in the preparation and handling of Compilations, but without allowing us to postulate that the systems of representation used for retrieval forestall in any logical way those which will prevail in theoretical constructions. This was the sense of figure 6, where Compilations have been displayed as a possible but not indispensable phase of a process wholly directed at Explanations.

The relationship between the two categories of symbolic systems, IL and SL, holds in fact in the reverse order, from SL to IL, for the simple reason that scientific Compilations can only be of use, whatever the field concerned, if they keep a record of the different ways in which the same facts are being apprehended and described in theoretical constructions of current interest. This is obviously true of archaeology, where the same object can give rise to different representations, according to the goals of the study (technological analysis, chronological attribution, functional interpretation, etc.), and to the paths that have been selected in order to reach them. The information language should

seriation, in which one proceeds from an IL or 'etic' representation of a set of data to an *empirically valid* theory (typology, chronology) that may be regarded as an 'emic' or SL reformulation of the same data, inferred from the initial description. The words in italics are here essential: we must have some reason to believe in the cognitive value of the product before we can mention it as an example of a *successful* IL→SL transformation. An unprejudiced analysis of the many exercises of that sort that have been carried out in the last fifteen years does not warrant much optimism in this respect; it also shows why cases of success – there seem to be a few – should be considered from an operational viewpoint as happy accidents, in so far as we do not know *a priori* where and how to reproduce them, rather than as the outcome of a well-formed reasoning that could be applied to other corpora within predictable limits (see below § 4.2.1). On the linguistic antecedents of this belief in a possible 'catalysis' of etic into emic features, or on the 'continuum' which is supposed to underlie the transition from the former to the latter, see the positions of Hjelmslev and Shaumian, respectively, recalled in Gardin 1967: 29. The doubts which I expressed then on the applicability of these views in archaeology or cultural anthropology (or indeed in any science) now seem to me much too shy; hence the above reformulation in stronger terms.

reflect this diversity, through either of two means: it may list explicitly the correspondences established between different specialized terminologies related to the same objects (synthetic approach), or it may provide a basis such that any scholarly designation can *a priori* be reduced to a particular combination of IL terms, within a certain range

Figure 11 The necessary relations between IL and SL. *I*: the information language used in Compilations C_c is not only a reservoir of data for *future* reformulations in the scientific language of Explanation C_e (path *c*, as in fig. 6), but also a reflection of positions taken in *past* Explanations with respect to the way archaeological materials should be described and understood (path *d*). *II*: a reciprocal relation is thus established between IL and SL, giving birth to the cyclical process described further on, in which the successive states of the two interdependent semiological systems mark out the progress of knowledge towards an ideal point ω where IL and SL are fused (see fig. 15).

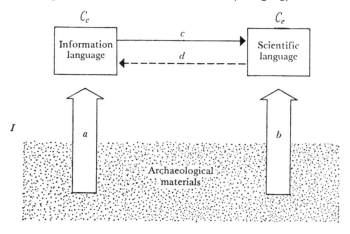

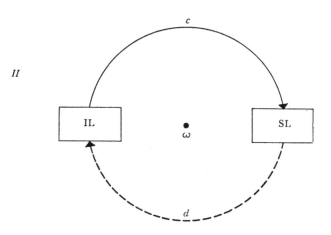

of approximation (analytic approach).[20] In both cases, the dependence of IL on SL stands out clearly, without impairing the autonomy of the former, as argued above: figure 11 shows this ambivalence of IL, both rooted in SL and yet free to invent new formulations for its own practical purposes.

3.4 *The ordering of IL representations*

Our definition of Compilations (§ 2.3) can now be made more complete through the addition of a short, but important specification, in italics: 'sets of *IL*-propositions interrelated in various ways, describing material remains that have been brought together in a systematic whole so as to facilitate the study of ancient peoples'. The indexing sheets which are used for recording objects on punched cards, magnetic tapes, etc., provide clear examples of what is meant here (fig. 12): the words or symbols written on each sheet constitute an IL-proposition, as understood in this definition. Any number of sheets related to a set of objects which the compiler has treated as a whole form a Compilation, C_c. An electronic file made up of 10,000 propositions of this kind, relating for example to a set of potsherds collected on a given site, is a Compilation in the same sense as a printed catalogue of the same finds, described in a non-coded language. And these descriptions themselves are again IL-propositions, even if they are couched in outwardly natural terms, as shown in § 3.3.2: they follow conventions that are *not* those of natural language, unless we are ready to allow that archaeological knowledge plays no part in the drafting of a proper description . . .

A substantial difference exists, however, between the two forms of compilation, with respect to the order in which the IL-propositions are presented to the user. In the case of an electronic file, this order is, as we know, of relatively minor importance: or rather, we have to distinguish three moments in the ordering process, which make it possible to rearrange the data at will in a large number of ways: (*a*) The ordering of IL-propositions as they are entered in the file (input); (*b*) The ordering of the same data within the file itself (internal organization); (*c*) finally, the ordering of part or all of the data as extracted from the file and presented to users in the form of print-outs or display screens, in response to their particular needs. The French word for computer, 'ordinateur', clearly conveys the fact that the basic function of the machine is here to produce those various rearrangements or orderings of the data, rather than to perform computations in the strictly arithmetical sense: the ultimate goal is not to end up with *one* preferential order, but rather

20 Abundant illustrations can be found in the codes mentioned above (note 9): the Code for the analysis of paintings on Greek vases is a good example of the synthetic approach (Salomé 1979), while the Code for the analysis of Ornament is an extreme manifestation of the analytical one (Gardin 1978a).

Types	A	φ	...		p q r	r 1	r 2
Body	B	top ... | ... bottom ... | ...		transition ...	H/W ...	T/B ...	aperture ...
Base	C	a e	profile ...	slope	transition ...	dimensions ...	number ...
	D	y	ext. ...	int. ...		transition	...
Neck	E	φ	profile ...	transition ...		dimensions ...	
Rim	F	inflection ... slope ...		int. ext.	i u o	end ... end ...	details ...
Handle — Type	G	φ	af at a'	ef et e'		number ...	< = >
Handle — Location	H	upper point ...		lower point ...		w ...	
Handle — Shape	I	profile ...		i u o	w b g	slope ...	
Handle — Section	J	...		details		...	
Handle — Details	K	...	f t n	decoration ...		dimensions ...	
Spout — Type	L	φ ... n		location ...	k t h	dimensions ...	
Spout — Shape	M	upper side ...		lower ...		i u o	
Spout — Section	N	p q r	a e j	details ...		decoration ...	
Details	P	...		φ 1 2 ...		decoration ...	
General features	Q	dimensions ...		< = > − +		material ...	
	R	technique ...		texture ...		colour ...	
	S	decoration ...				colour ...	
Special types	Z	φ 1 2 3 ...			n	p q z	
Origin	...						
References	...						

to contrive any number of arrangements suited to the user's specifications c, irrespective of the circumstances of input a, while the internal organization b is only to be regarded as a means to expedite the transitions from a to c.

In the case of the printed catalogue, on the contrary, the order of descriptive propositions is generally unique. It can be a reflection of the acquisition process, i.e. a chronological input order, as in a above (as in some inventories of archives or libraries). More often, however, the IL-propositions are grouped on the basis of the number of identical or neighbour terms which they have in common; the resulting classification, which plays the role of order b above, then becomes the major way of access to the materials in the Compilation (e.g. catalogues of objects classed by dates, origins, materials, functions, etc.). The retrieval process is easy only when the elements or themes on which searches are conducted can be expressed in the terms of the adopted classification; but this restriction may be deemed too strong. The compiler must then add to the catalogue one or several indexes in which other elements or themes are considered, so that the user may collect new series of data, which the organization of the catalogue has caused to be scattered among various classes. Such rearrangements under different index entries have the same function as orders of type c in the preceding case; but they are necessarily limited in number, and cannot therefore anticipate all the searches which users will wish to conduct in the compilation, even within the limits of the selected language of representation.

This parallel between computerized data bases and the more traditional printed catalogues shows that there is no need to linger over the *theoretical* problems of classification in the case of Compilations. Since the function of the two varieties is identical, and since we can do without *a priori* orders in the first one (data base), it follows that the use of classifications and indexes in the second (catalogue) is only intended as an answer to *practical* difficulties that are peculiar to the printed catalogue (fixed location of IL-propositions and their constituent terms, limitations on the combinations of elements that can form classification headings or index entries for use in retrieval, etc.). In other words, there is no such thing as a *theoretical* problem of classification in the case of constructions C_c; and the issues that are raised under this heading can only deal with matters of practical convenience rather than epistemological foundation: given a set of objects and the kind of services which their compilation is to render, what is the most efficient way of organizing the descriptive propositions, taking into account the constraints inherent

---

Figure 12 (*opposite*)   Example of an indexing sheet used for describing archaeological materials in terms of an 'analytical code', i.e. an information language suited to retrieval operations on punched cards or computers (adapted from Gardin 1976: 103).

in the printed forms of exposition?[21] The preferences that may be given at one time for a geographical or a chronological order, at another time for a classification presented by the author as a functional typology (§ 4.1.2) etc., should in no way be considered theoretical options, which would be at variance with the conception of such works. On the other hand, all utilitarian justifications are admissible, as long as they refer to the practical purpose of the compilation; it only remains to assess in each case whether the proposed order meets that purpose. The evaluation methods available to that end have been known and used for many years in the world of scientific information in general; they seem, however, to be mostly ignored in archaeology, so that a few words may be now added on what those methods are and what they do.

3.5 *Evaluation problems: the genesis and updating of Compilations*

Let us leave aside for the moment the way a language of representation is built, for a given compilation, and examine instead how we can measure the adequacy of this language, after it has taken shape. The analogy drawn earlier between the classification systems used in libraries and the representational languages implemented in archaeological compilations (§ 3.3.1) will help us once more to understand the general approach. Suppose we are in an archaeological library looking for documents containing plans of houses built in Sicily in the 2nd millenium B.C.; and let us assume that this library has been organized by subjects, according to a classification scheme in which the nearest heading for our question would be for instance: 'Bronze age: islands of the Western Mediterranean'. It is unlikely that the documents classified under this heading will all contain plans of houses, and more unlikely still that all the houses described will be from Sicily, and dated between 2000 and 1000 B.C. In other words, when going through the documents found, the reader will discover that only some of them answer the question; others are irrelevant, because they deal with remains that are not houses, or with houses that belong to other time and space categories. In the jargon of information science, this irrelevant fraction of the list of references is sometimes called the 'noise' of the information system for the question under consideration, on the basis of a metaphorical, largely unfounded analogy with the meaning of this term in the mathematical theory of information. Obviously, the noise should be minimized as much as possible; the way to do this is by refining the classification or indexing

---

21 Let us be fair: this question arises *also* in the case of electronic files, in so far as the internal organization of the data may in part depend on the kind of retrieval operations that are anticipated; only, the obligation to answer it is more pressing in the case of printed catalogues, for the reasons that I have just recalled. I had this relative freedom of organization in mind when I proposed to define Compilations as 'sequences of IL propositions *interrelated in various ways*', etc.

language. In this case, for instance, one could first *subdivide* the geographical terms, so as to be able to designate Sicily alone, among the islands of the western Mediterranean; secondly, *change* the system of chronological classification, which could be a decimal system indicating millenia and centuries rather than broader periods like the Bronze Age; lastly, *add* to the Space and Time categories a subheading specifying the kinds of remains concerned, in order to form compound indications of a narrower scope, as the following: 'Bronze Age: Islands of the Western Mediterranean: Architecture'.

However, even if we finally end up with a classification that has been refined to the point of containing exactly the heading wanted – for instance, 'Sicily: 2nd Millenium B.C.: Houses' – it does not follow that the outcome of the search will necessarily be satisfactory. The subject headings are used as indicators of the *overall* contents of books, they do not single out all the geographical origins, all the time periods, all the objects which may be mentioned in them for any particular reason (comparative studies, discussions on origin, diffusion, function, etc.). Documents that are concerned *in part* with the subject may therefore have been classified under other headings (e.g. Neolithic, Danubian lands, Social organization), even though they contain archaeological and historical materials that are more or less directly related to our question. These missing references, when they can be observed, constitute what may be called symmetrically the 'silence' of the information system. One way to reduce the 'silence', with this example, would be to introduce into the classification two different levels of analysis, corresponding to the distinction just made between the main or major subject on the one hand, and secondary or incidental topics on the other.[22] It is likely that one would then have to go one step further than the classification of books on shelves according to their main topic: a subject index would also be necessary, to take care of the secondary topics. In other words, the language of our classification would develop into a richer and more flexible indexing language; but the status and function of both would be the same within the broader category of information languages as defined above.

The evaluation of information languages is performed in all circumstances along these lines.[23] In short, the idea is to determine, in the

22 Or again, if the 'silence' was due to the fact that some of the elements specified in the question were not mentioned nor even 'included' in the classification (in the same sense as Sicily is said to be included in the Mediterranean islands, or houses in Architecture), one would have to add new terms to the classification, at the proper level of generality.
23 All the handbooks on information science have a chapter on evaluation methods, rightly considered as the unique way to ground our judgments on the adequacy of information systems: see for example Cros, Gardin & Lévy (1964: ch. 5), Vickery (1973: ch. 1), Meadow (1973: ch. 7), etc. Opinions differ, however, as to the kind of formulas that best measure the efficiency of such systems, in terms of relations between

course of using a Compilation, the extent of the two kinds of dysfunction illustrated above – 'noise' and 'silence' – when carrying out searches on specific subjects, and then to identify the deficiencies of the information language (code, classification, index, etc.) which are to be blamed. In order to be able to perform evaluations, one has to resort to standard lists that indicate for each of the test questions the materials or documents held relevant in those under consideration; noise and silence are measured in each case by reference to a standard list of this sort. The method is admittedly quite pragmatic; but there is no room for any other. This is why we insist on regarding Compilations as mere practical tools for collecting materials under more or less precise descriptive headings, while rejecting the thought that practicality or precision could be regarded in this case as tokens of the *theoretical* merits of the work, even when the language of representation seems to be highly sophisticated.[24]

Another consequence of the relativity of the whole process is to destroy the fiction of an 'ideal' language of representation, for any given category of archaeological remains, such that no other one could be found more efficient for retrieval operations of any sort. The refutation at this point is easy: depending on whether the users, who are ultimately the 'judges' of the language, will want to apply it to the handling of excavation archives, or to the retrieval of objects scattered in various collections and museums, or to the production of taxonomic series regardless of origin and location, etc., their definition of any 'ideal' representation is likely to vary, even though the materials concerned may be identical. In other words, it is not only legitimate but advantageous that the same objects give rise to different descriptions, in Compilations that are intended for so many distinct purposes or user groups; and the evaluation process makes no sense if it does not take the latter into consideration, in terms that have to be carefully specified, and therefore highly specific as well.

The evaluation of a Compilation, in the above sense, can take place at two different moments and with two different goals in mind: either while the language of representation is being developed, for the purpose of assessing what the descriptions should be, given the uses to which the Compilation is to be put; or later on, when modifications are deemed necessary as a consequence of fresh observations or discoveries. In the first case, the evaluation techniques are instrumental in the reasoned

noise and silence, quantified in different ways: inventories of the proposed measures can be found in De Prospo *et al.* (1973), Farradane (1974), etc. But those tactical differences in no way overrule the obligation to abide by the same strategy of empirical evaluation, when embarking upon Compilations of some magnitude.

24 I am not sure that I have always been immune myself from a specious belief in the epistemological worth of Compilations for which I was in part responsible (Allard *et al.* 1963, Christophe & Deshayes 1964, Digard *et al.* 1975); hence a number of recent clarifications which should put an end to possible misunderstandings on this point: Digard (1975: vol. 1, pp. 10–16), Gardin (1977a).

genesis of the language of representation; whereas in the latter they constitute the mainspring of its evolution, as the quantitative and qualitative progress of knowledge makes *updating* necessary (fig. 7, p. 34). The two patterns are not in fact very different; they both illustrate the 'vital' function of evaluation, literally speaking,[25] since without it all compilations would sooner or later be discarded, having lost touch with the changing world of ideas and facts that sustain the movement of science (fig. 11, p. 54).

It is all the more remarkable that the subject of evaluation should hold such a small place in archaeological literature, and more generally in the humanities which are the favourite domain of Compilations. One seldom sees inventories, or catalogues in which the semiological system can be shown to be the product of much thought about the use for which it is intended, or about the empirical evidence of its adequacy. This strange silence may be explained in several ways: it may be the legacy of an era of collectors and antiquaries, when 'bringing materials together' was more important than finding a rationale for their description; or it may be a result of the comfortable habit of relying on pictorial presentation, despite the inconsistency of this behaviour on the part of a scientist, as stressed in § 3.1 (p. 33); or again it may be due to the weakness of learned societies in the humanities, compared with the strength of scientific associations in disciplines like physics, engineering, chemistry, etc., which have recently played such an essential role in the development of information tools. There are many reasons to believe, however, that this legacy of traditional scholarship will gradually give way to intellectual attitudes and organizational patterns of a different brand. I have dwelt elsewhere on the basis for this forecast, as well as on the kind of changes that may be expected (Gardin 1975). Does it mean to suggest that only benefits are to be reaped from such an evolution? That is quite a different matter, to which I shall return in the concluding pages of this book (§ 7.3).

25 A function that has been perfectly acknowledged in information science, as witnessed by the merging of the two aspects in the more recent studies on 'the *design* and *evaluation* of information systems' (Swanson 1975).

4
The analysis of explanations

By way of transition, let us first recall the way in which archaeologists usually proceed in assessing the utility of a given Compilation: it is by playing the familiar game of comparisons or 'parallels'. Considering a given object, and a Compilation C_c relating to the same category of materials, we describe it in the terms of the language used for the same purpose in C_c, and then look for its 'parallels', i.e. for the objects that have an identical or similar description in C_c. If we think that the list is too long, that is in part irrelevant, we infer that the analytical grid is too loose (or our question badly phrased); conversely, if the list is held to be incomplete, because it does not mention objects that we regard as relevant, the inference will be that the grid is too fine (or our question badly phrased). We can also follow the reverse course, starting with a symbolic representation (i.e. a description formulated in the language used in C_c), in order to construct a set of fictitious objects that are compatible with this representation: depending on whether we regard this set as too heterogeneous or too meagre – or possibly both – we shall determine the kind of modifications needed in C_c, in the sense of refining or broadening the grid. Tests of this sort are quite common, and it is easy to show that they provide the usual mechanisms of validation for all Compilations, in the natural sciences as well as in the humanities (Gardin 1969); they imply, however, some trust in the judgment of the creators or users of C_c when they resort to qualifications such as 'irrelevant', 'incomplete', 'heterogeneous', 'meagre' . . . Which means that the evaluation of Compilations in fact relies on a science of *classification* that we need to investigate further.

Such will be the starting point of our analysis of explanatory constructions in this chapter – or in abridged form Explanations, C_e – as defined above (§ 2.4). We shall indeed observe, as many before us, that the classification of material remains is one of the exercises that archaeologists seem to favour most, and that it can be regarded as a primitive form of Explanation, to the extent that the status of the proposed classes is not the same as the status of the orders adopted in Com-

pilations (§ 3.4), *depending on the circumstances of the respective constructions.*

4.1 *Typological constructions*

'If I were permitted to focus upon a simple issue and treat it as the focal
point of the complex and tricky business of archaeological theory and its
developmental course, I should single out the concept and operation of
classification' (Chang 1967a: 4). I share the same view, except for the
expression 'focal point', which may be misleading: classification is
neither the centre nor the goal of theoretical constructions in archaeology, according to our definition (§ 2.4), but only the initial phase of a
reasoning process that is directed towards other ends. True, there are
cases where a distribution of objects or monuments into classes is
presented as the final product of a so-called typological effort; but the
authors of such works would certainly claim that they have achieved
more than a mere catalogue. The first question to consider is therefore
the following: what is the difference between the ordering of materials
in a Compilation and a typology of the same materials in an Explanation?

The answer naturally depends on the definition of the word 'typology'
– a hopeless task if ever there was one, judging by the diversity of the
constructions that bear this title, as well as by the numerous studies
devoted to the 'typological concept' (Krieger 1944) in the last thirty
years (for a summary of the 'typological debate', see Hill & Evans 1972).
I shall therefore refrain from taking any definite stand in relation to this
abundant literature; the definition which follows does not pretend to
represent a common denominator among those which have preceded it,
but only to express the characteristics that I shall need in order to
answer the above question. I shall provisionally call 'typology' *any
classification of material remains used as the basis of inferences relating to facts
that are not included in the initial representation of those materials.* Let me first
illustrate this rather abstract definition with a few simple examples.

Example 1. Suppose we are dealing with a collection of potsherds coming
from a stratigraphic excavation that have been initially classified on the
basis of intrinsic properties exclusively (e.g. material, techniques, shapes,
decoration, etc.); and let us assume that correlations have later been
observed between some of those classes and the stratigraphical origin of
the corresponding sherds. The natural bent of archaeologists will be to
infer from such correlations a chronological ordering of the classes, which
was not explicitly contained in the initial description.

The situation would be the same if this order were the product of a
seriation procedure in which extrinsic data had played no part (e.g.
data such as the stratigraphical allocations above), provided that the

archaeologist had some reason for interpreting this order chronologically.

In both cases, the final order of the construction is 'typological',
following our definition, because it ascribes to the proposed classes a
historical meaning which they did not have in the initial Compilation.

Example 2. Suppose now that we are preparing a catalogue of sculptures
located in various museums but mostly of unknown origin. This latter
fact does not preclude the building-up of an initial classification, that
may be termed centripetal, in which only the analogies and differences
observed in the objects themselves are taken into consideration, to the
exclusion of any external data; the resulting order then falls into the
C_c category. But let us assume that we later discover elsewhere, for
instance in excavations, a number of sculptures that can be ascribed to a
precise origin (region, city, workshop, etc.), and which present some
similarities, in terms of empirical or formal 'measures' of any kind, with
given classes of C_c. The archaeologist will probably infer a geographical
or more generally topical interpretation of the latter, by which I mean
that he will present these classes as distinctive of various 'locations',
in the more abstract sense of the word (countries, towns, schools, workshops, artists, etc.); he may then go one step further, and consider each
class as a regional or stylistic 'type', in the narrower sense which we shall
discuss below (§ 4.1.2).

Example 3. Lastly, let us consider a catalogue of heterogeneous tools –
knives, hammers, axes, etc. – collected on various sites, and presented in
a number of morphofunctional categories (e.g. blades with a transversal
edge, with a longitudinal haft-hole) which are supposed to reflect a
logical organization of the world of Tools more or less independent of
time and space (as in Christophe & Deshayes 1964). By studying the
'context' in which some or all of the objects have been found (e.g.
kitchens, workshops, farms, etc.), one may be led to formulate hypotheses on their respective functions in one or several human groups, and
thereby to propose a more meaningful classification, from an anthropological viewpoint. This new classification can be considered as a
typology, in terms of our provisional definition.

This last example shows that the concept of 'types' is here understood
on more than one level: it applies not only to the constitution of homogeneous groups of *objects* on the basis of their attributes, both intrinsic and
extrinsic (4.1.1), but also to the definition of classes of a more abstract
nature – e.g. *assemblage, culture, technocomplex*, etc. – whose elements are
made up of the preceding groups, arranged according to various criteria
(see § 4.3). Strictly speaking, we should therefore have proscribed in the
following pages the use of unduly restrictive terms such as 'objects', or
'attributes', and adopted instead a more general vocabulary for designating respectively the *entities* that are to be classified, the *elements* which

form the basis of the classification, and the *groups* produced by the classification procedure – granted that more or less standard names can be given to the manifestations of each category according to the level of archaeological conceptualization, as illustrated in the table below (the designations used from level 2 onwards can be replaced by others to

Levels of integration	Elements	Entities	Groups
I	attributes	objects (aggregates of attributes)	types
2	types	assemblages (aggregates of types)	cultures
3	cultures	–	–

suit different systematizations of archaeological units). I have, however, preferred to use the more suggestive terms of level 1 only, with the understanding that the analysis which follows holds also for any higher level.

4.1.1 *Intrinsic and extrinsic attributes*
The characteristic of typological constructions, in our three examples, is that the final classification is determined by attributes that were not present in the initial representation of the materials. Attributions of Time in the first example, Location in the second, and Function in the third, have been introduced after the materials had first been described in terms of their immediate physical properties; they were in each case the outcome of operations related to the terms of these descriptions, but which called on hypotheses or data external to the latter – *hypotheses*, for instance, in the case of a seriation, where it is assumed that a sequential order based on step by step similarities indicates an evolution in time; or external *data*, on the other hand, when relations are established between some of the materials or attributes under study and extraneous objects or facts, as a basis for spatial or functional attributes.

Figure 13 illustrates this transition from the more immediate attributes, in C_e, to the reasoned attributions that characterize typologies in C_e. A simple and apparently correct way of understanding the transformation would be to say that it consists in going from the *intrinsic* properties of archaeological objects – their material, their shape, the pictographic signs which they bear, etc. to *extrinsic* characterizations such as their date, origin, destination, etc. The temptation would then be to reify the opposition by drawing an absolute distinction between categories that are supposed to be essentially intrinsic (Technology, Morphology, Signs in the broad sense: inscriptions, ornament, signatures, etc.) and others that are extrinsic by definition: Time, Place or Location, Function (utilitarian, sociological, symbolic, etc.). This viewpoint may, however, land us in difficulty. First, it is not exceptional for intrinsic features to provide information of the most explicit kind on the date, origin, and function of archaeological materials. Such is the case in particular when inscriptions mention in a perfectly unambiguous way the *time* when a monument was built (e.g. tombs dated by an inscribed stele referring

Figure 13   The transition from the compilatory orders adopted in C_c (for documentation or retrieval purposes) to the explanatory orders proposed in C_e (taxonomies, typologies, etc.), through the application of classification procedures based on methodological postulates or on external evidence unused in C_c. This transition consists most of the time in inferring new extrinsic attributes (origin, date, function) from the intrinsic properties listed in C_c (path 2), occasionally from the extrinsic ones as well (path 4); but it can also consist in redefining the classification adopted in C_e in terms of new (arrangements of) intrinsic properties alone, after a reconsideration of the intrinsic (path 1) or extrinsic (path 3) features listed in C_c. The feedback loop at the bottom thus portends the relativity of the contrast between orders C_c and C_e through time (see fig. 15).

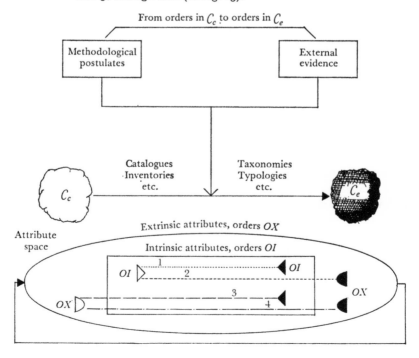

to a known era), or the *place* where it was made (e.g. coins bearing the name of the mint), or even its *function*, in the broad sense here given to that word (e.g. painted scenes with legends indicating the names of the actors, the kind of event in which they are taking part, etc.) . . . It would be tricky to maintain in this case an opposition between, for example, the intrinsic features relating to the form of inscriptions (i.e. the palaeographic features exclusively) and the extrinsic attributes provided by their substance: the transformation schematized in figure 13 would then amount to nothing more than reading and understanding the written text. The more 'natural' course is therefore to include these attributes among the intrinsic data.[1] In other words, a catalogue of steles arranged in a chronological order on the basis of inscribed dates is not, to me, a typology, nor is a catalogue of coins classified by mints, or a catalogue of paintings grouped according to the titles which their authors have given them.

A second objection to the absolute view suggested above is that, conversely, there are many situations in which intrinsic features are not immediately perceptible, and where they can only be determined through reasoning which has the same function as that illustrated by figure 13. This is what happens for instance in the case of fragmentary objects or monuments, where the archaeologist attempts to restore complete forms, decorations, texts, etc., or, more generally, intrinsic properties through comparison with other materials. Restitutions in that sense can formally be assimilated to typological constructions: the goal is indeed to allocate objects to classes that are not immediately derived from the initial description; but these classes are still defined in terms of intrinsic properties (Form, Signs, etc.), and this contradicts our tentative distinction.

We therefore have to qualify the latter: the transition from C_c orders to C_e typologies cannot be reduced to a search for extrinsic attributes, above and beyond intrinsic properties, since that search may take place in a space of properties that contains features of both categories at each end of the process (fig. 13). The so-called intrinsic characterizations that

---

1 I realize how relative this concept of 'nature' may be: let the reading of our inscriptions be difficult, hypothetical, controversial, we shall immediately cease to consider that the corresponding attributions belong to the intrinsic part of the description; they will be regarded rather as the result of an explanatory construction C_e, in which one goes from intrinsic features – palaeographic, iconographic – to extrinsic attributions in terms of space, time, meaning, etc. However, it could be shown that this alternative is but another manifestation of the changing status of distinctive features in scientific constructions, depending on whether they reflect hypothetical interpretations or the established order of things, at a given time (see above § 2.5). There is therefore nothing wrong in considering the reading of an inscription sometimes as an intrinsic characterization, when it is not open to discussion, sometimes as an extrinsic one if other readings are being proposed.

regularly occur in C_c can also determine typological orders in C_e; whereas conversely the so-called extrinsic categorizations that are normally the end-product of C_e can also be present in C_c. Consequently, what defines a typological construction is rather the addition or the substitution of new descriptive categories to those of the initial representation, as a result of reasoning that calls on hypotheses or data external to the latter, but without any necessary difference in nature between the initial and the final categories.

Let us have a closer look at the different situations which may then arise, using the following abbreviations:

OI orders based on intrinsic features alone, chosen in any of the following spheres:

P the 'physics' of objects, i.e. material constituents, features relating to the techniques of fabrication or decoration, etc.

G the 'geometry' of objects, i.e. shapes, features relating to dimensions, profiles, volumes, etc.

S the 'semiotics' of objects, i.e. ornament, iconographical representations, signatures, inscriptions, etc.

OX orders based *also* on extrinsic features, chosen in any of the following spheres:

T Time, i.e. chronological indications of all kinds, concerning various phases in the history of archaeological objects (genesis, transformation, disuse, re-employment, etc.)

L Location, understood in a broad sense, so as to include not only spatial or geographical attributions proper (toponyms), but also affiliations to anthropological entities of various sorts (creators or manufacturers: workshops, schools, societies, cultures, etc.)

F Function, also understood on several levels: physical or material (e.g. destination of a tool), sociological (e.g. allotment of edifices or rooms to different activities: political, religious, etc.), ecological (e.g. adaptation of sites to environmental constraints), symbolic (e.g. meaning of iconographical representations), etc.[2]

2 For a justification of this admittedly very wide sphere, see § 4.3.3. More generally, our triads $\{P, G, S\}$ and $\{L, T, F\}$ are here intended as mere *illustrations* of the meaning given to 'intrinsic' and 'extrinsic' attributes, respectively; any other arrangement would meet the purpose, within each of the two families. As an illustration of this latitude, let me point out that I have here omitted one of the dimensions used in chapter 1 for eliciting the basis of current divisions of archaeology into specialized fields, namely H, the human entities under study (§ 1.1). For the purpose of the forthcoming argument, suffice it to say that the values or states of the H variables or attributes can generally be expressed by particular combinations of L and T (on this point, see below § 4.3, beginning). The same is true of most stylistic attributions, by virtue of the broad meaning here attached to variables L and T; on possible criteria for separating stylistic and functional attributes (as in F above), see Dunnell (1978).

Path 1: transition from OI_i to OI_j

Suppose we have a catalogue of ceramics intuitively grouped in broad classes on the basis of physical constituents (e.g. coarse *vs.* fine clay, glazed *vs.* unglazed surfaces) and geometrical shape (e.g. open *vs.* closed body, large *vs.* small base); we may think fit to look for other possible classifications of the materials in terms of similar P and G attributes, but through quantitative methods of higher repute than our impressionistic groupings. The situation then can be described as that of a transformation $OI_i{\rightarrow}OI_j$, where both the initial classification (OI_i) and the final typology (OI_j) are defined in terms of intrinsic features only, without any reference to attributes T, L or F.

But is the resulting classification OI_j a typology? If we stand by our former definition of typologies (p. 63), the answer would tend to be a negative one: we have done no more than substitute one classification for another, without drawing more anthropological inferences from the one than from the other, so that we still find ourselves in the realm of constructions C_c, prior to the explanatory exercises of which the typological game is an example, if a primitive one. Conversely, if we consider figure 13, the answer may be positive: the transformation is at least subject to a hypothesis, implicit or explicit, according to which an order based on a mathematical classification procedure is, *a priori*, 'better' than any order founded on intuition – failing which the $OI_i{\rightarrow}OI_j$ exercise would here make no sense. But this postulated superiority cannot be claimed while remaining in the sphere of constructions C_c, since we have demonstrated that in this sphere ordering as such is of little import, so little that it could in fact be dispensed with altogether, or made to fit practical constraints that have little to do with the explanatory goals of typologies (§ 3.4). We therefore have to connect the alleged superiority of OI_j with its higher explanatory power, at least potentially, that is until empirical findings have confirmed (hopefully) the rightfulness of the postulate.

Which of the two conflicting viewpoints shall we choose? On the one hand, it seems reasonable to claim that a class of which we know, so to speak, the genetic formula, has more 'reality' than one based solely on the feelings or impressions of compilers, heedless of the demands of explicitness. On the other hand, it is *also* reasonable to claim that if this 'real' class cannot be correlated with empirical data, in any of the T, L, F spheres defined above, its formal virtues lose much of their value. In other words, which of the following should we prize more: classes that are well-formed in mathematical or logical terms, even when we are unable to 'make any sense' out of them, literally speaking, or classes that do have some cultural meaning, but no formal basis? The alternative has been a subject of embarrassment to many theoreticians, in several fields of scientific observation. To take but one illustrious archaeological example, K. C. Chang has long fought with this very issue, without much success. After denying that 'types' could be defined without referring to *specific* interpretative goals, Chang proposes a distinction between two kinds of types of which only the first one meets this requirement: whereas 'relative types' are tied to behavioural patterns characteristic of a given social or cultural system, 'objective types', as Chang calls them, are defined on the basis of 'cross-cultural and cross-social criteria that are, to the best of our knowledge, universally valid and applicable' (Chang 1968: 4). Since an archaeologist is usually concerned with the remains and history of *specific* societies, he should normally pay attention to relative types alone; as for the others, we can only postulate or hope that they will be 'useful in establishing categories out of which relative types are to be isolated' (*ibid.*) – which is another way of crediting them with the *potential* explanatory virtues mentioned above.

My own conventions in this matter will be the following: first, I shall separate the optional, contingent and utilitarian orders in Compilations, the unique function of which is to provide access to information, from the classifications derived in part from theoretical hypotheses – either methodological, as in the above example, or historical, as we shall see below – whether the latter be well-founded or not.[3] Then, I shall abide by the usage which consists in calling typologies or typological all classifications of the latter kind, irrespective of the way in which they have been derived. However, I shall designate as 'neutral' typologies or neutral types – rather than 'objective', a term which I find confusing[4] – the products of any ordering process conducted from OI_i to OI_j, as discussed in this section, neutrality being understood with respect to the T, L, F attributes, which are not brought into play here.[5]

3 Incidentally, the hypothesis made above concerning the *a priori* superiority of mathematical as opposed to intuitive classifications does not seem to be defendable in any way, rational or empirical (see below § 4.2.1); but this personal opinion has no bearing on the principle of the argument developed in this section.

4 Objectivity in our context may mean either of two things: either an avoidance of personal, 'subjective' bias in descriptions and classifications, or the existence of relations between abstract concepts and empirical facts. Chang's 'objective types' are objective only in the first sense, whereas the same expression, to me, rather conveys the second meaning (see § 2.3).

5 This designation is a concession to usage: I would rather have reserved the name 'typologies' to classifications that convey some information in any of the T, L, or F spheres (as in cases 2, 3 and 4 below), and used another word, for instance 'taxonomies', for the intrinsic orders hitherto considered, that have no immediate meaning, historical, geographical, or other. But it has become customary to consider such orders as types in their own right (e.g. Clarke 1968: 187–229), and to embrace under the general title of 'numerical taxonomy', on the other hand, all the classifications that have been obtained mathematically, whether they have a cultural meaning or not. Moreover, the contrast between 'taxonomies' and 'typologies' has already been given quite another sense (Rouse 1972: 52–3); for further views on these matters of terminology, see below, § 4.1.2, fig. 23.

Path 2: transition from OI to OX

Let us now turn to the case where the same collection of potteries as above, initially classified on the basis of intrinsic attributes *P* or *G*, is reorganized according to categories of the *T*, *L* or *F* groups, taken separately or combined. This kind of transformation will be more familiar to the reader: the goal is to determine classes of objects which present a more or less homogeneous distribution with respect to time (*T* types), space (*L* types) – or more often both (*TL* types) – or which present a certain functional unity, in physical, social or symbolic terms (*F* types), in a given geo-chronological setting (*TLF* types). This is the typological game par excellence, played here in an inductive sense, from effects to causes: starting from the premise that the variability of intrinsic *properties P, G, S* is related to the *circumstances* in which objects and monuments have been made and used (where, when, who, why, how, etc.), the archaeologist tries to infer from the former, suitably ordered, insights about the specificity of the times when some classes of pottery were made but not others (*T* types), the specificity of regions or work-shops characterized by different productions (*L* types), the specificity of behavioural patterns associated to a practical function, a political goal, religious activities, etc., and which are reflected in the relative uniformity of objects (*F* types).

The outcome of the exercise is a classification *OX* obtained by cor-relating two sets of variables: extrinsic variables, first, which determine the labels of the proposed classes (e.g. *Neolithic* pottery from . . ., *Norman ware* at the time of . . ., *Funerary vases* in . . ., etc.), and then, intrinsic variables which provide elements for the differential definitions of those classes (fig. 14). The course followed in such cases is always roughly the same: the archaeologist establishes 'parallels' between certain objects characterized by intrinsic features *only* (*P, G, S*), and others that he regards as 'comparable', but for which he can *also* propose extrinsic attributes (*L, T, F*). The latter – the 'type-fossils' in Childe's somewhat old-fashioned terminology (1956: 34) – are usually thought of as lying outside the set of materials under study; in fact, they can also be found within the set when features *L, T* or *F* have been attributed to some at least of the objects classified in *OI*. In both cases, the game of analogies is played in the same way, as a means to transfer the *L, T, F* attributes of the 'type-fossil' to the objects that have comparable *P, G, S* properties. If the process can be extended step by step to a sizable portion of the set, the initial classification *OI* may finally give way to a true typology *OX* that will be all the more valuable as it will count features of the *L, T* or *F* brand.

It is not an exaggeration to say that archaeology is massively engaged in this exercise, and that most of the explanatory constructions of the discipline can be reduced to logical sequences of this nature. To many, the formal monotony of the process may be blurred by the semantic

Figure 14   The transition from classifications based on intrinsic properties *alone,* for documentary purposes, to typologies based *also* on extrinsic attributes. The upward arrow indicates the reverse transition from typologies based on known extrinsic attributes to their rationalization in terms of intrinsic properties.

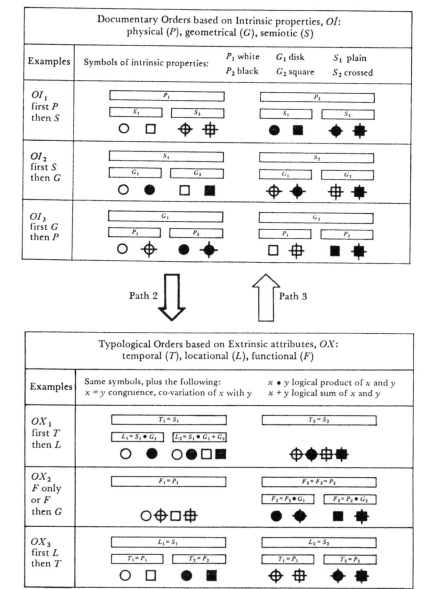

diversity of current interpretations, first on the *TL* axis (events, phases, periods, . . . styles, cultures, schools, etc.), but more so on the broader *F* avenue (modes of production, social organization, religious beliefs, meanings of obscure texts and images, etc.); it is further concealed by the multiplicity of attributes that are liable to be called in, under *P*, *G* or *S*, in order to establish the variability of archaeological materials according to *T*, *L* or *F*. Nevertheless, it remains true that the reasoning is fundamentally the same behind its multifarious manifestations;[6] the fact that it is now assisted or simulated by mathematical and computing techniques does not lessen the monotony of the process.[7]

Path 3: *transition from OX to OI*

A reverse course is possible in the privileged case where attributes *T*, *L*, *F* are known at the start, so much so that they form the basis of the initial order in C_c. Let us go back to the ceramics of our previous example and assume that we are informed not only of their origin in time and space (attributes *T*, *L*), but also of the ways in which they were made and used, in various circumstances (attributes *F*). Our problem then is to find among the intrinsic properties *P*, *G*, *S* of our pots those which show maximum co-variation with the *T*, *L*, *F* classes in C_c. The typological game is here played in the deductive sense, from causes to effects: the typologist seeks to bring out the material consequences or reflections of historical affinities that have been established independently. The product of the construction is then a classification *OI* where types are defined in terms of intrinsic features chosen on the basis of their relationship with more or less coextensive classes in the initial order *OX*.

The interest of this *OX→OI* transformation is that it provides a representation made up of features that can be postulated to have a cognitive or 'explanatory' value, because of the way in which they have been selected: taken one by one or in combination, they help in distinguishing classes of objects that have a different meaning, in any of the usual spheres of interpretation *L*, *T* or *F*. If new objects exhibiting the same features are discovered, we shall then be authorized to propose

6 . . . and behind the innumerable paraphrases that are used to disguise the endless iteration of the same basic operation, namely the establishment of a parallel between *x* and *y* (objects or features, entities or elements): see on this point the legitimate criticism passed on my own rhetorical endeavours in a plain *OI→OX* construction which did not require them (Chevrier 1959).

7 Exposing the monotony of a mental process, as against the variety of its end products both in substance and form, is not the same thing as questioning its utility: let me stress again that the goal of the present book is not to promote new reasoning processes of a more subtle kind in archaeology but only a better understanding of existing ones, in terms of formal and therefore necessarily monotonous patterns – whereby the usefulness of the kind of operations discussed above is not denied.

similar attributes which, if empirically verified, will confirm the diagnostic value of *OI*. This validation process, an indispensable step in the progress of typological constructions (see below § 4.5), can be considered as a return to path 2: the intrinsic properties which now define our classes in *OI* are used as a basis for attributions that lead to another order (or another formulation of the same order in terms of tentative extrinsic categories), *OX*. In fact, the two courses are complementary, and they are usually followed in turns, in a trial and error fashion which does not make it possible – nor indeed desirable – to retrace with precision the history of the oscillations that have led to a given *OI* or *OX* order, as found in archaeological literature.

Path 4: transition from OX_i to OX_j

It is in this mixed or combined sense that the fourth and last case should be understood; for the transition from one system of extrinsic attributes to another is of interest only if it goes through the universe of intrinsic properties once more, so that the changes that take place in the course of this transformation can be assessed. Going back to our imaginary collection of ceramics, let us assume that it has first been organized in an *OX* way, on the basis of space and time attributes (e.g. 'Region L_1, periods $T_1, T_2, \ldots, T_n$; region L_2, periods $T_1, T_2, \ldots, T_n$, etc.'), and that the study of the resulting classes reveals parallel variations in the manufacture of the ware: composition of the clay, firing techniques, surface decoration, etc. The typologist will then be tempted to replace the geo-chronological order by a 'functional' one, in our broad sense of the term, in which a number of intrinsic properties are brought into relation with the *L*, *T* distribution of potteries (in its original or in a revised form) so as to give it an additional meaning with respect, for instance, to the history of technology. The transformation effected in this case is indeed of the kind $OX_i \rightarrow OX_j$, but it only makes sense if we include passage through the intermediate phase *OI* which alone justifies the process: $OX_i \rightarrow OI \rightarrow OX_j$.

Things would not be different if our goal, conversely, was to replace a functional typology ignorant of space and time by a classification taking more account of regional and chronological variations; or again if we decided to re-interpret in chronological terms a seriation that was first presented as a model of diffusion in space, etc. In all such cases – which are numerous in archaeology – it can easily be shown that the change in the system of reference, extrinsically, goes with modifications or additions in the system of representation, intrinsically. This is why the arrow of path 4, in figure 13, passes through the space of intrinsic attributes; and it is also the reason why we may consider this path as a combination of the two preceding ones, taken in the following order: first $OX_i \rightarrow OI_j$ (path 3), then $OI_j \rightarrow OX_j$ (path 2).

If we now go to figure 15, we shall see that this combination is equivalent to a complete cycle or loop $OX_i \rightarrow OX_j$: path 4 appears then as an epitome of the typological approach, in which we continuously call into question past or present organizations of the archaeological record that refer to extrinsic, historically meaningful data (OX_i), in an effort to enrich or replace them by others (OX_j) that have wider or firmer roots in the universe of intrinsic data, OI.

Figure 15   The alternation of intrinsic orders (triangles) and extrinsic orders (half-disks) in the progress of typological constructions, through a succession of operations along paths 2 and 3 aimed at replacing or complementing 'established' orders (in white), as reflected in current Compilations, by tentative orders (in black) which are presented in Explanations as making 'more sense', literally speaking, in terms of extrinsic or intrinsic features. The spiral representation hints at the theoretical convergence of the process at an imaginary point ω where our dichotomies (OI vs. OX, C_c vs. C_e) are no longer necessary. The continuous line q–r–s represents a complete cycle $OX_i \rightarrow OX_j$, which is the definition of path 4.

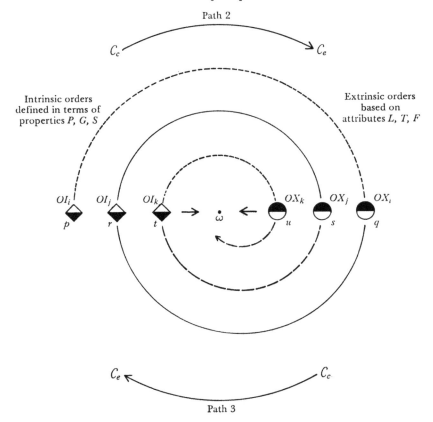

4.1.2 *The intermediate status of typologies*

Seen in this light, the typological approach can be reformulated in a simple though somewhat abstract way, which deepens the tentative definition given at the beginning of § 4.1. The goal remains the drawing of 'inferences relating to facts that are not included in the initial representation' of the materials, but the mechanism of those inferences is now more transparent: it consists in *a systematic matching of intrinsic properties with extrinsic attributes*, through constant to-and-fro motions between the two sets (paths 2 and 3), so as to base the largest number of attributes L, T, F on the smallest number of observations P, G, S (path 4).

At first sight, this revised definition may seem to create confusion, in two contradictory ways: either because we take it as applicable to most of the catalogues and inventories considered in the preceding chapter (C_c), or because we regard it as suited to all explanatory constructions (C_e), rather than only to the typological ones among them. I shall take those two objections in turn.

(A) It is true that a large number of Compilations take the form of classifications based on combinations of intrinsic and extrinsic features. Let us consider, for instance, the three following examples: (a) a catalogue of coins grouped by periods, dynasties, etc. (extrinsic attributes T), it being understood that chronological attributions are here based on reasoning (comparative data) rather than on explicit legends (epigraphical data); (b) an inventory of archaeological materials arranged by sites and layers (extrinsic attributes L) with plates showing the finds from each stratigraphical unit, accompanied by short descriptions of some or all of them; (c) a museum presentation of several thousand tools set out in functional groups according to their intended use (agriculture, woodwork, transportation, etc.: extrinsic attributes F), irrespective of differences in origin (space, time, cultures, etc.). Shall we say that these compilations are typologies under the terms of our definition, since for each of the proposed classes in OX we also have summary descriptions referring to various intrinsic attributes: material, shape, iconography, etc.?

The answer depends, I would say, on the scope and purpose of those descriptions. If, in example *a*, intrinsic data given for each class of coins do not go beyond an immediate reading of the epigraphical and iconographical elements found on each member of the class, we can hardly consider that 'types' have thereby been defined. The situation could be different, however, if some or all of the classes were subdivided into more homogeneous series, each characterized by an explicit combination of such elements: it is not uncommon to speak of those series as 'types', in a loose sense, which is not incompatible with our definition provided that the intrinsic characterizations be sufficiently detailed, and genuinely distinct between the series.

In the same way, in example *b*, no one will claim that the assemblages associated with the various sites and layers have a typological status. Nevertheless, it may happen that the stratigraphical units have been selected in such a way that each assemblage is in fact distinctive of a given geo-historical or cultural group. If this is the case, and if the differential characterizations are explicitly stated (rather than left for the reader to discover through the plates alone, which obviously falls short of our requirements), there is no reason why the compilation should not again be considered as a typology, at least in the broad sense suggested above (§ 4.3, example 3), where typological classes can be formed at different levels of integration in such a way that an assemblage may bear the same relation to its constituents as a type to the attributes which define it.

Lastly, in example *c*, the cross-cultural nature of the functional classes – agricultural implements, woodcarving tools, vehicles, etc. – would tend to deter us from equating the latter with types related to specific regions, periods, or human groups. However, functional differentiations are not any more straightforward than attributions of space and time, so that it would be absurd to deny them a cognitive value equal to that of geo-chronological types, though in another sphere – the sphere of technological evolution, for instance, considered on a world-wide scale from the emergence of man up to the present day. Moreover, one only has to discover within some of the functional groups a number of series that have different distributions in time and space to be inclined to carry the classification further, until one has typology as understood by anthropologists and archaeologists.

It is therefore true that the boundary is not always clear between the classifications found in Compilations and those that claim to be typologies. The examples just discussed suggest that we may place it differently depending on the methodological requirements which we associate with the word 'systematic' in the definition proposed at the beginning of this section. It is not enough to arrange material remains in groups L, T, or F, and provide summary descriptions in terms of features P, G, S to qualify as a typologist in any technical sense of the word: the relation between the groups and the descriptions must be established through procedures that should enable anyone to go unhesitatingly from the observation of features P, G, S to the prediction of attributes L, T, F, or conversely from the observation of attributes L, T, F to the prediction of features P, G, S. The classifications and descriptions that are found in current Compilations usually do not go far in this direction.

(*B*) The converse question bears on the place of typologies among the explanatory constructions of archaeology in general; for it may be argued that the latter are all based on the 'systematic matching of intrinsic properties with extrinsic attributes' that was presented above as the distinctive mark of typologies. Let us only remember the definition of Explanations given earlier (§ 2.4): sets of propositions relating to past events or ways of life, formulated *on the basis of the properties exhibited by a given body of material remains*. A relationship is here postulated between intrinsic properties and the inferences that are drawn from them, concerning practices or events which clearly have the same formal status in Explanations as extrinsic attributes in typologies. Hundreds of examples immediately present themselves: (*a*) the reconstruction of commercial routes in the Mediterranean and Near-eastern regions during the Neolithic period, based on a spectrographic analysis of obsidian objects found from Iran to Sardinia (Dixon, Cann & Renfrew 1968); (*b*) the explanation of the changes observed in the decoration of Arikara pottery (Missouri valley, eighteenth century) through the evolution of residence rules resulting from contacts with Dakota Indians and European immigrants (Deetz 1965); (*c*) the hypothetical reconstruction of agricultural cycles in Central Europe, from a careful study of Neolithic settlements and their successive occupations in time (Soudsky 1966), etc. . . . In all such cases, the mental process is the same: the starting point is a collection of observations relating to material data (properties P, S or G, prevalent in examples a, b, c respectively), which are then brought into relation with space and time distributions (attributes L, T, either given or inferred) in order to lead to the terminal propositions of the construction, regarding particular aspects of the behaviour of ancient peoples in the areas and in the periods mentioned (inferences on the F axis, according to our loose acceptance of 'functional' interpretations: economic activities in a, social organizations in b, agricultural techniques in c, etc.) [8]

Granted that these examples are representative of the kind of constructions which archaeologists undertake by way of Explanations, it would indeed seem logical to consider that typological constructions are a mere subset of the latter. Two differences may however occur. One of them is that a typology necessarily refers to a plurality of objects, by definition (§ 4.1), whereas in an Explanation, the set of objects may be reduced to one. An author may strive to shed some light on a particular object (unpublished, misunderstood, unidentified, etc.), without necessarily ascribing it to a particular type. However, a careful analysis of this kind of construction shows that the difference is illusory: for most of them do in fact resort to comparison between the object under study and others that have something in common with it, which is tantamount to the constitution of series in support of given phases or parts of the interpretation. The inclusion of the object in such series thus plays the same role as its affiliation to a type in the process of archaeological

---

8 The 'terminal propositions' should normally be thought of as the conclusions of the explanatory construction; but others may prefer to regard them as the *hypotheses* which the construction has to establish, under the terms of the hypothetico-deductive model. Those epistemological quibbles will be taken up in due time (§ 7.1.1), they are of no import in the present discussion.

Explanations; consequently the tentative difference put forward above need not detain us longer.

The other difference will prove more substantial: namely, the fact that typological constructions frequently stop at attributions in the *L* and *T* range (space and time), whereas explanatory constructions normally tend to go some steps further in order to reach the sphere of anthropological or historical interpretations. More specifically, we tend to reserve the typological qualification for constructions whose major goal lies avowedly in the *L* or *T* spheres, and to omit it in the case of more ambitious constructions where the definition of *LT* types is only a starting point or an intermediate stage in the process that leads to an explanation in the *F* range. The basis of that explanation is necessarily typological, as hinted at in the preceding paragraph; but it is now implicit in the overall architecture of the Explanation.

This vision of the place of typologies in the realm of explanatory constructions links up with the positions adopted by other archaeologists on the same subject, even though the arguments and the terms may differ. I shall mention for instance Fritz & Plog (1970), who stress the same convergence between classification and Explanation, once a certain level of conceptual ambition is reached, and propose consequently

Figure 16 The various kinds of archaeological classifications differentiated in § 4.1 and their equivalents in former systematizations. The thick line in each column indicates the position of the major dichotomy, conventionally represented as an absolute one in this table, even though it is best understood in a relative sense as shown in fig. 15.

	Proposed distinctions \ Past equivalents	Rouse 1960	Swartz 1967	Chang 1968	Fritz & Plog 1970
Compilations	Documentation-oriented classes (§3.4): classifications	Descriptive types	Classes	Objective types	Classifications with a formal and contextual referent
Compilations ↓	Neutral types: taxonomies (§4.1.1, Path 1)	*Taxonomy*: Descriptive types	*Analysis*: Classes	Objective types	Classifications with a formal and contextual referent
↓	Spatio-temporal types: typologies in this restricted sense (§4.1.2)	*Taxonomy*: Historical types	*Analysis*: Analytic types	Relative types	Classifications with a formal and contextual referent
Explanations	Functional types: interpretative constructions (§4.3)	*Analysis*: Cultural types	*Interpretation*: Functional types	Relative types	Classifications with a functional referent

to distinguish two kinds of classifications: those which rest only on observable empirical facts, 'formal and contextual' – equivalent to our *LT* typologies above – and those which also deal with function ('the kind of use that a particular artifact or feature had in the past . . . the behaviour of constructing and using it') – equivalent to our typologies *F* – thereby acquiring an explanatory quality (1970: 407); also Swartz, a few years earlier, with his opposition between analytical types with a space–time meaning (1967: 490) and functional types, defined 'on the basis of suspected common use' (*ibid.*, 493); or again Rouse, with his subtle distinctions between 'historical types, formed in order to establish differences of time and space' (1960: 318), and cultural types based on 'modes', that is, 'any standard, concept, or custom which govern the behaviour of the artisans of a community' (*ibid.*, p. 313), etc.

(*C*) Figure 16 summarizes the correspondences between these various segmentations of the universe of archaeological classifications. Its value lies essentially in showing that a de facto agreement has been reached for some time, beyond terminological differences, concerning the substance of the more basic distinctions. My own systematization is therefore by no means original: its only departure is that it does not entail rigidly contrasted definitions, which in practice turn out to raise difficulties, but only differences in emphasis or degree that become manifest gradually, as one goes from one kind of order to another. We should, moreover, keep in mind that these distinctions change through time, as the typologies or interpretations accepted at any given moment normally affect the substance and order of subsequent compilations (fig. 15). An unreservedly relativist position therefore seems more appropriate, where the important matter is the understanding of the overall *movements* of constructions on a continuum, rather than the assigning of pigeon-hole positions to all of them.

The foregoing observations finally lead us to propose a somewhat more restrictive definition of *typologies*, which emphasizes the intermediate position of these constructions somewhere between the utilitarian documentary orders in C_c and the more ambitious explanatory orders in C_e: *any ordering of material remains based on a systematic matching of intrinsic and extrinsic attributes, out of which the author seeks to derive information concerning first and foremost the situation of those remains in space and time, broadly understood.*

4.2 *Logicist analysis of typological constructions*

We now have to examine the way in which typologies understood in those terms are built. According to our methodological requirements, subsumed under the word 'logicism' (§ 1.3.5), the problem should be stated as follows: by which sequence of explicitly defined operations does one go from an initial apprehension of archaeological objects to a typology of the same? I shall begin by underlining an obvious difference with the situation illustrated in figure 7, concerning the genesis of Compilations. The goal here is not to produce a system of representation, coupled or not with a classification of the materials, for the sole purpose of making retrieval operations easier; we now have to build up, *through the same two means used differently* (representation and classification), an organization of the material that should tell us something about their situation in space and time, as required by our definition. This change in our objectives is bound to influence the decisions that we have to take at each stage of the chain discussed in chapter 3: selection of the materials (§ 3.2), adoption of a representational language (§ 3.3), selection of an order of presentation (§ 3.4), or, better, of a method capable of generating the order which will be regarded as the most productive (§ 3.5).

Concerning the rationality of the initial selection, there is indeed little to add, *mutatis mutandis*, to the observations of § 3.2: the author of a typology should normally indicate the reasons which have led him to choose certain objects and ignore others when collecting the raw materials of his construction. Unfortunately, it has became the custom to belittle this obligation, as if the criteria of this selection went without saying, or as if they were dictated by circumstances over which the archaeologist had no control. We shall provisionally put up with this usage, by proceeding *as if* the selection was a kind of 'natural' field of observation, which could always be circumscribed in a straightforward way, without resorting to any definite selection procedure; this position will obviously have to be qualified later (§ 5.1.2).

As for the rationality of the language of representation, it is here again closely related to the goal of the construction; in fact, as in the case of Compilations (§ 3.3), the success or failure of the exercise depends largely on the adequacy of that language, so much so that any selection of attributes can be regarded as a good one, 'reasonable' in the etymological sense of the word, if it leads to the definition of types that are well circumscribed in time and space. Description and classification should thus be considered to be two inseparable facets of the typological process, each one 'authorizing' the other in the prospective or retrospective acceptance of the word depending on the sense of the relation. Such at least is the position which I shall endeavour to vindicate after having examined the prevailing strategies of typological construction exemplified in archaeological literature, on the joint grounds of descriptive analysis and synthetic classification. Three such strategies seem to emerge, according to the degree of freedom which the typologist is willing or compelled to observe in the selection of traits and the delimitation of classes. For the sake of convenience, I shall give a name to each of them, which I shall justify in the following sections:

– free constructions (§ 4.2.1)
– guided constructions (§ 4.2.2)
– imposed constructions (§ 4.2.3)

4.2.1 *Free constructions: taxonomic orders*

The typological constructions which I call 'free' are those in which the selection of traits and the classifications of objects are not determined or influenced by any *a priori* knowledge of the distribution of one or the other in space or time. The collection is then processed as a set of entities which have no L or T attributes, and the intrinsic properties of which are not themselves conducive to such attributions, even of a relative kind (by relative attributions, I mean any proposition of the kind: 'object or feature X should or should not be put in the same L or T group as object or feature Y', for any explicit reason: stratigraphical origin, morphological or technological heterogeneity, etc.). This is the the case of typological constructions built *in terra incognita*, when the archaeologist is supposed to know nothing of the geographical, chronological, or 'cultural' coordinates of the objects under study. Situations of this sort, in my opinion, are rare; or more exactly, I believe that the archaeologist seldom behaves as if he were totally without a clue as to the L or T attributes of the objects or features which he is studying. The distinctive features which he selects, in particular, are more often than not the expression of more or less articulate hypotheses about their potential value for the discrimination of such attributes, rather than the product of a supposedly neutral vision, devoid of any such preconceptions. By way of proof, I shall mention the fact that observers who belong to different 'cultures', or who exercise their intellectual faculties differently in the same society, do not by any means come out with the same groups when asked to produce a 'natural' classification of a given collection (Carroll 1964). Further, one only has to read the texts which accompany 'free' typologies, in the above sense, to be convinced of the paramount importance of the author's presuppositions, implicit or explicit, in the apprehension and organization of the data (e.g. Higham 1972, where the 'initial model formulation *in terra incognita*' in fact consists in describing and ordering archaeological materials of unknown dates into a number of cultural phases that are the direct product of a preconceived evolutionist model).

This first kind of construction would not therefore have detained us longer, if it had not benefited lately from a renewal of interest due to the progress of mathematical methods of classification and seriation in archaeology. The connection between the two factors is easy to understand: when they resort to such methods (numerous examples in Hodson, Kendall & Tăutu 1971: 30–290; Doran & Hodson 1975: 158–284), archaeologists frequently proceed *as if* nothing was known of the extrinsic attributes associated with some or all of the monuments under study. The game consists in computing classes or serial orders on the basis of intrinsic features alone, listed in a data matrix for a given set of objects (or assemblages, etc.). The construction then develops *as if* the formal merits of the ordering procedure[9] made it unnecessary to raise questions about the more or less arbitrary nature of the descriptive data to which it is applied. This can be seen for instance in the somewhat naïve use which has been made of cross-cultural codes, basically designed for retrieval purposes only, in projects of mathematical classification or seriation related to the remains of highly specific cultures.[10] This method of typological research, if it is one, does not seem very promising to me: for it rests on a number of unverified epistemological postulates, to say the least, regarding: (*a*) a 'natural' congruence of information languages, such that ultimately any one of them could serve as a tool for typological research, provided it was taken to be sufficiently discriminating, detailed, precise, or any other adjective of this kind; (*b*) a de facto, if not de jure homomorphism between the 'etic' units of initial descriptions and the 'emic' units of typological definitions (§ 2.5); (*c*) the cognitive value of the computed orders, or, more exactly, the possibility for any competent archaeologist to discover an empirically valid interpretation for each of the computed orders; (*d*) last but not least, the univocal character of such interpretations, and the reasons why we should formulate them in terms of L and T attributes alone, for the sake of our definition, instead of admitting that the computed orders may *also* be the product of F factors that are independent of L or T (e.g. homologies resulting from ecological or technological constraints which transcend cultural boundaries; for an excellent analysis of the confusion which prevails in this area, see Speth 1972).[11]

Are we not then asking too much of the 'nature of things', especially since the things with which we are dealing are not the work of Nature, nor of a unique Creator credited with a pervading concern for consistency and order, but rather the products of a multiform human

9 Let me recall that I am using the word 'ordering' (or in French 'ordination') in a broad sense, which covers both classification and seriation processes of any kind (mechanical or 'manual', mathematical or empirical), as against F. R. Hodson, for whom 'ordination' seems to mean seriation only, through formal means: Doran & Hodson (1975: 167).

10 To take but one example, the Code for the analysis of Pottery shapes, established in 1956 as a tool for handling large bodies of documentary data on punched cards or magnetic tape, reappeared twenty years later in nearly identical form for quite another purpose, namely automatic classification experiments in various sections of ceramology: Roman amphoras, Etruscan bucchero, Medieval ceramics (references in Gardin 1976: 8–9).

11 As much as confusion, the matter is one of inconsistency: it is not uncommon for an author to plunge into all kinds of statistical calculations in order to establish the non-random character of co-variations observed between objects or features that have been selected in an unspecified if not arbitrary fashion, while the same author argues in other publications that any non-trivial interpretations of such phenomena are bound to be risky, on account of the multiplicity and imbrication of the factors that could 'explain' them.

Culture whose material remains do not seem to warrant any of those extraordinary postulates?

To sum up, this first strategy for building up typologies has, to me, no firm epistemological basis, and therefore little practical value (for another critical analysis, see Thomas 1972b). I am of course well aware of the fact that a number of mathematicians have chosen to defend it, for obvious reasons (e.g. Benzecri 1973); and also that as many archaeologists are ready to believe in its heuristic virtues, for want of more palpable returns. The arguments presented here should however help to explain why I was earlier reluctant to admit that classes derived in this fashion should be considered as archaeological types at all (§ 4.1.1, path 1) and why a more neutral designation seemed then in order (note 5), as hinted again in the title of the present section.

4.2.2 *Guided constructions: induced typologies*

A typological construction is 'guided' if, in contrast to the preceding situation, the selection of attributes, or even the assignment of certain objects to given classes, is determined by what the archaeologist already knows about the kind of materials under study. Speaking of attributes, first, he will choose those which he takes to be related in some way to the goal of the construction, on the basis of reasoning or experience. If for instance the goal is to separate classes of objects that belong to different human groups, it will be wise to describe the former in terms of attributes or traits that are supposed to be distinctive of the latter on whatever ground (field observations, previous knowledge, logical or physical determinants, etc.). Then, speaking of objects, we will require in the same way that available attributions be incorporated in the typology, at least in the relative sense indicated above: 'X should belong to a class that comes chronologically before the class of Y', 'X and Z fall into necessarily distinct geographical groups', 'Y and Z may (or should) belong to the same chronological class', etc. (fig. 17) In other words, the overall movement of the construction no longer proceeds from the real or simulated disorder of the perceptual data to any formal order that the taxonomist sees fit, as in the preceding section; we start here from a few *partial* orders observed or postulated in the space of objects and attributes, and try to derive a *total* order which will be in conformity with those empirical constraints.

The reader will have recognized here the course which archaeologists usually follow when dealing with material remains of which the L, T attributes are not totally unknown, but rather suggested in an indirect or incomplete way by field observations or comparative data. And yet the logical steps in this very common process remain largely obscure, the reason being that typologists seldom take the pains to put into words the successive options which give shape to their constructions (still less the basis of such options), as is done for instance in systems analysis or artificial intelligence in the form of explicit decision procedures. This contention may cause some irritation: are not all the elements needed to reconstruct the genesis of a typology to be found in the explanations given by the author himself on the matter? The answer, unfortunately, is no: any attempt to take an author at his own word leads to difficulties and frustrations of all kinds, but certainly not to a 'chain of explicitly

Figure 17   The inductive generation of typological orders. Suppose that for reasons of his own, the classifier of W, X, Y, Z decides to take into consideration only two morphological attributes, with two possible states each: BASE/'Disc' as on Y, or 'tripods', as on W; and BODY/'open', as on W, or 'closed', as on Y. He may then generate order no. 1 $\{(W, X)(Y, Z)\}$ based on the first attribute alone, or order no. 2 $\{(W, Z)(X, Y)\}$ based on the second, but obviously not a third order such as $\{(W, Y)(X, Z)\}$ based on the form of the RIM. Let us assume further that our classifier may rely on external evidence to postulate various relations between objects, or features, e.g. 'the disc appears in time before the tripod' (therefore W and X are older than Y and Z), 'X and Z are of different origin', 'Y and Z are contemporaneous'. A simple reasoning shows that only X and Z are contrasted both in Space and Time, whereas, according to Time, W may go with X, and Y with Z. Order no. 2 is then excluded; the only possible 'typologies' are either order no. 1 $\{(W, X)(Y, Z)\}$, or more atomized classifications such as $\{(W, X)(Y)(Z)\}$, $\{(W)(X)(Y, Z)\}$ and $\{(W)(X)(Y)(Z)\}$, which are all compatible with our external constraints. Obviously, more 'types' could be defined under other empirical constraints, or with a different code (or both).

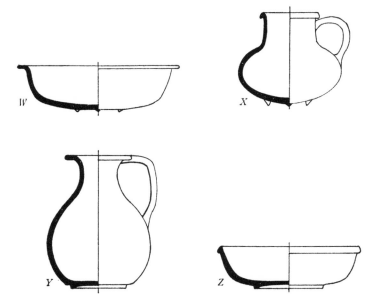

defined operations' conducive to the proposed typology; the few endeavours of this kind that have been reported in the literature are in this respect illuminating, especially since they concern established constructions by well-known authors, in the most diverse sectors of archaeology or art history: the classification of Greek archaic sculptures by Gisela Richter (Borillo 1970), the classification of Owasco pottery in North America by Ritchie and MacNeish (Whallon 1972), the classification of Cistercian churches by Dimier (Lagrange 1973), etc. A possible remedy to such formal weaknesses is to seek refuge in the strength of mathematical reasoning, along either of two possible courses. The first one consists in remaining within the system of the empirical construction under study, by clinging both to the language of representation and to the typology proposed by the author, so that the role of calculus is here limited to reproducing the author's behaviour in the typological process. The other tactic, on the contrary, takes only the basis of the construction into consideration, that is the raw materials and the 'empirical constraints' relating to them, as defined above; and an original classification is sought, according to formal methods which do not then pretend to reproduce the author's process, nor even his findings. Mathematics here takes the place of discursive reasoning, and its products are considered as substitutes or complements to empirical constructs, with the added prestige gained from 'well-formedness' in this case.

The first of the two ways amounts in fact to a change of strategy: the empirical typology is then considered as a *datum*, and the game consists in finding a method which accounts for the transition from given individual descriptions to given synthetical types through 'a chain of explicitly defined operations' of whatever kind, mathematical or other. This approach is deductive in as much as the operations (and if needed the additional descriptive data) that are required in order to give a formal footing to the construction are in fact derived from the typology itself; we shall return to this case in the following section.

Consequently, we only have here to consider the second approach, which may be conversely termed inductive, to the extent that the reasoning process goes in the same direction as in empirical constructions, namely *from* the initial set of data *through* more or less articulate operations *to* the resulting typology. The 'guided' constructions announced in the title of the present section are those which proceed in this fashion, within the limits imposed at the outset by a number of known empirical facts – in contrast with the 'free' constructions considered earlier – and with more or less precision in the definition and use of the central operations. Mathematical methods of classification can no doubt be of help in this latter respect; but they must also fit in with the known empirical constraints, failing which they lay themselves open to the same epistemological criticisms as were raised in the case of the free constructions, in the preceding section.

4.2.3 *Imposed constructions: deduced typologies*

The typological constructions which I call 'imposed' are those in which classes are determined by L and T observations, either extrinsic (e.g. excavations, written sources, etc.) or intrinsic (e.g. inscriptions, legends), which may occasionally be challenged (e.g. stratigraphical interpretations, textual criticism, palaeographical decipherings, etc.), but the implications of which, in terms of space and time attributions, are not open to doubt once they have been established. The work of the typologist then consists in selecting intrinsic features, P, G, S that seem to bear some relation to the 'imposed' L, T classes, and in defining the order in which these features should be taken as classification criteria in order to generate the target classes, or acceptable approximations of them. This part of the procedure is a kind of rationalization, where the typologist takes a given order as a datum in order to draw a number of implications from it with regard to the description of the objects concerned. We could therefore hope that the reasoning would always be explicit and clear, in this privileged situation; nothing of the sort is, however, to be found in archaeological literature, as witnessed by the amazing diversity of competing systematizations offered in sectors of archaeology or art history where the LT groups are perfectly established – for example, in branches of numismatics where there is no mystery concerning the places and dates of issue, or in the study of architectural monuments that are also unambiguously positioned in space and time, or again in the countless constructions customarily considered as art history, but which are designed exactly as in archaeology, their goal being less to establish LT groups (usually given at the outset, under one name or another: schools, workshops, styles, etc.), than to build up a systematization or rationalization of the observed differences between them, in terms of intrinsic features that everyone seems to perceive in his own way.

Not that the existence of competing systematizations is in itself condemnable: it is no wonder, after all, that opinions differ as to the features which 'distinguish', in iconographical or palaeographical terms, the coins of classical Athens from those of Ionian cities in the same period; or that questions should be raised concerning the essential differences between a 'pre-classical' or a 'classical' pyramid in Maya art; or that so many divergent papers should be written or read on the contrasted merits of Titian and Tintoretto, or any other groups of works objectively circumscribed as far as L and T attributes go, but of which art historians relentlessly try to formulate the specificity as they see it, in a never-ending flow of learned papers. The embarrassing fact, at least for our present purport, is that the relation between material objects and written discourse is in most cases so obscure, or so loose when it has been cleared up, that we may doubt whether there even exists any logicist chain that could describe it adequately. I have mentioned earlier a few recent studies which give an idea of the price that has to be paid, in terms of intellectual effort, in order to give some rational foundations to typological constructions that are considered for the sake of the exercise as irrefutable, or 'imposed', in the sense of the present section. Besides the relative ponderousness of the mathematical or logical machinery that must be brought into operation, three distinct obstacles are met: (*a*) either we accept resorting to statistical expedients that have no relation whatsoever with the typologist's empirical approach which we are supposed to elucidate (as in Whallon 1972); (*b*) or else, in order not to deviate from this task, we must be ready to put up with complex logico-semantic tools that are only applicable to the construction under study, and which must be redesigned whenever we move to another one (as illustrated in Gardin & Lagrange 1975); (*c*) unless of course we are led to the more radical conclusion that there is no 'computable' relation, in the mathematical or logical sense of the term, between what the archaeologist *says* of types and monuments, and what he *does* when he invents the ones as a way to account for the distribution of the others in time and space (as shown by Borillo 1970 and Lagrange 1973).[12]

These difficulties, however, are not such as to discredit the endeavour: the scientific claims of archaeology will hardly be taken seriously, anyhow, as long as we have not grown into the habit of grounding on explicit and reproducible reasoning – mathematical *or other* – the definition of the space and time series on which most of our explanatory constructions are based. Admittedly, we shall not reach that stage in looking for the rationale of established typologies when it is fairly obvious that the ways in which they have become 'established' are not those of reason alone. A more efficient strategy is to combine in the same process, as types are being generated, the requirement of empirical validity and the requirement of formal consistency. Experiments along this line are only just taking shape; they offer a pleasant contrast to the past usage of typologies borne out by facts, but formally flimsy, as well as with the modern usage of well-formed taxonomies that are little more than that (e.g. Guénoche & Tchernia 1977). Their two-fold merit, empirical and logical, is the fruit of a cyclical process of construction by trial and error, where induction and deduction both come alternatively into play (as indicated on figure 15) until the typology provisionally

12 There is no inconsistency in the fact that I should again refer to these studies, *à propos* of 'imposed' constructions, after having first mentioned them *à propos* of 'guided' constructions: the reason is that they are related to both inasmuch as they deal with typologies that have been 'induced' in the way described in § 4.2.2, but for the purpose of assessing how similar typologies can be 'deduced' in the sense of the present section. Nor is it alarming that we should here refer to Gardin & Lagrange (1975), even though the rationalizations attempted in this work concern studies of single objects rather than typologies: I have stated earlier the reasons which made this difference immaterial for our present purpose (§ 4.1.2, *B*).

considered as the most meaningful in terms of L and T correlates (order OX) is mirrored in a descriptive–generative system fully defined in terms of properties P, G, S (order OI).

4.2.4 Synopsis

The reader will have noticed the parallelism between the modes of construction just discussed and the paths earlier considered when we were assessing the respective role of extrinsic and intrinsic attributes in

Figure 18 A synoptic view of the modalities of typological constructions or reconstructions discussed in § 4.1 and 4.2, respectively.

The ways to typologies according to relations observed within or between OI and OX (§4.1) 1	Constraints* Degree 2	on Description 3	on Ordering 4	Typological products (§4.2) 5
Free classifications = path 1, $OI \rightarrow OI$. 1	null	O	O	*Taxonomic classes* Neutral types, pseudo-types (§4.2.1)
Guided classifications = path 2, $OI \rightarrow OX$. Constraints on the selection of all or some descriptive traits (col. 3), and/or on some classes (col. 4) 2	partial	◐ ● 2a / O ◐ ● 2b	O / ◐	*Induced types* obtained by selecting an order which agrees with empirical constraints on some classes and/or some or all traits (§4.2.3)
Imposed classifications = path 3, $OX \rightarrow OI$. Constraints on all classes (col. 4) and on all or some descriptive traits (col. 3) 3	total	O ◐ 3a / ● 3b	● / ●	*Deduced types,* obtained by selecting an order which agrees with empirical or formal constraints on all classes, and some or all traits (§4.2.3)
Logico-empirical classifications = path 4, $OX \rightarrow OI \rightarrow OX$. Constraints as in lines 3 and 2 above, successively (cf. fig. 15, spiral $q–r–s$) 4	Configurations as in lines 3a and 2a or b, successively, until configuration 3b is reached			*Logico-empirical types,* obtained by selecting an order which is both well-formed and in agreement with empirical data (§4.2.4)

* Either empirical constraints which guide or impose original typologies, or formal constraints observed in the rationalization or reconstruction of such typologies (§4.2.3).

Symbols

O   no constraints on the initial selection of traits (col. 3) or on the final classes (col. 4)

◐   constraints on some traits (col. 3) or classes (col. 4)

●   constraints on all traits (col. 3) or classes (col. 4)

the genesis of typologies (§ 4.1.1). The two presentations are in fact complementary visions of the problem of typological construction, depending on whether we handle it in terms of the current distinction between intrinsic and extrinsic orders (§ 4.1), or according to the sharper requirements of logicism (§ 4.2). Figure 18 indicates how the two viewpoints are interrelated (col. 1), while providing a summary of the various modes of construction or reconstruction[13] distinguished in both cases (cols. 2 to 5). The convergent outcome of the two analyses is indicated in line 4, namely the eminence of constructions that we shall call later logico-empirical, in order to convey the dialectical movement which gives birth to them, in a never-ending search for better compositions of *both* formal *and* empirical requirements (§ 7.2).

4.3 *Interpretative constructions*

By 'interpretation', generally speaking, I understand here the process by which meaning is attached to any kind of order, such as a series of 2, 3, . . ., *n* objects formed on the basis of their similarities (seriation) or a class of objects attributed to the same time and space unit (classification). Consequently, interpretative constructions are those in which the author goes beyond the formal phase of ordering in an attempt to *explain* the meaning of the proposed series or classes. Typologies are in this respect somewhat ambiguous, for the reasons discussed above (§ 4.1.2): they normally take into account a number of empirical constraints which confer to them, by construction, a potential explanatory value (the attribution of objects to identical L or T units would otherwise make no 'sense'), but this meaning is not self-evident and distinct reasoning processes are needed in order to bring it out, once the typology has been established. It is to the nature of those processes that we shall now address ourselves.

Let us first recall and amplify the two reasons already given for considering typological constructions as a kind of prerequisite to the interpretation of archaeological data (§ 4.1.2, *B*). One of them is in the form of a syllogism: (*a*) according to our definition of Explanations, the interpretation process necessarily consists in connecting material data with 'past events or ways of life related to particular individuals or groups' (§ 2.4); (*b*) but those individual or groups, H, can only be

13 I have made a point of bringing together in the same table the conditions observed in the genesis of original typological *constructions* and those which prevail in the case of *reconstructions* aimed at a formal grounding of established typologies. The homology of the two situations lies in the identical constraints observed in both, concerning the language of representation (col. 3) and the product of ordering (col. 4). The only difference is that these constraints are related to archaeological considerations in the case of original constructions (empirical constraints), whereas they are nothing more than the rules of the rationalization game in the case of reconstructions (formal constraints).

apprehended through specific space and time coordinates, L, T (see below); (c) therefore, the archaeologist cannot study the history of behaviour of any individual or group H unless he has first singled out the material remains that present the L and T attributes of H. A research project on the cities founded by Alexander, for instance, presupposes that we are able to recognize in one way or another the class of urban sites which are eligible as such, on the basis of their LT attributes, as well as some intrinsic properties P, G, S. In the same way, we shall hardly be in a position to study the pastoral economy of the Normans if we are unable to distinguish, among the material remains that may have a bearing on this kind of activity, those which present the L and T attributes of Normanism, etc.

One could object that the attribution of L, T (or H) specifications to material remains does not necessarily constitute a typological act. To which my answer will be – and this is the second of the two reasons – that attributions of this sort seldom crop up alone: they are usually coupled with various comments on the intrinsic properties of the remains concerned, put forward in order either to justify the extrinsic attributions, or to demonstrate the specificity of the intrinsic properties in the proposed L, T or H units. In both cases, the constitution of *series* is inevitable, for purposes of comparisons: external series in the former case, upon which attributions are based in order to constitute the initial set of materials (urban sites that may qualify as Alexander's foundations, traces of pastoral activities that may qualify as Norman, etc.); and internal series in the latter, as a basis for a systematic presentation of the materials (description and ordering), which commands or prefigures the subsequent interpretation. Whether these pre-interpretative or pre-interpreted series be considered as types or not is of little importance: the indisputable fact is that the mechanism by which they are generated, when we care to look into it, turns out to be necessarily one of those which have just been discussed under the cover of typology, whether in a broad or in a restricted sense. This is why I have chosen to consider that all interpretative constructions presuppose a prior phase of typological or quasi-typological ordering.

4.3.1 *Primitive interpretations: convergence, influence, inheritance*

The constructions referred to under this title are those in which the interpretation does not go beyond attributions L, T or H of the sort just discussed, even when they would seem to aim at a higher explanatory level. Supposing for instance that we discover in a number of Bronze age sites in Central Asia several pottery types that are quite common in Indus valley settlements of the same period; we may immediately summon a variety of hypotheses calculated to 'explain' the phenomenon: economic expansion, conquests, migration, commerce, etc., in one direction or another (Lyonnet 1977), but we do not in fact 'demonstrate' any. Or again, having observed that certain architectural forms that were current in Persia under the later Sassanians Kings (sixth–seventh century A.D.) persist on the Iranian plateau long after the Islamic conquest, whereas they tend to disappear in Mesopotamia and Western Persia, we may be led to many different 'explanations' such as the strength of corporative traditions in certain geo-historical areas, the influence of ecological factors (climate, available materials, etc.), the lagging of evolution in the more distant provinces of the Islamic empire, the vigour of cultural resistance to Arab rule in Persia, etc.; but such explanations are in fact hypotheses, none of which can be regarded as grounded *unless one has taken the pains to demonstrate why the others should be dismissed.* In other words, in those two standard examples, interpretation is nothing but a paraphrase of similarities or dissimilarities observed between monuments that have different space and time attributes, but a paraphrase which should always be taken as *one among others*, and which is credible only in so far as we are prone to ignore this simple fact.

It would indeed be interesting to draw up a list of the more current paraphrases of this nature that are to be found in archaeological literature. Not that we would discover anything that could not be anticipated by the exercise of common sense alone; still, a systematic display of the various factors called upon to explain similarities or dissimilarities cannot fail to awaken us to two or three truisms of which archaeologists do not all seem to be quite aware.

(*a*) The first one is that although these factors are numerous, they can nevertheless be reduced to a few recurrent categories of explanations, the striking characteristic of which is rather that they should be so few, and thereby so monotonous. Figure 19 is a recapitulation of the more common interpretative factors as I see them, arranged in the manner of a flow-chart so as to emphasize that the adoption of any one of them implies in principle a refutation of the others. The division into three branches, headed Convergence, Influence, Inheritance (fig. 19, top) is only intended to reproduce the traditional distinctions between the three major lines of interpretation known as Functionalism, Diffusionism, Evolutionism, respectively (fig. 19, bottom). The meaning given to these conventional headings should be clear from the examples of explanatory factors (circumstances, phenomena) listed under each.

(*b*) Conversely, if the 'decision tree' of archaeological explanations proves somewhat primitive, it is none the less sufficiently ramified to illustrate how extraordinarily restrictive any unique interpretation is, considering the number of options which it shuts out. This accounts for our doubts regarding constructions in which the only arguments that are put forward are those which support a given interpretation, without anything being said of the reasons why others should not be given the same credit. This scepticism is certainly not foreign to the feeling of boredom mentioned in our preface as one of the motives for undertaking the present book: interest soon dries up for constructions that amount to stereotypes, especially when the poverty of their logical form is not offset by the wealth of their historical substance.

(c) To these two truisms should be added a third observation, less evident but equally to the point, concerning the faith one may have in interpretations of the kind listed in figure 19: it has to do with the wavering status, not to say more, that is implicitly assigned to *dissimilarity*, as opposed to similarity, in most of the so-called comparative constructions. The following examples will help in understanding both the nature of the phenomenon and its epistemological import. Oriental archaeologists all know that the Achaemenian kings of Persia led several military campaigns in Central Asia, at the same time that they were extending their rule in the direction of Egypt and Greece, following which this vast region was divided into a number of satrapies (Bactria, Sogdiana, Margiana, etc.) placed under the authority of Persepolis. On the basis of these facts – established by the convergent testimony of ancient texts and inscriptions – archaeologists have come to believe that these provinces must have been subject, during the two or three centuries of Achaemenian rule, to the 'influence' of the superior Persian civilization, especially as regards material culture: architecture, sculpture, metalwork, etc. And a number of archaeological indications have indeed been found in support of this belief, in the form of various examples of Persian craftsmanship found in Central Asian sites of Achaemenian times. There is a noteworthy exception, however: the *pottery* made in Bactria, Sogdiana, etc. in the same period forms an amazingly homogeneous assemblage which shows no connection whatsoever with the contemporary ceramics from Fars to Khorassan, the only points of contact being in the boundary areas on the eastern fringe of the Iranian Plateau (Cattenat & Gardin 1978). Two courses are then open to us: either we uphold the idea that the positive testimony of texts and of the more 'noble' categories of

---

Figure 19 (*overleaf*)   The more common categories of 'explanation' in archaeological constructions, rooted in the observation of similarities. The figure reads as a kind of flow chart, from top to bottom and left to right, with the major classes of explanations inscribed in lozenges. Schematically, the archaeologist has to make a YES or NO decision for each class, which takes him downward or to the right, respectively, until he reaches a list of factors (circumstances, phenomena) that contains a plausible explanation. In fact, elements from different classes are often mentioned jointly, in a complex or at least compound sort of explanation (hence the fusion of the vertical lines, at the bottom of the diagram): the 'yes or no' alternative is a mere graphical convention, which would better read 'yes, but why not also', or any other expression of the usual laxity of arguments presented along those lines.

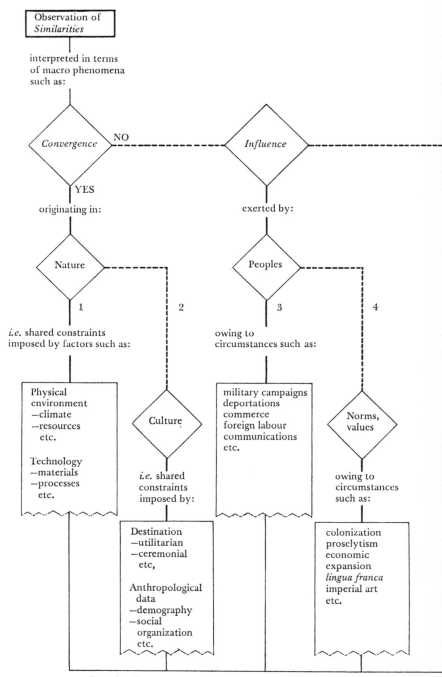

Observation of
Similarities

interpreted in terms
of macro phenomena
such as:

Convergence — NO — *Influence*

YES

originating in: exerted by:

Nature   *Peoples*

1   2   3   4

i.e. shared constraints   owing to
imposed by factors such as: circumstances such as:

Physical
environment
—climate
—resources
  etc.

Technology
—materials
—processes
  etc.

Culture

military campaigns
deportations
commerce
foreign labour
communications
etc.

*Norms,
values*

i.e. shared
constraints
imposed by:

owing to
circumstances
such as:

Destination
—utilitarian
—ceremonial
  etc,

Anthropological
  data
—demography
—social
  organization
  etc.

colonization
proselytism
economic
expansion
lingua franca
imperial art
etc.

Functionalism   *Diffusionism*

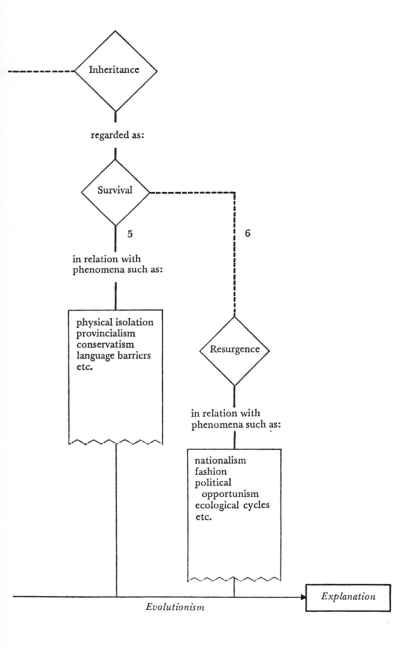

regarded as:

5   6

in relation with
phenomena such as:

physical isolation
provincialism
conservatism
language barriers
etc.

in relation with
phenomena such as:

nationalism
fashion
political
  opportunism
ecological cycles
etc.

Evolutionism

Explanation

monuments has somehow more weight, *in this particular case*, than the dissimilarities observed in the domain of pottery; or we decide conversely to interpret those differences as the sign of a cultural disjunction – which is the pattern followed *in other cases* – even if we then have to revise our understanding of written documents. Whatever option we may prefer, the same question arises: on which criteria, according to which rule do we decide that dissimilarities are or are not meaningful, for any given explanation? Or again, what are the 'particular cases' in which dissimilarities are meaningless, as opposed to those in which they are put forward as proof of an explanation, when exactly the same category of materials is involved?

Archaeologists have not shown much concern for this question, except through general considerations on the dangers of the argument *a silencio*, which, however, does not operate on the same basis as the argument *a differentia*. What is in fact lacking is another decision tree similar to the one shown on figure 19, but here rooted in the observation of *dis*similarities (top left), and with branches leading to the various possible explanations of *difference*, instead of analogy. One of these would have to be the 'zero' explanation, corresponding to the case when differences are alleged to be meaningless, that is, ascribed to the hazards of human industry. We could not fail to discover then that this interpretation is in fact *more* exacting than any other, in so far as it amounts to asserting that none of the factors leading to similarities (decision tree no. 1) are applicable 'in this particular case', while also declaring inapplicable all the factors of dissimilarity (decision tree no. 2). I can hardly think of any archaeological situation in which I would be bold enough to take such a stand.

The term 'paraphrase' which I used earlier thus takes on its full meaning: it is not enough to mention a more or less copious array of historical or natural facts to 'explain' why a given monument or feature is absent or present in selected *L*, *T*, *H* units of the anthropological space–time. However brilliant and scholarly these interpretations may be, they belong to a commonplace logic and semantics of *plausibility* – the word 'commonplace' having here no negative connotations (see below, § 7.2) – rather than to the realm of necessity as understoood in disciplines that impose stronger requirements with respect to demonstration and truth. It is surely right and proper these days to call on ecological or social factors in the interpretation of archaeological variability, rather than on historical events of a seemingly more *ad hoc* kind; but we should not delude ourselves, the *manner* of the intellectual exercise has not radically changed together with the jargon, and there is not much difference, from an epistemological viewpoint, between the harder sociological and ecological determinants of modern explanations and the softer 'influences' of the traditional ones. The word *primitive* associated to the latter, in the title of the present section, does not therefore refer to their substance, but only to the more superficial and somehow unfinished form of the argument as disclosed above.

4.3.2 *Normative interpretations: ideas, beliefs, cultural values*

The constructions just considered could be called primitive for another reason: they usually rest on the examination of relatively homogeneous series, which do not lend themselves readily to interpretations of the richest sort – urban sites, instruments of pastoral activity, potsherds, etc. Archaeology, as we have earlier recalled, strives to embrace more diversified sets, in the hope of discovering formal units analogous to 'types', but defined at higher levels of integration: assemblages (sub-assemblages), cultures (sub-cultures), communities, societies, etc. (see § 4.1) Does the interpretation of such aggregates raise the same issues as the interpretation of typological series in the strict sense, limited to a single category of materials or to isolated distinctive features?

Before answering the question, two observations are in order, that are hardly open to discussion. The first one is that the larger aggregates do not have the same definition for everyone: not only do the designations vary from one author or one school of thought to another, but also the ideas expressed as to the content that should be given to anyone of them, in order to provide a suitable ground for the more ample archaeological and historical developments. It would be irksome, and hardly useful for our present purpose, to review all the systematizations that have been proposed in this area, in the last ten or fifteen years (e.g. Leroi-Gourhan *et al.* 1966, Chang 1967a, Deetz 1967, Clarke 1968, etc.). Moreover, the exercise would only have value if it went beyond the unfortunate frontiers of 'western', or more specifically Anglo-Saxon, archaeology, in order to take into account other contributions to the same debate, rooted in different experiences and traditions, especially in the USSR (see in particular Institute of archaeology of Leningrad 1970, and among the various communications collected under this title, those by Artamonov, Grjaznov, Klejn, Masson, Tretjakov, on the concepts of 'culture', 'ethnos', 'society', etc.; see also the publications that followed these discussions, e.g. Kamenetskij 1970, Klejn 1970, 1971, Klejn *et al.* 1970, etc., and more recently Bromlej 1977, Pimenov 1977). Failing this, we can only underline the most obvious common trait of such constructs: the various aggregates of material remains are arranged in a small number of categories or 'levels', each of which is supposed to reflect norms of behaviour that are characteristic of human entities of different scope, from the individual (craftsmen, masters) to society, culture, etc., through all kinds of intermediate groups that receive different names. One may sometimes be inclined to scorn the tone of self-evidence in the presentation of such systems (e.g. 'human cultural behaviour occurs on *four* levels', Deetz 1967: 108, italics mine): they have none the less the merit of revealing clearly the goal of the exercise, which is to determine, through the regularities and variations displayed by archaeological remains, aggregates of data that seem to follow formal rules of distribution – in particular the rules of Gaussian distribution – and that can be interpreted for this reason as the expression or consequence of 'norms' in force in the human groups associated with them. These norms will be understood differently according to the nature and size of the group; but they always presuppose, even if only implicitly, a voluntarist view of human affairs, according to which our behaviour is governed by ideas, values, beliefs or motivations that are supposed to be shared by all the members of the group – a pattern of interpretation that comes directly from sociology or ethnology as it stood twenty or thirty years ago (Kluckhohn 1951, Kroeber 1952, White 1959, etc.).

It can easily be shown that the patterns of interpretation considered in the last section, for a more elementary class of Explanations, already imply the existence of norms: stating that the individual character of rural settlements in Corsica is 'due to' the Mediterranean climate, or to Genoese domination, or to insularity at large, comes to the same thing as postulating a 'normative' action of those same factors, in a statistical if not in a psycho-sociological acceptation of the word.[14] Hence now our second observation: the presuppositions and mental operations that govern the interpretation of archaeological variability are of the same kind at any level of integration, irrespective of the nature, scope, and complexity of the aggregates selected as the basis of explanation. A semantic organization such as that of figure 19, for instance, illustrates the kind of conceptual tools that are used not only in bringing out the meaning of a rather elementary comparative or typological series, but also in explaining the extension of a much more elaborate assemblage through time and space.

The answer to the question raised at the beginning of this section should therefore be somehow balanced. On the one hand, it is true that constructions aiming at the discovery of complex historical or anthropological entities, on the basis of the variability of archaeological remains, resort to interpetation processes that are formally identical to those which we discussed in the preceding section, under their traditional titles:

14 The statistical acceptation alone is sufficient: there is nothing wrong in calling on norms, in a cultural context, even when the individuals who reveal them through their behaviour are not aware of them. The analysis of linguistic behaviour is the standard example of this kind; but human action as a whole is amenable to similar systematizations, in which regularities are 'explained' by norms which may perfectly exist only in the anthropologist's mind: see for instance the exchange of conflicting ideas on this theme in the *American Anthropologist* (1964, 67, no. 1) in parallel with the preparation of a special issue on the subject, which was to revive the quarrel (Hammel 1965) – and more particularly the short article by Burling (1964) the title of which aptly summarizes the vanity of the whole debate.

functionalism, diffusionism, evolutionism (fig. 19). On the other hand, the originality of such constructions is that they take into consideration larger numbers of comparative series or typological classes, selected because of the potential significance of their conjunction (or disjunction) in given *L*, *T* or *H* units. The epistemological quality of these Explanations therefore rests on *two* conditions: not only should the interpretation of each of the elementary series or classes be rid of the weaknesses earlier discussed (§ 4.3.1), we must also draw correct conclusions in explaining their conjunction (or disjunction), on the basis of a distinct conceptualization system.

4.3.3 *Dynamic interpretations: behavioural systems*

The methods hitherto discussed have two characteristics in common: first, they tend to give more weight to analogies than to differences, in the interpretation of variability (§ 4.3.1); secondly, they make for the construction of static models, where analogies are brought into relation with behavioural norms considered as sorts of invariants peculiar to human groups of varying nature and scope (§ 4.3.2). The two features are probably interdependent: were *differences* to be taken into account as systematically as analogies, we would be led to give more thought to the reasons why the material products of human activity *change* through time and space, rather than confine ourselves to explanations of their conformity. This is precisely the course now recommended by a number of archaeologists, legitimately anxious to reintroduce a little life in those immovable patterns of interpretation. Their stock argument lies in the notion of 'system' or 'process': the explanation of variability should not consist only in ascribing it to static factors, natural or cultural; we must also elucidate the system according to which any modification of those factors brings about changes in human behaviour that are reflected in a general redistribution of variability.

The more zealous supporters of this approach (Binford 1965, 1968a, b; Binford & Binford 1968: 14–18; Flannery 1967, 1973; Clarke 1968: 38–40, 101–30; Watson, LeBlanc & Redman 1971; Plog 1973, etc.) are prone to present it as distinctive of a new school, to which they give the name of 'processual (or process) archaeology', or again 'systemic (or systems) archaeology'. Rather than concentrating on the historical or sociological agents of material production, the stress is now on the systems which seem to regulate the changing effects of the one or the other; to put it in Flannery's fine words, 'the process theorist is not ultimately concerned with "the Indian behind the artifact", but rather with the system behind both the Indian and the artifact' (1967: 20). A model example of the kind is the study undertaken by D. H. Thomas in a valley of Nevada, a few years ago, in order to verify a theory earlier formulated by Steward on the ecological determinants of a number of economic and social behavioural patterns ascribed to the Shoshone Indians, prior to the Conquest (Thomas 1972a). The method consists in inferring the kind of remains that should be observed in the field, as well as their distribution, if those patterns did indeed obtain, considering the natural resources available in the region, the acquisition techniques that could be used at the time for procuring them, and the archaeological traces that should thereupon result. Various systems (or subsystems) are thus constructed, which set in motion the three categories of variables mentioned – ecological, socio-economic, archaeological – in such a way that their combined action can be computed through a simulation process. The discrepancies observed between these formal predictions and the empirical facts collected in the field ultimately provide an estimation of the construction as a scientific theory. The end-product in this case goes beyond the statement of a causal relation between ecological and anthropological data on the one hand, and archaeological data on the other; it takes the form of a system in which this relation is not only stated but quantified (in a logical or numerical sense of the word), so that we may predict the behavioural variations induced by any modification in the environment, however minor.

The constructions built on this pattern are already countless (abundant examples presented or cited in Clarke 1972, Renfrew 1973b); most have in common, besides the 'systemic' orientation, two features clearly visible in the Thomas study. One of them is a marked taste of natural determinants in the broad sense (ecology, geography, biology, dietetics, etc.), rightly regarded as omnipresent regulating agents in the processes of cultural change (see especially Ucko & Dimbleby 1969, Tringham & Dimbleby 1972); the other feature is a no less judicious emphasis on the plurality of systems (or subsystems) that are at work in the processes, in contrast with the fallacious monism of normative constructions in the sense of the preceding section.[15] Since we agree with both positions, the only question of interest concerns their alleged novelty, asserted with more or less vigour by the protagonists, according to their temperament: I confess that I am on the side of those who would challenge this assertion, for the following reasons. First, it is all too easy to discover in the 'pre-

15 Some archaeologists carry their fondness for systems to the point of drawing up *finite* lists of *the* 'subsystems', 'parameters', 'dimensions', 'paradigms', etc., that go into phenomena of cultural change: thus, for Renfrew (according to Moberg 1975), Subsistence, Metallurgy, Technology, Social Systems, Symbolic and Projective systems, Differentiation, Integration, Energy; for Clarke, Morphology, Anthropology, Ecology, Geography (1972: 6–7), etc. Clearly, no agreement has yet been reached either on the meaning of the terms between inverted commas or on the number or nature of the universals of systemic analysis in archaeology; any such agreement would besides be most alarming . . . and I may now be forgiven for the prudence or weakness of the polysemic symbol *F* under which I have chosen to subsume so many different parameters of dynamic processes, in a formal rather than substantial sense of the word Function (§ 4.1.1).

systemic' archaeological literature quite a number of explanatory constructions where natural determinants play an essential part: Gordon Willey has stressed this before me (1968: 208), with the authority of a man who has taken an interest in the ecological paradigm long before it was given that name (Willey 1953, 1956). In the same way, no one in his right mind would dare contend that with the 'processual' school archaeology discovered the composite nature of the factors which can contribute in an independent or joint way to the variability of cultural facts, material or other: Julian Steward in his time (1955) was grappling with the same problem, through other methods and in different terms, while the structuralist school was attempting in its own way to disentangle the various systems which govern the behaviour of man in society (Lévi-Strauss 1958). Last, but not least, the phraseology developed in systems or model-oriented archaeology is often but a rhetorical transformation of interpretative statements that were expressed long before, only in other forms, perhaps less . . . systematic? I have cited elsewhere a few examples of this trend (Gardin 1974c: 344-5), while taking care to emphasize that the editor of the book in which I found them was himself well aware of the trick: 'Whether we appreciate it or not, we always *operate* conceptual models in the interpretation of observations. We all resemble the Molière character who was delighted to find that all his life, unknowingly, he had been speaking prose' (Clarke 1972: 3).

Upon which David Clarke added: 'we should make these operational models *explicit* and *testable*' (*loc. cit.*, italics are mine). The cardinal virtue of systemic or processual archaeology should indeed be in this effort, if it is to depart from constructions that are admittedly less methodical in their genesis as well as in their form, but which do not otherwise differ with respect to their substance or to their goals. The following section will bear on each of these two requirements, respectively: the explicitation (§ 4.4) and the verification (§ 4.5) of interpretative constructions in archaeology.

4.4 *Logicist analysis of interpretative constructions*

Let us observe first that the three modes of interpretation discussed above are not as radically different as their classification in terms of 'schools' may suggest. The kind of postulates and facts which support the rather elementary patterns of functionalism, diffusionism or evolutionism, for instance (§ 4.3.1) are again present in the more synthetic constructions of culture history or historical archaeology (§ 4.3.2). In the same way, explanations in terms of dynamic processes and systems are for the most part reformulations in a more articulate or analytical language – in the sense of David Clarke's analytical archaeology – of phenomena of interaction which preceding schools had not failed to perceive, but had mentioned in other rhetorical forms (§ 4.3.3). Any unprejudiced person can convince himself of these 'homologies', in the etymological sense, by observing how easy it is to translate the findings of a construction regarded as characteristic of a particular school into the phraseology of another, without losing anything as to the *substance* of the interpretation. When for instance James Deetz (1965) describes the 'dynamic system' through which he connects stylistic variations in Arikara ceramics to changes in the rules of residence of this people, following contacts with Europeans, we can immediately think of a 'normative explanation' which would say exactly the same thing in the language of historical anthropology: we might for instance call on a theory of cultural contacts to account for the observed correlation between the growing heterogeneity of the archaeological materials, throughout the eighteenth century, and the progressive dislocation of the social group which produced them. From this point, we are in a position to reformulate the interpretation in classical 'diffusionist' terms: all we have to do is to mention the probability of a relationship between the pressure exerted by Europeans on the Indian population of Arizona and Nebraska in the eighteenth century and the decline of traditional patterns on Arikara ceramics in the same period, as the residence groups responsible for the perpetuation of those traditions were disintegrating.[16] The differences of *form*, however, are far from negligible: the most significant one, to me, lies in the degree of concern shown for proper definitions of the logical and semantic operations which account for the transition from the initial material data (the *explanandum*) to the final conceptual propositions (the *explanans*) – or vice versa, depending on whether we proceed through induction or deduction (fig. 20). Let us first examine the case of induction, from *explanandum* to *explanans*: the most commendable methods, in the perspective of this book, are not necessarily those which end up with a dynamic model of interpretation, but in a more general sense those which attempt to make explicit all the links of the chain of inferences which connect the empirical observations with the interpretative propositions derived from them, whether the latter be couched in systemic terms or not. In other words, the explicitation requirement (i.e. the requirement that our explanatory processes be made explicit) is not the privilege of any particular school of thought, as the title and substance of recent manifestos might lead us to believe (Watson, LeBlanc & Redman 1971); it is applicable to all kinds of interpretations, under any of the three broad classes distinguished in the last sections. This pervasiveness of the trend is illustrated by a growing number of studies on the inferences that can be rightfully drawn from various categories of archaeological materials: funeral objects and

---

16 For a more elaborate presentation of the same syncretic views, see
    Rouse (1977), where a detailed example is given of commutations
    between different formulations of the same explanatory theory, in
    West Indian archaeology.

monuments (*World Archaeology* 1975, vol. 7, no. 1), houses (Reynolds 1975), animal remains (Ziegler 1973), etc. The authors concerned are certainly not all prepared to place their effort of explicitation under the banner of the systemic revolution in archaeology.

The same remarks hold for the inverse approach, from the *explanans* to the *explanandum*: the idea here is to discover possible archaeological manifestations of the concepts that enter into the fabric of explanations, beginning with the more basic – e.g. the attempt by Ascher & Ascher (1965) to quantify the concept of 'industry' in prehistory – and ending with the more abstract notions that characterize the relation of man

Figure 20   Paths of interpretation in archaeological constructions: (*a*) either from empirical data to explanatory statements, upward (induction); (*b*) or from theoretical hypotheses to their material substantiation, downward (deduction). The architecture can be represented in both cases as a pyramid of propositions $P_1, \ldots P_{n-1}$ derived from descriptions P_0 or from hypotheses P_n, respectively, in order to establish logical connections between the two sets.

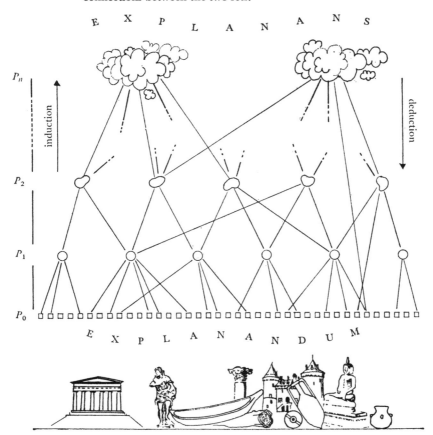

with the environment – e.g. the 'domestication' of animals (Collier & White 1976) or plants (Renfrew 1969), or the structure of society, on any particular level, political (Trigger 1974), social and economic (Masson 1976), etc. In all such cases, the goal is to state explicitly the material criteria which are instrumental in the definition and therefore in the recognition, or inference, of the behavioural facts, norms, or systems to which archaeological explanations refer (Watson 1976); or again, to put it in a more modern or modish form, our concern is with the 'transformations [that enable us] to build a bridge between the operation of a past cultural system and the location and interpretation of data in the archaeological record' (Schiffer & Rathje 1973: 169; see also Schiffer 1976: 12–17).

Clearly, we have here linked up with the logicist project, as defined at the beginning of this book (§ 1.3.5): where could we grasp the mechanisms of archaeological reasoning better than in those 'transformations' from the realm of material observations to that of theoretical propositions? And are they not the ultimate measure of the epistemological quality of constructions, forceful when the transformations are clear and convincing, weak when they are ill-defined and open to discussion? This is true, it should be noted, of *all* the constructions which one may think of, irrespective of their value according to anyone's judgment: all of them are indeed amenable to an analysis which merely aims at eliciting the underlying transformations, in the above sense, when they are not explicitly stated. We have thus reached a point where we can ignore the distinctions made in the preceding section, since the logicist requirements are the same for the most diverse constructions, e.g. for palaeo-ecological explanations, whether they be based on the 'traditional' postulate of adaptative behaviour, or on the more 'modern' concept of ecosystem (Burnham 1973); for bio-archaeological constructions, even when the natural determinants put forward by some are strongly controverted by others (Sahlins 1976); for reconstructions of ancient religious customs or beliefs carried out in the most dissimilar contexts, for instance the Palaeolithic throughout the world (Leroi-Gourhan 1964), *vs.* the Roman period at Palmyra (Seyrig 1934–66), without any danger that the irreconcilability of the remains and sources considered in each case will make the comparison of the reasoning processes less instructive. The following considerations are therefore applicable in principle to any form of Explanation, including those which do not meet everyone's approval, because of their alleged doctrinal errors or empirical inadequacy.

4.4.1 *Architecture of propositions*

As in the case of typological constructions (§ 4.2), we shall leave aside the problems related to the selection of the set of materials, following criteria and procedures which will be considered later (§ 5.1.2). The reason is that the nature and number of the remains which form the empirical basis of a construction have no bearing on our present purport: the interpretative operations are of the same order whether the selection ends up with a single object (as in studies on the meaning of a scene, the function of an edifice), or ten thousand. Further, in the latter case, we may disregard for the same reason the kind of aggregates that are being 'explained' (e.g. a hoard of coins, the objects found in a tomb, the monuments of a given city), in so far as the interpretation follows in all circumstances the same course, indicated in figure 20. I shall therefore use this diagram as a guideline for the presentation of my views regarding the kind of intellectual operations that are set in action in the central part of the picture.

(*A*) Let us begin with the more usual situation, in which the interpretation process follows the upward arrow, from the material remains to the 'conclusions' that are derived from them. Most archaeologists operate in this direction, simply because the circumstances of observation do not leave them any other choice (salvage excavations, surveys in unknown territories, etc.); and we shall see later that the reverse course, downward (from theoretical hypotheses to their empirical verification), is more often than not a mere rationalization of constructions that have in fact evolved in the upward sense (7.1.1). The initial propositions, then, are the descriptions, that is, the words, phrases, or symbols used to indicate, in a more or less systematic language, the properties of the body of materials on which the construction will be based; let us call such propositions P_0. The choice of P_0 is obviously critical, since the content of the subsequent propositions $P_1, P_2, \ldots$, which will lead to the final 'conclusions' P_n is largely dependent on the content of P_0. For this reason, the formulation of P_0 should in fact be regarded as the first step of the interpretation process. However, it is customarily viewed as a distinct operation deserving a different name, Description, prior to Interpretation proper, on the tacit assumption that it enjoys some sort of autonomy within the overall construction. Most archaeologists seem to work on this assumption, judging by the way they traditionally present Explanations in the literature (see below, § 4.4.2); and the situation is not different when they resort to modern methods of data analysis, which would tend to reinforce if anything the apparent separation of the two phases, *first* Description, *then* computation and reasoning processes (§ 4.2.1). The alternative, however, need not detain us very long, since we may choose to reduce it to a matter of convention, on the understanding that descriptions themselves are necessarily the products of an interpretation (§§ 3.3.3, 3.5). Suffice it to acknowledge that the descriptive propositions P_0, whichever way we look at them, constitute the semantic foundations of our conceptual pyramids.

The construction then proceeds through successive operations of *derivation*, the first one of which marks the change of perspectives which characterizes Explanations: the corresponding propositions, P_1, do not concern material remains any more, as did P_0, but the peoples who made, used, transformed or destroyed them. The articulation P_0–P_1 thus plays a special role in archaeological constructions: it acts literally as a hinge between the two perspectives contrasted in the first chapters of this book, Compilations on the one hand, oriented towards monuments (as P_0), and Explanations on the other, oriented towards peoples of the past (as P_1). More specifically, the transition from P_0 to P_1 is the object of the 'C-transforms' (C for Cultural, as opposed to N, Natural) proposed by Schiffer (1972) in order to explain 'the spatial, quantitative, and associational attributes of archaeological materials as a function of the depositional behaviour of the cultural systems that produced them' (Schiffer & Rathje 1973: 170; see also Schiffer 1976: 14–15). I have earlier drawn attention to the growing number of studies recently published on the systematization of inferences $P_0 \rightarrow P_1$, for various categories of material remains: tombs, houses, fauna, etc.; it would be an error, though, to reduce the mechanism of interpretation to this unique operation. The propositions that are offered as the 'conclusions' of any given constructions are not all *directly* derived from P_0, far from it; most of them are the product of inferences drawn from intermediate propositions which relate to human events or behaviour, as P_1, but only as a step between this initial derivation (P_1) and the ultimate conclusions (P_n).

Figure 20 gives an idea, deliberately simplified, of the overall architecture. It will be noted that as we move closer to the terminal propositions P_n, we are entitled to draw elements from any of the previous levels, down to P_0 included. In other words, the elements of any proposition P_i may come not only from its immediate antecedents P_{i-1} but from any proposition $P_0, P_1, \ldots, P_{i-1}$, formulated at an earlier stage in the construction. By 'spreading out' reasoning processes in this way, we may already discern and display their articulations more clearly than through linear discourse; but this is not all. Most derivations of the type $\{P_0, \ldots, P_i\} \rightarrow P_{i-1}$ give rise to written comments on their justification, which should be given a place in the overall structure. Suppose for instance that we observe in a survey various signs of an alternation of irrigated and unirrigated periods, over a long span of time, which we bring into relation with historical (e.g. invasions) or ecological data (e.g. climatic changes). These data should not be regarded as parts of P_0, since they do not belong to the initial set of observations provided by the survey itself; yet, they are indisputable constituents of the construction, called in at various intermediate stages $P_1, \ldots, P_{n-1}$ in order to reach conclusions P_n on the differential characteristics of settlement throughout the ages, in the region studied (example in Gardin & Gentelle 1976, 1979). We must consequently expand figure 20 to the point where it will account for external data of this kind, and for their respective positions in the design of the pyramid $P_0, \ldots, P_n$.

(*B*) Before we give a detailed example of such a pyramid, in the following section, let us turn briefly to the second situation envisaged earlier, in which propositions are derived in the other direction, from P_n to P_0. This is the hypothetico-deductive course, one of the tools of the 'scientific revolution' which champions of the new archaeology seem to cherish most (Binford 1968b, Hill 1972, etc.). The starting point here is the statement of propositions P_n,[17] relating to events or to behavioural patterns that are postulated as so many hypotheses on the history and ways of life of ancient peoples, to be verified in the field. The method of verification consists in drawing from P_n a number of implications or 'deductions' in the form of propositions $P_{n-1}, P_{n-2}, \ldots$, relating to the same universe of discourse, until we arrive at a category of statements P_1 which can be translated in terms of probable or necessary archaeological correlates, P_0; then, confronting these 'predictions' with the observed empirical facts, we measure the value of our initial hypotheses, which, if verified, become the 'conclusions' of the construction, as in the previous case.

Notwithstanding their apparent symmetry, the two approaches are not interchangeable. A simple proof is the fact that if a proposition P_n has been inferred from an archaeological observation P_0, it does not follow that the observation of P_0 is necessary for the validation of P_n in the reverse order. Or again, the graphs which schematize the processes of archaeological reasoning, in the manner of figure 20, are such that the paths followed in order to go from P_0 to P_n do not necessarily coincide with those which take us from P_n to P_0. We may for instance infer phenomena of demographic growth (P_n) from particular variations observed in settlement patterns (P_0), going 'upward', without thereby implying that these variations are a *necessary* manifestation or proof of the reality of such phenomena, going 'downward'. A reformulation of this trivial and long known fact in terms of the theory of finite sets would only give it an air of technicality, without adding anything to its significance for our purpose. The important point, however, is that the conceptual networks which underlie or guide the interpretation are made up of the same sort of elements in both cases; we are therefore entitled to take a comprehensive view of the logical and semantic tools that are set to work in all kinds of explanations, whether inductive or deductive. This will be the object of the next section.

17 For the sake of convenience, I shall keep the same index numbers as those of fig. 20, notwithstanding the resulting anomaly: P_n now designates the 'initial' propositions, read from top to bottom, and P_0 the 'final' ones.

4.4.2   *Logico-semantic organizations: a case study*

A convenient way to approach the subject is through the analysis of a particular category of explanation which follows most clearly the pattern summarized in figure 20, namely the interpretation of iconographical monuments. The starting point in this case is a more or less elaborate *description* of various 'objective'[18] traits, P_0, on the (usually tacit) assumption that it contains the elements needed for understanding the meaning of the image. The terminal is the statement of that *meaning*, P_n, the product of the author's 'comments'. These are therefore to be considered as the vehicle of a transformation $P_0, \ldots \rightarrow P_n$, from the *explanandum* (description) to the *explanans* (meaning), in agreement with our diagram (fig. 20). To this extent, iconographical analysis seems a convenient field for the study *in vivo* of the mechanisms of such transformations, half-way between the more primitive space–time attributions of typologies and the more ambitious ecological or anthropological constructions.

In order not to protract the demonstration unduly, I have selected an example already presented elsewhere in more depth, so that the reader may if necessary consult the full exposition (Gardin & Lagrange 1975). The construction appears in a short but penetrating article by J.-P. Roux (1971), a turcologist, on a relief now in the Konya Museum which has been the subject of various interpretations, none of which satisfies the author (fig. 21). The monument is a relatively small stele (0.55 m × 0.50 m), probably coming from the region of Konya, which all past commentators – and also Roux himself – attribute to the twelfth–thirteenth century A.D., when Anatolia was under the rule of the Seljuk dynasty. In order to establish his own interpretation of the scene, the author begins with a description which does not pretend to mention all the features displayed by the stele, but only, to quote his own terms, 'those which can serve our demonstration'. The novelty of this position is worth noting: the description P_0 is quite explicitly presented as having no *raison d'être* other than to found a given construction $P_0, \ldots \rightarrow P_n$, aimed at discovering the meaning of the scene, P_n. Here is the text of P_0 (leaving out the fragments which concern the stone as such): 'two figures of different height are facing each other, both wearing identical long double-breasted coats, fastened by knotted belts. The taller one, to the left, is seated on a plain chair, perhaps a folding-chair: on his right fist, covered with a glove, sits a large bird; his left hand is holding the chin of the smaller figure. The latter figure, to the right, is standing, with his left hand tucked into his own belt, and his right hand into the belt of the seated man.' Next comes a summary of previous interpretations of the scene, with indications of the elements which the author chooses to retain or to reject, and of the reasons for his choices. The accepted

---

18 The word 'objective' being here taken in the first, vague sense indicated above, note 4 of this chapter.

elements are, essentially, the identification of the seated figure as the *Seljuk sultan* and that of the bird as a *hawk*; the rejected ones are the global explanations of the scene, namely 'an episode in the training of a hawk', or 'a conversation between a mystical master and his disciple', etc. The terms in italics are then used as the basis of two inferences: if one of the figures is the *Seljuk* sultan, then the subject of the scene must bear some relation to the *traditions of Turkish peoples* such as we know them through written sources of the same period; on the other hand, the presence of a trained *hawk* suggests that the scene has something to do with *hunting* – but, according to the author, not with hawking as such, since the 'static and solemn character of the relief' would rather connote some kind of *ceremony*.

Let us stop for a while at this intermediate stage of the construction. Three groups of traits or properties have been singled out, at the level P_0 (fig. 22): (*a*) a first, unspecified group, which accounts for the reading of the seated figure as the *Seljuk sultan* (it is likely that the

Figure 21   The relief in the Konya Museum discussed by J.-P. Roux in the article analysed in § 4.4.2 (reproduced with permission of *Revue des Arts Asiatiques*).

Figure 22   A schematic reconstruction of the empirico-inductive process described by J.-P. Roux in his interpretation of the relief shown on fig. 21. Graphic conventions as on fig. 20; the question marks on level P_0 indicate that the elements of the description (hatched squares) responsible for a given P_1-inference are not stated.

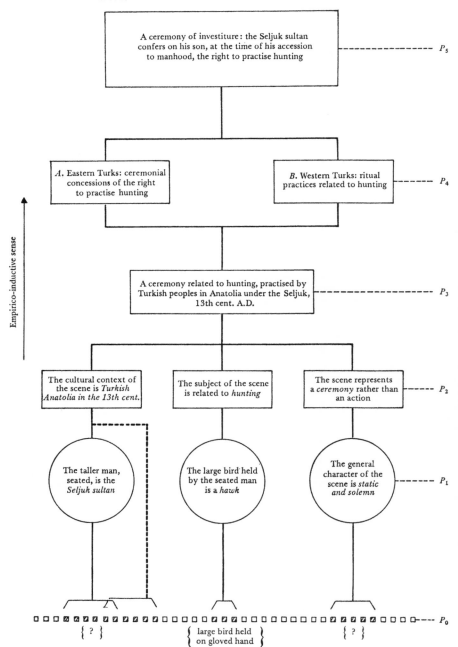

extrinsic attributes of the stele play a part in this interpretation); (*b*) a second group, specified ('large bird on a gloved fist'), which accounts for the reading *hawk*; (*c*) a third group, again unspecified, which accounts for the two-fold qualification *static and solemn* on which the inference 'ceremony' is based – the underlying traits being in this case stylistical rather than morphosemantic. The three terms or expressions in italics thus constitute the propositions of the first level in the interpretation process, P_1. Each one of them is then taken as the root of another set of inferences, at level P_2: we go from the 'Seljuk sultan' (or perhaps more correctly from the extrinsic attributes that I have mentioned as the probable source of this reading) to the hypothesis of a scene bearing a relation to the cultural context *Turkish Anatolia in the thirteenth century*, from the 'hawk' to *hunting*, and lastly from the 'static and solemn' aspect of the scene to the idea of a *ceremony*. The combination of these three notions then leads to a reformulation, at level P_3: the scene presumably represents a ceremony related to hunting, particular to the Turkish peoples who were living in Anatolia at the time the stele was made.

The next step consists in searching through the historical sources that might contain information on the hunting traditions of the Turks. J.-P. Roux discovers a few, which he summarizes in the following way: (*a*) the practice of hunting was 'subject to a superior authority, it was effected in the name of the chief, with his permission, by virtue of a mandate which he had conferred'; (*b*) the concession of this right took place at puberty, and gave rise to a 'ceremony of investiture in which the principal officiant was . . . the shaman, the father, or the chief'. However, the Turks to which Roux's sources refer are not the 'Western Turks' settled in Anatolia at the time, but the 'Eastern Turks' who were roving in Central Asia, several thousands of kilometres away, prior to the migration of some of them towards Persia and the Mediterranean regions, from the eleventh century on. The author must therefore explain how he can attribute to the former practices that have been observed only among the latter: this is done through a kind of probabilistic syllogism which may be summarized as follows: (*A*) some written sources indicate that the *Eastern* Turks performed a ceremony in which the seat of authority (religious, social or political, according to the case) conferred on adolescents, when they reached adult age, the right to practice hunting; (*B*) but then, we know from other sources that hunting was also for the *Western* Turks the object of ritual practices described in less detail, but which indicate the same subordination of this activity to certain rules, in the region and at the time of our stele. (*C*) We are thus entitled to suppose that one of those rites was the ceremony of investiture performed two or three centuries earlier by the remote ancestors of the Seljuks in Central Asia.

Figure 22 summarizes this part of the construction, starting from level P_3 where we had stopped. The examination of written sources provides the elements of propositions P_4, in the universe of discourse imposed by P_3: namely the facts A and B, as above. By matching one with the other, we are led to proposition P_5, which marks the outcome of the inductive phase of Roux's interpretation: 'the scene represents a ceremony of investiture in which the Seljuk sultan confers on his son, at the time of his accession to manhood, the right to practice hunting'.

Roux's construction does not end here; for proposition P_5 is presented at this stage as a mere hypothesis, induced from *some* only of the elements mentioned in P_0. We now have to verify that it is compatible with the other elements of the description as well. The author settles down to this task by showing how this hypothesis 'succeeds in explaining several characteristic details' of the stele, unmentioned in the inductive phase of the construction – such as for instance: (*a*) the 'portable aspect of the chair on which the sultan is seated, and which we can imagine placed in the open, on a hunting ground', (*b*) the way in which the same figure presents the hawk, 'symbol of a triumphant hunt, and probably also of imperial power . . ., to the young man about to go hunting for the first time'; (*c*) the fact that this figure is of smaller height than the sultan, 'because he has not yet reached the size which only initiation can bestow'; (*d*) the similarity of the clothes worn by the two figures, because they are 'of the same lineage, and engaged in the same activity'; (*e*) lastly, the gestures of the smaller of the two, who is 'holding his belt with one hand, and that of his father with the other, because the knotted belt connotes dependence, obedience, submission'. Figure 23 summarizes the semantic relationships, thus established *a posteriori* between the hypo-thetical explanation of the scene, P_5, and elements of the description P_0 that had not been used in the genesis of the explanation. This last phase can be considered at first sight as a *validation* of the hypothesis, in as much as we can verify that its 'predictions' are in agreement with the empirical data: we shall, however, be led to cast doubts on this viewpoint in a moment. Meanwhile, a number of lessons can be drawn from our schematization of Roux's construction, and our reordering of its logical phases.

Let us first point out that despite the author's explicit will to include in the description only those iconographical traits that were to be used for the interpretation, there is no strict one-to-one correspondence between the elements mentioned under each title. One of the features listed in the initial description, for instance, plays no part in the explanation, namely a gesture of the seated figure who 'with his left hand . . . holds the chin of the man standing in front of him': no allusion is made to this gesture, either in the generation of the hypothesis, or in its validation. The reverse phenomenon, a more embarrassing one, is also present: some of the iconographical traits that underlie the interpretation are not explicit in the initial description, nor even in the subsequent comments. A first case of this sort concerns the interpretation of the

seated figure as the 'Seljuk sultan', or more generally as a person of royal
status: taking it for granted that the 'Seljuk' qualification is here derived
from the intrinsic properties of the stele, on which traits does this
reading rest? The author does not raise the question, merely declaring
that 'for want of more decisive proofs, the quasi-unanimity of scholars
. . . compels our adhesion'. But the arguments put forward by the
preceding commentators hardly state more explicitly the list of intrinsic

Figure 23   A schematic reconstruction of the hypothetico-
deductive process described by J.-P. Roux in his 'validation' of
the proposed interpretation.

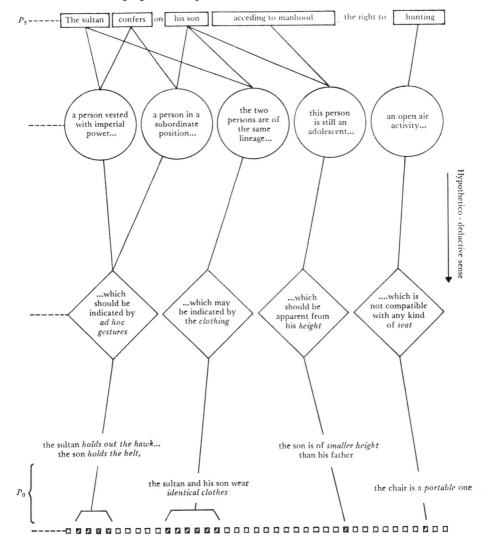

features which impose or compose the royalty of the seated figure; and the fact that no other reading has been suggested amounts to a kind of proof *ad absurdum* the weakness of which is self-evident. The second case of inexplicitness is still more instructive: when the author mentions the 'static and solemn character of the relief', it is left to the observer to appreciate the iconographical traits that substantiate this qualification. The reason is simply that the author's description bears exclusively on the semantic components of the work, not on its stylistic aspects; it deals with the *meaning* of the basic forms carved on the stone, rather than with their *execution*, or with the *impressions* to which they may give rise, according to the viewer's training or sensibility. This fact is all the more striking in that the monument under consideration is an image, not a text: everything is set, however, as if the interpretation process was a kind of discourse analysis applied to a text P_0 which referred only incidentally to an image, everyone being free to 'visualize' its content, literally speaking, in his own way. In other words, if all that is required for apprehending the description P_0 is common sense, one should be careful to note that the persons whose common sense is called on are the *readers* of the text P_0 rather than the *viewers* of the monument. The conventions that govern the graphical rendering of the elements mentioned in P_0 play no part in the construction, or at least not explicitly, so that Roux's interpetation should in principle be applicable to any image representing 'two figures of different height facing each other, wearing both the same long double-breasted cloak . . .'

Figure 24 shows the oddities which may result from this apparent indifference to the relations between image and text, or to put it in more general terms, between the empirical world and the propositions which are supposed to describe it. In fact, Roux's construction is certainly not independent of the apprehension of many intrinsic features which the author merely assumes 'go without saying', and of which he therefore says nothing: let us recall once more the unstated stylistic features which underlie the qualifications 'static and solemn', in the transition from P_0 to P_1, as well as those which, combined with extrinsic attributes, lead to the qualification 'Seljuk' and the ensuing inferences (fig. 22). To convince oneself of the cogency of this point, one has only to imagine what the interpretation of the same image might have been if the stele, instead of finding its way to the Konya Museum, had once been transported to Mexico by an enlightened collector, and then been bequeathed to the Museo de la Culturas, with the caption 'unknown origin' . . .

These examples are enough to suggest the kind of extremes to which we would be carried if we took the requirement of explicitation literally, in the analysis of transformations $P_0 \rightarrow P_i$; and it would be wrong to believe that this requirement raises difficulties only in the allegedly special case of stylistic analysis (e.g. 'Seljuk' art, 'static and solemn' style, etc.), in contrast with semantic analysis. Formally speaking, the difference between one and the other is merely a matter of degree; and it is easy to realize that the elicitation of correspondences $P_0 \to P_1$ (or $P_1 \to P_0$ in the hypothetico-deductive direction) entails in both cases an elucidation of the mechanisms of pattern recognition which is a logicist project in its own right, and a formidable one at that (see § 1.3.3).

The foundations of the reasoning process in fact seem to become clearer as we reach the upper levels of the construction. No one will contend that it is illegitimate to establish a relationship between the hawk and hunting, between the static character of the scene and the ceremonial

Figure 24 One of many ways to visualize the relief studied by J.-P. Roux, on the basis of its description alone, according to a given set of semiological conventions.

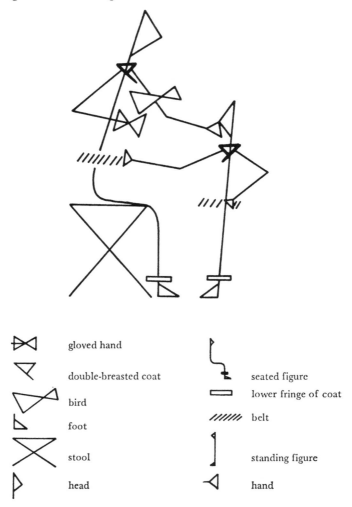

interpretation, etc. (fig. 21), or again, going backward, between the hypothetical difference in the age and status of the two figures and the observed asymmetry of their size and attitude (fig. 22), etc. The basis of these inferences is an organization of knowledge which is again supposed to be shared by all readers, in either of two ways: either we postulate a kind of 'universal' semantics, or at least a semantics that is so widespread among our potential readers that we need not bother to vindicate the inferences drawn from it; or we refer to specific events or facts which have no reality beyond the limits of a more 'local' area – in terms of space, time, people (L, T, H) – known only to specialists of its present or past history (ethnologists, historians, etc.). In the first case, the justification of an inference is again supposed 'to go without saying'; and our author is indeed silent about it (e.g. from the hawk to hunting, from the adolescent prince to his smaller height, etc.). In the other case, on the contrary, a critical apparatus is called forth, in the form of footnotes indicating the factual or written sources that are held to support the proposed relationship (for instance, between gestures 'to the belt' and their connotations of 'obedience' *among certain peoples of Asia*; or between the 'portable seat' and the fact that *Turk or Mongol princes* used to watch 'in the open' the hunting parties of their subjects, etc.). This distinction between universal and local semantics should however be understood in an eminently relative sense: for one thing, the concept of universal semantics is a pure fiction,[19] and we should only be talking of semantic organizations of a more or less local scope, between the imaginary poles of a conceptual order restricted to a unique 'culture' (local in this sense), or conversely extended to a hypothetical 'nature' of things, immutable through time and space (universal in this sense). An easy way to decide where we are supposed to stand in this continuum consists in observing the position taken on this matter by the author himself, in so far as he chooses to leave certain inferences unvouched for (that is, not backed by explicit arguments), while others are made to rest upon the evidence of well-specified material or textual data (Gardin & Lagrange 1975: 51).

In the case of our transformations $P_0 \rightarrow P_1$, however, we may occasionally wish to question the inferences of the first category, those which go without saying: is it self-evident, for instance, that the 'static and solemn' aspect of the picture – once we take it for granted – imposes a

19 At least in the pragmatic sense here given to this expression, not to be confused with the 'universal semantics' construed by logicians, from Carnap to Bar-Hillel, in which the concepts are defined by their analytical content rather than through empirical references (Bar-Hillel 1970: 190): the way in which archaeologists make an *implicit* use of semantic universals of a most *informal* kind has of course nothing to do with a semantic calculus in a logical sense, as we shall stress further on. More generally, it will be wise to consider that all the terms or expressions which seem to be derived from logic or linguistics are here taken in a metaphorical sense.

ceremonial interpretation, rather than an explanation through the funeral function of the stele, which could then be held merely to represent 'an episode of the defunct's life' as one of the previous commentators had suggested? In the same way, is it self-evident that the 'portable' aspect of the chair on which the man with the hawk is seated indicates that the scene is taking place in the open, rather than being merely a characteristic of the furniture or of the way to represent it in this particular cultural context?

Etc., etc.: one only has to put the question in those terms to discover the correct answer. If inferences of this sort are dealt with as if they needed no justification, it does not mean that we are invited to regard them as *necessary* in any way, by virtue of a compelling universal order of things. Only, the author trusts that they will seem at least *plausible* to every one, by virtue of a common referential order, so that he may be exempted from having to justify them. The flaw in this position, however, is that it takes no account of the fact that other inferences are usually just as plausible, under the same terms, leading to mutually exclusive interpretations. In other words, the 'self-evidence' of a given relationship depends not only on its plausibility, but also on the *non or lesser plausibility of others* which may occur to the reader, at any stage in the argument, by virtue of a conceptual organization of the universe which contains them all.[20] Needless to say, this hidden face of the seemingly most indisputable inferences seldom receives much attention in archaeological Explanations; I shall refrain from labouring the hypothesis of a possible relation between this flippancy and the blossoming of interpretative constructions in the study of human affairs.

The same point was already made earlier, in the terms suggested by the more abstract figure 20: at any vertex of the graph which represents the relations between one concept and another, in a given construction, there usually branch off several arcs corresponding to different inferences between which a *choice* has to be made, so that the movements observed in this conceptual space seldom have much to do with implication or deduction in the strict sense. This limitation remains true even when we proceed from top to bottom in our diagrams, following

20 The same point was taken in more detail in § 4.3.1. Excellent examples of this situation are given by George Cowgill (1975), *à propos* of historical explanations based on demographic hypotheses or data. Constructions of this sort make an explicit or implicit reference to 'factors of growth', which observations relating to our own societies lead us to question; however, we often tend to regard them as based on sheer common sense, for the sole reason that our attention has not been drawn to the counter-examples. Thus the *selection* between complementary or contradictory paths is an essential aspect of the interpretative process in the historical sciences (but just as noticeable in the physical or biological disciplines, for that matter); on the epistemological consequences of this requirement in historical explanations, see Scriven (1959: 461–3); and for archaeology in particular, the recent and thorough study by Smith (1977).

the hypothetico-deductive direction, as may be seen in figure 23. The distinctive features mentioned in the lozenges, at the bottom, are clearly not deduced from the hypothesis, P_5, in the same fashion as we would deduce for instance that if a 'sultan' and his 'son' are mentioned in P_5, then the image must contain forms which we describe in P_0 as 'human figures', at least 'two' in number, etc. The reference to the 'sultan' implies the presence of a man, but the reference to a 'ceremony' having something to do with 'hunting' does not imply that this man should be seated, nor that, if seated, his chair should be a portable one; the mention of the 'son' implies the presence of another figure, but not that the latter should wear the same clothes as the sultan, etc. In fact, the plurality of possible inferences, from P_n to P_0, is the reason why each of them can be regarded as additional *information*, as defined in the theory related to that concept; but it is also the reason for the relative weakness of deductions or predictions of the 'one among others' sort, since their empirical verification is necessarily of limited value as far as the validation of the hypothesis is concerned. If for instance any of the predictions considered in figure 23 (lozenges) had *not* been verified, it is unlikely that the author would have regarded his interpretation as disproved on the basis of that fact alone: one can readily imagine that a scene in which 'the sultan confers on his son . . . the right to practise hunting' might be staged in many other ways, e.g. with the sultan standing, or seated on an imposing throne, with the prince clad in a different garment, etc. Conversely, if we choose to read figure 23 in the other direction, from the bottom upward, we are bound to come across situations that are equivocal in the etymological sense: the portable seat suggests other circumstances than the exercise of open air activities alone, the identical clothes other reasons than kinship, etc. (for a comprehensive treatment of these basic logical issues with special reference to archaeological reasoning, see Salmon 1975, 1976, and Smith 1977).

This last observation takes us back to a characteristic of semantic networks that has already been discussed, in connection with figure 20, namely the fact that while it is true that we can view the construction as a to-and-fro movement between the *explanandum* and the *explanans*, the separation between the 'upward' and 'downward' operations is in fact largely arbitrary. J.-P. Roux assures us that he has used a number of traits P_0 for deriving the hypothesis P_n, in the upward direction (fig. 22), and others to verify the latter, in the downward direction (fig. 23); without challenging his word in any way, I would rather feel that the second group has *also* played some part in the genesis of the hypothesis, if only in an unconscious way. One could even go so far as to invert the two diagrams, at least by way of a methodological exercise, in order to show that the paths of figure 23 could be followed in the upward sense, for deriving the hypothesis, and those of figure 22 in the downward sense, for verifying it . . . We shall return to this point later, in connection with the status of validation in general in explanatory constructions (§ 4.5); meanwhile, let us only bear in mind that we are entitled to cumulate all the traits found in the P_0 propositions of both diagrams, and present them either as the inductive basis of the construction, or as the deductive manifestations of its validity, depending on our preference for the ways of invention or the ways of proof. Whatever the case may be, the alternative, to me, is not worth a holy war.

To which many will probably object that I am thereby dodging the historical or psychological aspect of the picture: if it is 'true' that Roux's construction was first tentatively built and then reinforced in the two-stage process which he describes, why not reconstruct this process in the form of two oriented graphs which respect this distinction, as in figures 22 and 23? My first inclination would be to answer, indeed, why not, since we have just established that it matters little whether we distinguish these two phases *or not*, in the logicist formulation of the process . . . but we are then running two risks. One of them is that the terms of 'validation' or 'verification' will be taken a little too seriously: Roux's construction does not rest on a firmer basis, in this two-faced presentation, than it would if we chose to formulate it through a unique cumulative diagram, as suggested above; and we need to take a quite different view of the meaning of these two terms, in the broader context of the succession of archaeological constructions over a span of time, rather than within the limits of any given construction (see § 4.5). The second risk is that the contingency of the distinction, from an epistemological standpoint, will be forgotten: it may be interesting to know that Roux was *first* led to his hypothesis by a certain path, *then* strengthened in the same course by another – although I must confess that I am still just as unconvinced of the psychological reality of this distinction as of its epistemological value – but I fail to see why and how we should separate the two phases in a schematization of the logicist foundations of any scientific construction.

My last remark concerns a serious limitation in our own diagrams. If we regard figures 22 and 23 as particular 'interpretations' of the general sketch of figure 20, in the sense which is given to the term in logic, we must admit that the interpretation does not go beyond the vertices of the graph; no labels are attached, on the other hand, to the arcs that connect vertices with one another. A quick glance at the two figures mentioned is enough to realize the extreme heterogeneity of the corresponding relations. (*a*) Some of them belong to the realm of componential *definitions:* for example, the relation between the 'hawk' and the group of terms (i.e. traits) listed at the bottom of figure 22, 'bird-large-held on-fist-gloved'; or again the relations shown on figure 23 between the attributes mentioned in the lozenges and the groups of terms or traits in description P_0. (*b*) Other relations are more in the nature of *association of ideas*, such as those which hold for instance between an element and its function (from 'hawk' to 'hunting', in fig. 22), or its usual setting (from 'hunting' to 'open air activity' in fig. 23). (*c*) Others still connect abstract concepts with their *symbolic manifestations*, as for instance the relations between vertices within circles and lozenges, respectively, in figure 23. (*d*) The classical Saussurian opposition between *paradigmatic* and *syntagmatic* relations is also present: the division of Turks into 'Western' and 'Eastern' is an example of the former, whereas the combination of 'ceremony', 'hunting' and 'Turkish context', as formed at level P_2 into a synthetic proposition of level P_3, is an instance of the latter (fig. 22).

Clearly the anatomy of archaeological constructions should include a systematic inventory of their constituent *relations*, just as needed as the inventory of *entities* in the analysis of the underlying intellectual processes; for it is through the reasoned combination of the former with the latter that all Explanations are formed. Obviously, the rules of the game cannot be stated precisely as long as we have only one word to go by, 'inference', to designate the manifold relations that we establish between the conceptual units of the construction, in networks such as those of figures 22 and 23, in order to account for its generation or for its verification, respectively. Suppose now that both the relations and the rules have been defined, for a given construction: the network which expresses them takes on its two-fold function, semantic and logical – *semantic* because the vertices indicate the concepts which are set to work in the interpretation process, and *logical* because the arcs indicate the relations that hold between them, underlying the operations of derivation (inference, reformulation, rewriting, etc.) inherent in this process.[21]

4.4.3 *Problems of formalization*

The consequences of the logicist requirement on the interpretative constructions of archaeology should now be clear: it imposes an explicitation of the logico-semantic organizations of knowledge – both general and specialized knowledge, or 'universal' and 'local', in the operational sense proposed above – that underlie the build-up of these constructions. The single example analysed in the preceding section

21 Needless to say, I am not here contending that the deliberately simplified figs. 21 to 23 illustrate *the* way of organizing knowledge for the purpose of logicist reconstructions. Possible objections regarding for instance the shortcomings of binary reductions when dealing with *n*-place predicates, the relativity of most logical distinctions (e.g. between paradigmatic and syntagmatic relations, definitional or functional, etc.), or any other formal matters of this sort, should therefore be deferred until more is known of the true architecture of specific reconstructions, as found in archaeological literature (references in § 4.2.2, 4.4.1, 4.4.2), as well as of the more general discussions already published on the same issues, in a broader perspective than that of archaeology alone (e.g. Cros, Gardin & Lévy 1964: 40–75, Gardin 1965a, 1967b, Bely *et al.* 1970, etc.).

may seem to provide a very narrow basis for contending that *any* interpretation presupposes a referential organization of that sort, and that *all*
such organizations display the same structure, as suggested by figure 20.
I am nevertheless ready to take such a stand, for no other reasons than
those which have led me to sketch out diagrams of this sort in the present
book (§ 4.4.1). Several questions then crop up: since we know that there
is a limit beyond which the explicitation of our mental processes is of
little methodological value, as illustrated above, to what point should
we carry the obligation to display the logico-semantic organizations
(abridged hereunder *LSO*s) that support our constructions? To what
extent does this effort contribute to making the latter more 'scientific'?
More generally, what is the place of *LSO*s in the progress of archaeology
toward the formalization of its theories? This last question summarizes
the purport of the present section.

My first observation will bear on the substance of LSOs, as illustrated
by the preceding example. It appears to be in this case so elementary,
so untechnical, that one is justified in questioning the utility of this tool:
are the materials and mechanisms of archaeological explanations always
as plain as all that? A tactful way to answer affirmatively is to associate
the qualifier 'natural' with the kind of semantics and logic that archaeological interpretations call on, through LSOs. By 'natural semantics',
we are given to understand a system of definitions and classifications
that is supposed to convey the knowledge shared by most speakers of a
given language, or group of languages, in turn called 'natural' in
contrast with the scientific languages used in narrower universes of
discourse (cf. the NL *vs.* SL opposition in § 3.3.3). In other words, if the
rationalization of archaeological constructions does not seem to require
semantic systems of reference of a very sophisticated sort, the reason
must be sought, I believe, in the fact that our theories are still relatively
primitive, rather than in any shortcoming of the rationalization process
itself. In the same way, 'natural logic' is the logic of operations which we
carry out in handling natural language, under any of the vague designations already mentioned – derivations, inference, transformations,
reformulations – without resorting to any special technique of a mathematical or more generally formal kind; and if the logical sequences that
lead to interpretative statements seem in turn amazingly primitive in
our reconstructions, the reason is again that there is no evidence of a
more sophisticated relational calculus in archaeology. In brief, as long
as our Explanations will take shape in the terms and according to the
rules of natural discourse, there is no reason why the elucidation of the
concepts and operations that underlie them should require a more
artful medium than the primitive LSOs suggested above.

But what proof can we give that logico-semantic organizations do
indeed represent the cognitive structures at work in our author's mind?
As a matter of fact, none whatsoever; but this admission is not very

damaging. For such is not the goal of the exercise: LSOs are not meant to provide a film of the successive stages of a construction, as they 'really' developed, but rather a kind of flow diagram indicating one way of reproducing the construction through a mechanistic sequence of operations that may have nothing to do with the author's own mental processes. The notion of simulation immediately enters our head: the objective of logicist reductions is in short to propose reasoning procedures of which we can say that archaeologists behave *as if* they were following them, even if unknowingly. The characteristic of this analysis, however, is that it tends to remain within the realm of a 'discursive logic' (Vignaux 1976), i.e. a logic of sequential statements formulated in natural language, rather than calling on mathematical quantifications and inferential processes (e.g. stochastic models) that seem foreign to the archaeologist's mental behaviour. For this reason, the concept of formalization here refers to the use of tools that are not mathematical in the standard sense, as opposed to the case of typological constructions – the formation of classes being more amenable to calculation than the derivation of interpretative statements – but rather more akin to linguistics, at least in the very broad acceptation of the term which a number of experts in discourse analysis seem to have in mind (Lakoff 1970, Mel'čuk & Žolkovskij 1970, Grimes 1975, Petöfi & Rieser 1973, Noël 1973, etc.).

This reference to linguistics is however highly deceptive. Let us first emphasize that discourse analysis has little to do with the methods of generative or transformational analysis in which a few archaeologists once thought fit to look for models of scientificity (Deetz 1967: 83–93; Muller, cited and discussed by Hymes 1970). The reservations aptly expressed by Dell Hymes about those early attempts at borrowing methods from linguistics also hold for all those which followed, as a result of transient alliances between historians, linguists or computer scientists (Robin 1973). More generally, it is quite vain to imagine that theoretical linguistics, or for that matter any other discipline concerned with the study of formal sequences (mathematics, logic, computer science), can ever provide us with a set of analytical methods that will bring forth the hidden meaning of any phenomena we may care to study. The persistence of naïve beliefs in panaceas of this sort is one of the oddities of the human sciences as they stand today (Gardin 1974a: 44–5; 1979: 399). As for so-called applied linguistics (or computational linguistics), the prospects are not better, for other reasons: the analytical tools that are proposed under this title are eminently *ad hoc* in nature, unamenable by definition to any such universalistic use, or abuse. While it is true, for instance, that we are now able to produce algorithms such that a computer will 'interpret' scientific abstracts with the same measure of success as the specialist of the field concerned (e.g. Bely *et al.* 1970), it is *also* true that those algorithms rely on semantic tools which have no value outside that field. The limitations are even more severe: these tools merely reflect the state of knowledge available *at a given time* for under-standing the meaning of certain texts, in the very peculiar sense which is given to the word 'understanding' in computational linguistics (e.g. Winograd 1972; Schank & Rieger 1974, etc.); but this state is by definition a changing one, in the sciences of man as in any other discip-line, so that we must be prepared to revise constantly the content of our rules of inference, as the substance of knowledge changes. The truly 'formal' part of interpretative processes, invariant throughout these modifications, finally turns out to be very meagre, compared with the scope and complexity of the semantic operations involved, especially since we have to include among the latter the assignment of definitions not only to individual concepts (vertices) but also to their relations (arcs), the grammarians' distinction between semantics and syntax being of no avail here (Gardin 1967b: 35–6; 1973: 154–8). In all such respects, the analogy is unmistakable between our 'logico-semantic' organizations, meant as the basic system of reference in the generation and verification processes of archaeological constructions, and the kind of tools which are being developed by specialists of the 'conceptual' or 'cognitive' analysis of natural texts of all kinds, with a view to its for-malization (Bobrow & Collins 1975, Norman *et al.* 1975, Schank *et al.* 1975, etc.); this very analogy will now help us in assessing the limits of the formalization trend in archaeology.

For one thing, the investigations just mentioned tend to depart from the relatively well-defined objectives and methods of linguistic analysis proper, and merge quite naturally with the analysis of cognitive processes in general, applied to any object – textual or other. The domain of research is shifting from the study of grammar to artificial intelligence; the big name in quotations is no longer Chomsky but Minsky, and the authors of 'language understanding programs' are now 'products of departments of computer science or psychology, rather than linguistics' (Damerau 1976: 109). Is the future of formalization thereby more secure? I do not believe so, for the following reason: this change in viewpoint or strategy, however sound in its principle, is likely to accredit once more the belief in the existence of *general* methods of textual analysis, even though they will not fare better under the banner of artificial intelligence than they did fifteen or twenty years ago under the banner of linguistics. The obstacle mentioned above is indeed exactly the same in both cases, namely the obligation to set up logico-semantic organizations of an extreme complexity (under a variety of names: cognitive networks, dependency trees, mental templates, etc.) in order to account for interpretative processes of the most elementary kind, with the sad certitude that we shall have to repeat the operation whenever we move to a different universe of discourse, however slight this difference may be. One of the earliest warnings of the sort was given as far back as 1960, in connection with the then flourishing studies on machine translation (Bar-Hillel 1960); nothing has invalidated the forecast, which the same logician was able to reformulate not long ago in still more radical terms (Bar-Hillel 1975). The alternative, ultimately, amounts to this: either we admit that our investigations should be limited to very special domains of cognitive activity, in order to elucidate the conceptual tools which command the build-up of scientific constructions in each one of them taken separately; or we persist in looking for the rules of a more general 'logic of discourse' beyond these limited fields of application.

We have many reasons to have doubts about the wisdom of this second path – e.g. (*a*) the unproductiveness or failure of all the 'general-purpose programs seeking to mimic the problem solving aspects of human CNS (central nervous system) activity over a rather wide field' (Lighthill 1973: 15); (*b*) the mystery which continues to float over notions such as natural logic, logic of argumentation, discursive logic, etc., currently presented in the last ten or twenty years as the privileged instrument of discourse analysis, but to which no one has yet managed to give an operational form suited to the reconstruction of cognitive processes of even the crudest sort, such as those which form the subject of this book; (*c*) the persistence of the same deficiency in the latest linguistic theories, even when they are meant to mitigate it (see for instance the recent speculations on 'network grammars', 'cognitive grammars', etc., Lakoff & Thompson 1975), etc. I would therefore wholly subscribe to the following unexpected conclusion of an experimental study centred on inference operations purposely chosen among the most elementary ones: 'it may seem strange to argue for a common-sense interpretation of the data, but elimination of constructs and formal models involved as explanations is the first step towards clearer understanding of actual cognitive processes' (Paris 1975: 83–4). To which the author adds the basis for such a courageous stand, on the part of an expert in formal reasoning: 'the truth-functional interpretation of material implication simply does not adequately represent subjects' comprehension processes because it explicitly ignores[22] the semantic relationship between the elements within the proposition ... Comprehension of propositional relationships is dependent, *inter alia*, upon the semantic relationship between the components of the proposition' (*op. cit.*, 89–90).

We are thereby running the risk of being insidiously taken back to the former path, that is, probing instead of cognitive processes in general, the idiosyncratic and changing LSOs that underlie a ridiculously small

22 The conjunction of these two terms may be regarded as a slip of the
    pen, but I would rather take it personally as an excellent though
    unorthodox way of stressing the apparent if not *explicit* will of many
    champions of formal or computational models of thought and language
    to *ignore* as much as possible the highly specific semantic constraints
    that limit the practical value of such models.

number of constructions peculiar to a discipline, a school, or even to a person alone. The 'formalization' of interpretative constructions in archaeology can therefore only mean, to me, the multiplication of very limited exercises of this sort, quite foreign to the higher ambitions which 'artificial intelligence' should indeed uphold, if the expression were to be taken seriously. For this reason I would agree with the opinion of J.-B. Grize, a logician whom I have already quoted, concerning the necessity of a distinction between *formalizations* in the strict sense, in which the proposed models are truly formal systems, relying in one way or another on the theorems of mathematical logic, and on the other hand, *schematizations*, defined as 'models generated through a discourse in natural language' (Grize 1974: 204). Clearly, the goal of logicism, as we have presented it in this book, is to produce schematizations rather than formalizations of archaeological reasoning; but if the scope of formal analysis is reduced to such a degree, what benefits can we hope to reap from it? Nothing more, ultimately, than a clearer vision of the enduring limitations of our constructions, at a time when it is becoming the custom to speak highly of their present or potential merits, in the name of newly discovered 'scientific' methodologies of various kinds. The exercise discussed in the previous section is in this respect illuminating: the reformulation of Roux's analysis in logicist terms does not increase the probability that his interpretation of the object is correct; supposing that the same exercise were repeated for each of the six previous interpretations opposed by Roux, we would still be unable to decide, on the basis of schematizations alone, which of them is the most likely. The gain is rather, conversely, in evincing a certain equivalence of the various constructions, in as much as they are all equally *plausible*, or even in some cases *compatible*, provided minor changes are brought to the underlying LSOs (the demonstration of this point consists in rediscovering Roux's hypothesis deductively, on the basis of the previous interpretations alone: Gardin & Lagrange 1975: 38–48). Thus, the value of logicist analysis lies ultimately in the relentless unveiling of the postulates and presuppositions that accompany each construction, and in the resulting power gained by archaeologists in locating with precision the parts of the architecture which they regard as fragile, if not unacceptable.

Let us imagine for a moment that all archaeological publications were presented – God forbid – in the form of schematizations in the spirit of figure 20, with all the necessary specifications concerning the labels attached to the arcs and vertices of the graph, as well as the logico-semantic rules of derivation from any level P_i to another, P_{i+1} or P_{i-1} (fig. 22 and 23, respectively); and let us suppose further that we cumulate the observed LSOs and rules in order to constitute the 'cognitive grammar' so to speak of archaeological constructions as they stand in archaeological literature. We can bet that the resulting picture would display the most freakish kind of architecture, in which the paths of well-formed constructions *with respect to this grammar* would be so numerous at each point of the cumulated graph that we would despair of bringing about any order in the overall interpretation process. In other words, we should find ourselves back in the situation described earlier *à propos* of the *non*-systematic interpretations, when we tend to regard an explanation as credible only in so far as we fail to consider others that are equally so, in terms of our underlying 'cognitive grammar' (§ 4.3.1, 4.4.2).

The conclusions reached in this section can now be summarized in three points. (*a*) For one thing, our logicist analysis, i.e. the schematization of explanatory constructions in archaeology, *is not* the formalization dreamt by some; but I fail to see how we could come close to the latter without having first gained experience in the former, unless we make a clean sweep of all the discursive forms of reasoning and restrict ourselves to statements and derivations formulated in the language of mathematics or logic alone. There seems to be little chance (or risk), to say the least, that anthropological disciplines will soon be ready to take that course. (*b*) On the other hand, even if reduced to relatively modest ambitions, the logicist project implies 'remodelling' efforts which certainly exceed the zeal of most archaeologists, even among those who attach due value to the scientific status of their constructions. But there is fortunately no need for the whole profession to be committed to the arid if gratifying exercises of schematization. What I have in mind is rather a specialization somehow parallel to the distinction made between the empirical *vs.* theoretical branches of any given discipline, in the natural sciences – the former occupying the 'unmarked' or unqualified pole of the opposition, as phonologists might say: physics *vs.* theoretical physics, chemistry *vs.* theoretical chemistry, biology *vs.* theoretical biology, etc. Theoretical archaeology, in this case, becomes the study of the abstract or formal aspects of constructions produced by empirical archaeologists, i.e. by experts in the interpretation of material data in specific geographical or historical areas.[23] The empirical branches of archaeology may very well progress without sharing all the requirements or goals of theoretical archaeology in this sense, even if they can be shown to suffer in the long run from a prolonged separation; and theoretical archaeology in turn loses the imperative

23 Long discussions could take place on the wisdom of this definition or designation. I wish only to say: (*a*) first, that I do not regard this matter as terribly important, provided agreement can be reached both on the substance and on the desirability of 'a critical study of patterns of archaeological reasoning', under this or any other name (Clarke 1973: 15, cited more fully on p. v); (*b*) second, that I am aware of the fact that the expression 'theoretical archaeology' is being used in the USSR in a much broader sense (Klejn 1977), for which I think however that the alternative designation used by Sher, 'general archaeology' (1976: 77–9), is more appropriate.

character which some of its champions have improperly given it in the last years. Its role surely is inquisitorial, but only in the etymological sense of the word, without any of the unfortunate judicial connotations that spring up whenever anyone pretends to direct the whole profession in this unique way. (*c*) The acceptance of this duality, lastly, is but the consequence of a truism that it is perhaps worth recalling: the most explicit constructions are of no avail if the resulting propositions do not stand the test of empirical facts. In other words, the scrupulous elicitation of the semantic data and logical operations that support an Explanation is not a sufficient nor even a necessary condition for conceding it a scientific value (see § 7.2). I shall now enlarge upon this last point.

4.5 *Validation of Explanations*

That the formal merits of a construction do not necessarily go hand in hand with its cognitive value should be self-evident; it may however be appropriate to reaffirm it, judging from the number of methodological exercises in which the pleasure taken in experimenting with a particular algorithm or computation technique seems to be greater than the will to obtain results that will stand the test of empirical verification.[24] The necessity of an ultimate recourse to empirical proofs is indeed inherent in any theoretical construction, whatever the discipline concerned; it is only more urgent in archaeology, for two reasons. The first one is that historical interpretations, as we have seen, are more in the nature of *plausible* orders of things than anything else (§ 4.4.2): it is not uncommon for the same objects to give rise to radically different interpretations, that are nevertheless all well-formed, i.e. each based on explicit and consistent LSOs.[25] The recourse to a wider array of factual criteria is therefore needed in this case, for want of any formal reason to prefer one interpretation to another. Secondly, we have to admit that the more systematic constructions currently proposed, in this primitive stage of theoretical archaeology, may easily be denounced as over-simplified, in comparison to the wealth of tangible data handled in the more traditional ways. Buffon, in the eighteenth century, had already pointed out 'the drawbacks suffered when we want to apply geometry and calculation . . . to objects of which we hardly know the properties well enough to measure

24 This remark is not addressed only to the experiments of others, but also to some of my early dealings with computers in archaeology: see for instance Gardin & Garelli 1961, a methodological exercise which should have been followed by applications, but never was, so that no practical results have been reached as far as assyriology is concerned.
25 To give but one example, I shall cite the illuminating case of two constructions concurrently developed by two archaeologists interested in the dating of the same tumuli, at Se Girdan in Iran: the conclusions reached, starting from the same empirical data, and using arguments that are readily amenable to logicist reformulations in both cases, differ by two or three thousand years (Deshayes 1973 and Muscarella 1973).

them; in all such cases, we are led to make assumptions that are always contrary to nature, to strip the subject of most of its qualities and transform it into an abstract entity that no longer bears any resemblance to the real one; and when we have much reasoned and calculated on the relationships and properties of this abstract being, and reached a conclusion which is just as abstract, we believe we have formed something real ... which produces an infinity of false consequences and errors' (cited by Thuillier 1976: 149; the English translation is mine). Archaeology is particularly prone to this weakness of incipient formalizations; the proof of the 'reality' of its mental constructs is all the more necessary.

How shall we produce that proof? The methods used for the validation of scientific theories are familiar to everyone, so that I need not go beyond a summary of a previous study, in which I discussed the validation of compilatory and explanatory constructions of the more systematic sort in the sciences of man (Gardin 1969: 34–8). For the sake of clarity, I shall again begin with the relatively simpler sorts of Explanations examined in the first part of this chapter, namely typologies.[26]

4.5.1 *Validation of typological constructions*

The essential function of typologies, according to our definition, is to assign the objects of a given corpus to classes that are brought into relation with specifications of space and time in the broadest sense (§ 4.1). The affiliation of an object to a type amounts then to an LT attribution, the L and T units being, however, defined in a wide variety of ways. In order to verify that these attributions are correct, a number of tests can be devised; I have proposed to group them into two categories, respectively characterized by the following titles: 'diagnosis' and 'counterfeit'.

(*A*) *Diagnosis tests.* We need here a number of standard objects of which the L and T specifications are indisputable, on any ground (inscriptions, extrinsic data, etc.): the typological definitions given in the construction under study will be used for ascribing them to a 'theoretical' LT unit (i.e. predicted on the basis of the intrinsic properties of the standard objects), which we shall then compare with the 'real'

---

26 It has been argued that the only satisfactory validation procedures in the behavioural sciences were those which made use of statistical tests, in one way or another, and that there was in fact little hope of validating theories unless they were couched in a mathematical language that made them amenable to such tests (MacEwen 1963). The following presentation is based on a different postulate, namely, that we can test the validity of propositions formulated in a non-mathematical language (*IL* or *NL*), in ways which are neither more nor less reliable than statistical tests, as suggested by our repeated use of them in the guidance of our behaviour in daily life, *as well as in scientific research itself.* The tests discussed below belong to that non-statistical group, exclusively.

attributions. This procedure is tantamount to an evaluation of the relevance of the classes proposed in the typological construction with respect to the derivation of inferences L or T: (*a*) if the tentative classification of the standard objects leads to a few correct attributions among others that are erroneous (a phenomenon identical to the 'noise' in the corresponding tests applied to Compilations, see § 3.5), the conclusion is that the proposed typology is not an adequate filter for the sorting of objects with respect to L and T, and that it must be further refined; (*b*) on the other hand, if the same classification never leads to the correct attributions (a phenomenon equivalent to 'silence', as defined in the same connection, *ibid.*), the inference is that the typology is wholly inappropriate, and that it must be reconsidered.

(*B*) *Counterfeit tests.* Suppose now that we have no standard objects of known L and T origin; we can then use the typological definitions as directions for the making of imitations which present all the intrinsic features listed in the definition of any given class, *other things being equal* (I shall come back later to this all but inconsequential clause), the imitation merely consisting in most cases in graphical or symbolic representations of the objects concerned. Those counterfeit products are then shown to experts who are asked to assign L and T attributes for every one of them – which means, if they are not taken in by the experiment, the L and T attributes which they believe to have been in the mind of the forgers. Assuming of course that the knowledge or connoisseurship of experts is a reliable standard, the success or failure of the test will indicate the discriminating power of the typology, in the realm of LT predictions for which it has been made: (*a*) if the counterfeits inspired by the definition of a single type are regarded as heterogeneous, i.e. open to different LT attributions, the conclusion is that the typology is too loose (phenomenon of 'noise'); (*b*) if on the contrary they are viewed as conformable to the original type, but hardly reflecting its 'real' diversity, the conclusion is that the definitions proposed in the typology are too restrictive (phenomenon of 'silence').

The latter kind of test is not as easy to set up as the former, for obvious reasons: the manufacture of convincing fakes, even graphically, is a difficult task which not all archaeologists are able to perform. Moreover, the clause *other things being equal* is in practice rather embarrassing: for the reproduction of an individual feature distinctive of a given class is one thing, the making or drawing of a whole monument that can be taken for a member of that class is another, of quite a different scope. An intentionally simplified example will help to reveal the difficulty. Supposing that in order to contrast romanesque and gothic architecture,[27] we rely on a few elementary oppositions such as 'round-arch'

---

27 In taking the adjectives 'romanesque' and 'gothic' as examples of space–time specifications, I am not misusing my own LT definition: see above, § 4.1.1.

vs. 'pointed arch', 'barrel vaults' *vs.* 'ribbed vaults', etc.: anyone can learn without too much pains how to draw if not how to make round and pointed arches, etc., considered in isolation, but it does not follow that we are able to produce representations of 'romanesque' or 'gothic' churches that will be regarded as acceptable or plausible constructs, under either label, with respect to all the unexpressed attributes that are covered by the 'other things being equal' clause (bonding of stones, outline of doors and windows, columns, buttresses, etc.). This clause is therefore a veiled way to acknowledge the incomplete character of many typological distinctions: they have value only within a given set of materials, and the intrinsic attributes upon which they rest are not necessarily those which we would consider if we had to contrast the set as a whole with other aggregates.

(*C*) This limitation is the reason why the counterfeit tests are or should be the necessary complement to diagnostic tests. For it may happen that the observation of suitably defined traits is enough to predict unerringly the LT attributes of standard objects (diagnosis), while the knowledge of the same LT-bound traits is farcically insufficient for any high-fidelity reproduction of these objects. The above example illustrates this situation to the point of caricature: if one were to assert that romanesque arches were all round and gothic arches all pointed, these two features would be enough to build up a 'typology' of romanesque gothic churches that would resist all diagnostic tests . . . but the counterfeit tests would immediately reveal the poverty of the construction.

4.5.2 *Validation of interpretative constructions*

Let us now turn to the more ambitious constructions aiming at 'functional' inferences (*F*), drawn from materials assigned to given LT units: destination of objects and monuments, sociological conditions for their production or use, historical circumstances of their decay, etc. (§ 4.3) If we reduce these constructions to their terminal propositions, in the sense earlier indicated (§ 4.4), the problem of their empirical validation can be formulated as simply as in the case of typological constructions, by calling on the same two means: measuring the predictive power of the construction, as in the diagnostic tests, and assessing its generative potentialities, as in the counterfeit tests.

(*A*) *Predictive power.* Let us consider for instance different types of architectural remains typical of a specific human group H, to each of which a distinct function has been assigned as a result of an interpretative construction of some sort (dwelling houses, stores, cultural monuments, etc.); and suppose we state in the form of a unique proposition P_n the sociological characteristics of architecture H, on the basis of those types. The first way to verify the validity of P_n is by referring to a set of comparable structures built and used by the same people H, and of whom we know, so to speak, the sociology: if the same archaeological reasoning, applied to those standard structures, ends up with the 'true' functional inferences, one can put some trust in the cognitive value of P_n. It is for validations of this sort that archaeologists sometimes resort to ethnographic observations, when they regard a given living group, with or without good reasons, as an heir to the cultural patterns in question. This course is no doubt dangerous, since we seldom are in a position to *prove* behavioural continuity from the ancient group H to its living descendants (see Chang 1967b; Watson, LeBlanc & Redman 1971: 49–51); but it has at least the same worth as this assumption. The same approach is on the other hand irreproachable when the standard knowledge refers to the very remains under study and to their 'function' in the group H itself: this is the case when we can draw jointly on archaeological and textual evidence, and use the one to bear out inferences from the other. An extreme situation of this kind is found in 'experimental' excavations or surveys conducted solely for the purpose of evaluating the reliability of interpretative constructions; a standard example is the study by Bonichsen (1973) of an Indian camp abandoned in modern times, in which he proved the discordance between the sociological inferences drawn by an archaeologist and the real organization of the camp as related by a former member of the group; or again a comparable effort by Ascher (1968) to show the misinterpretations which might creep into socio-economic explanations of the configuration of car dumps in the USA if they were to follow the archaeologist's usual reasoning patterns.[28]

The other, more classical way of verification through predictions is part of the hypothetico-deductive method, as mentioned above (§ 4.4.1, B): considering P_n as a hypothesis to be tested, we shall try to deduce from it as many consequences or implications as possible, on the basis of a logico-semantic organization of the same form, if not of the same substance as the one used in inducing P_n; and we shall observe in the archaeological record under study the degree of realization of these predictions. This was the course followed by J.-P. Roux, it will be remembered, in order to validate his hypothetical interpretation of the Anatolian relief (§ 4.4.2);[29] and I exposed then the reasons which made me doubt the soundness of this approach, notwithstanding the fact that it is held in great respect by most of the new archaeologists. Essentially, the root of my reluctance lies in the extremely 'spongy' character of the

28 The comparison by George Cowgill of demographic explanations relating respectively to ancient and contemporary societies, already mentioned, provides another interesting example of the consequences of validation tests in archaeology: see above, note 20.

29 Admittedly, Roux's interpretation P_n is not nomothetic; but the fact that it is presented as the product of an inductive process is not an argument against its possible treatment as the basis of an hypothetico-deductive process, as indeed shown by Roux himself in the final stage of his construction, namely Validation.

LSOs that are set to work in historical constructions, so much so that they can be tailored to fit anyone's requirements. I shall return to this fundamental point[30] in the final chapter of this book (§ 7.1.1, *B*); meanwhile, I shall satisfy myself with a conciliatory, hardly disputable position, namely that verifications based on this procedure have the same degree of credibility as the LSOs which support the deductions or predictions used in the proof.

(*B*) *Generative power*. Let us now adopt a different viewpoint, and consider P_n as a kind of descriptive–generative model of the archaeological reality under study: intended first as a symbolic system for the description and understanding of a given set of archaeological remains, this model can also be used to produce others, 'artificial' in this sense, which will exhibit all the intrinsic features considered relevant to the interpretation, *other things being equal*. Going back to the architectural remains of human group *H*, with its structural differences and specialized functions, we shall reproduce, both graphically and verbally, a number of architectural configurations compatible with P_n, and again call on experts to identify the human group in which these kinds of configurations obtain. If, to them, the 'artificial' structures bear little or no relation to the 'real' structures of group *H*, the conclusion must be either that the model is inadequate, or that the 'other things being equal' clause has been put forward a little too rapidly, as happened previously (§ 4.5.1, *B*), and that some of its implicit substance should be transfused into the model.

A concrete illustration of this approach is provided by a number of studies of ancient technology, where the archaeologist, after having determined the manufacturing processes responsible for the production of given objects, sets his hand to the fabrication of 'artificial' ones according to the same processes, in order to observe how they compare with the originals (e.g. Hester & Heizer 1973).

Mutatis mutandis, this is the kind of exercise which I was suggesting in an earlier section for the verification of Roux's iconographical interpretation: we had to produce an image which would display all the elements mentioned in support of the latter, other things being equal (that is, the other elements being similar, in some unspecified sense, to the allegedly

30 An easily demonstrable one, when time and space permit; in default of both, I shall have to assume that the many symptoms and examples of the plasticity of LSOs mentioned since the concept has been introduced (§ 4.4.2) are enough to establish my case. As a lighter piece of evidence, I shall mention the dazzling succession of short-lived hypotheses which currently attend the development of an archaeological excavation or survey, from day to day, as tentative explanations of the latest state of empirical observations: the fact that they may be at the same time numerous, mutually exclusive, ephemeral, and *yet all endowed with some kind of logico-semantic consistency*, is a sign among others of the kind of laxity which I am referring to, even granted that only a few of these explanations find their way to the published literature.

irrelevant features also present in the original relief), and observe whether it would also be read as a 'ceremony of investiture related to hunting', etc. (§ 4.4.2, and fig. 24)

We are clearly back in the realm of simulation, already visited in connection with the validation of typological constructions. The remarks which were made then still apply here, namely that even though the method raises many practical difficulties, it sets the kind of requirements that Explanations should eventually meet, in the way of validation: the proposed schematizations C_e, as defined in § 4.4.3, should be suited to the generation of fictitious objects or representations in harmony with the specifications of C_e (e.g. architectural structures designed in the manner of . . ., artifacts manufactured in the manner of . . ., scenes related to the concession of hunting rights composed in the manner of . . ., etc.), and calculated to suggest in turn historical or sociological interpretations similar to C_e. The discrepancies observed between the inferences drawn from the real and from the simulated data, respectively, give an indication of the validity of the construction used both in shaping the former and in forging the latter.

4.5.3 *A synoptic view of validation procedures*

The parallelism between the two pairs of tests discussed in § 4.5.1 and 4.5.2 cannot be ignored: the diagnostic test is a way to measure the predictive power of a construction (paragraphs A in both sections), while the counterfeit test amounts to measuring its generative power (paragraphs B). This congruence merely reflects the fact that the mental operations involved are of the same nature in the A and in the B groups, respectively: roughly speaking, we may contrast the two courses as analysis *vs.* synthesis, or again, in the more pedestrian language of schools, translation *vs.* prose. In the first case – diagnosis, prediction – the explanatory construction C_e is used as a system (or 'grammar', to press the school analogy) for proposing an interpretation of standard materials for which the correct L, T or F attributions are known (as in translation exercises with answers). In the second case – counterfeiting, generation – C_e is used as a system or grammar for producing objects or compositions (through drawings, symbols, texts) which should be acknowledged by experts as acceptable specimens of the L, T or F categories defined by C_e.

The virtue of this dichotomy is that it applies as well to the validation procedures used in the case of Compilations, C_c (§ 3.5). Suppose we have stored in a data base a number of descriptions relating to a body of materials M; in order to verify the adequacy of those descriptions for retrieval purposes, we resort in the same way to exercises of 'translation' and 'prose', as above. The 'translation' exercise consists in describing new materials M' with the same representation language as M, and in using the descriptive terms as search criteria in the data base, so as to obtain comparative series $M'-M$. The relevance of the parallels thus established by C_c, and the price paid in terms of 'silence' and 'noise', jointly indicate the efficiency of the compilation. Conversely, the 'prose' exercise consists in considering any number of expressions formed in the terms and according to the rules of the representation language, in order to compose for every one of them fictitious objects M'' compatible with these specifications, that is, amenable to the same description; the homogeneity or heterogeneity of the groups $M''-M$ thus formed, seen in the practical perspective for which the data base was built, again gives an indication of the efficiency of C_c.

The following table brings together the different validation methods which we have examined, both for Compilations and Explanations. The distribution into two classes (col. 1 and 2) accounts for the complementarity of the tests broadly defined as analytic *vs.* synthetic in this section, for *both* C_c and C_e. Further, the parity between the tests carried out *respectively* on C_c or C_e, in each class (lines 1 and 2), is indicated by the semantic affinities of the keywords by which they are designated; an appropriate summary of our table would be to combine them in the following definition: the validation of scientific constructions C consists in evaluating the *relevance* of *diagnoses* and the *acceptability* of *counterfeits* which are produced in accordance with the specifications given in C.

| Category of constructions | The complementary ways of validation through: | |
	analytical tests 1	synthetic tests 2
Compilations, C_c 1	Tests of relevance (parallels)	Tests of acceptability (fakes)
Explanations, C_e 2	Diagnostic tests (predictions, deductions)	Counterfeit tests (imitations, simulations)

5
Schematization

The reader will probably have noticed strong homologies in the argument of the two preceding chapters, respectively on Compilations and Explanations. (*a*) First came the emphasis on the necessary subordination of both categories of constructions to well-defined *Objectives*: it is impossible to come to a conclusion with regard to the quality or utility of a compilation without referring to its practical destination; in the same way, an archaeological commentary makes little sense if we ignore the cognitive purpose which it is supposed to serve, etc. (*b*) In particular, the *Selection* of materials which form the substance of archaeological constructions should be somehow the consequence of those Objectives: no one any longer dares take refuge in the traditional ideal of 'exhaustiveness', either because the endless accumulation of materials makes it an impractical task, even to the most zealous compilers, or because archaeologists are slowly awakening to its theoretical vacuity for purposes of typological or more elaborate interpretative constructions. (*c*) It was further stressed that the *Description* of material remains could not be regarded as an autonomous task, and that it had in turn to be subordinated to the Objectives of the construction, both in the C_c and in the C_e categories. (*d*) From this point on, archaeological reasoning was presented as a sequence of operations carried out on the terms of Descriptions: operations of *Ordering* on the one hand, customary though not strictly necessary in Compilations (§ 3.4), inevitable but of another nature in Explanations (§ 4.2); (*e*) operations of *Interpretation*, on the other hand, only present in the latter (§ 4.3 and 4.4). (*f*) Finally, *Validation* came logically last in both categories of constructions (§ 3.5 and 4.5), the methods used under that name being shown to be formally identical for Compilations and for Explanations (§ 4.5.3).

We are thus in a position to express through one diagram the basic structure of Compilations and Explanations, as it merges from these homologies. Figure 25 may serve the purpose; we shall examine first the lay-out of each part, in the above order (Objectives, Selection, Description, Ordering, Interpretation, Validation) (§ 5.1), and then insist on the commonplace nature of the diagram, which is but another way of representing the course of scientific constructions in general, irrespective of the object or fields concerned (§ 5.2).

5.1   *The general diagram of Constructions C_c and C_e*

5.1.1   *Objectives*

Let us notice first the position of box 1, *Objectives*, in figure 25: it is not only the initial one in the chain of operations from 1 to 6, but also the determining step in the whole construction, in as much as the following ones cannot be dissociated from the goal of the exercise. The selection of the materials, the way we look at them in our descriptions, classifications,

Figure 25   Schematization of the various aspects of archaeological constructions discussed in chapters 3 and 4, and their interrelations. The six aspects may be represented in a linear order, as *phases* of the C process (heavy line), but with three restrictions: (*a*) the nature of Objectives, in 1, directly affects the course followed under 2, 3, 4, 5, while providing the standard by which to test C^i, in 6; (*b*) for Compilations, the process stops at 3 or 4; (*c*) phase 6 should be regarded as a dynamic link between two successive states of the same construction C^i while it is being worked out (feedback arrow, upward), or between two successive or alternative constructions C^i and C^j standing in competition (feedback arrow, downwards). The linear order from 1 to 5 is therefore merely a static rationalization of archaeological constructions, *once completed*.

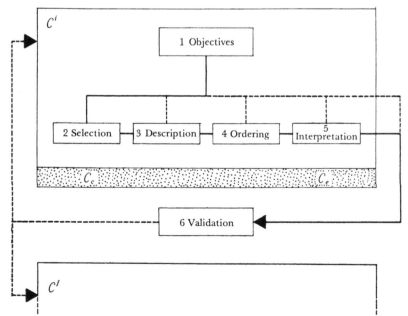

interpretations, and indeed our appreciation of the whole construction can hardly be decided or commented upon unless we have a clear view of the reasons why any of these operations should have been carried out at all. Such is the sense of the direct links from box 1 to boxes 2 to 6, vertically.

The starting point in any archaeological publication should therefore be an account of what it purports to achieve, or of the considerations that decided the author to undertake the work, whatever its place on the continuum from C_c to C_e. What I have in mind here is not the traditional prologue on the 'importance', 'richness', 'interest' of the sites or monuments which the archaeologist has chosen to study: although such statements have very little discriminatory power, archaeological literature is full of preambles of this kind, in which we may see an honest rationalization of the pleasure or pains taken in the study of particular materials, but certainly not a serious argument for the reasons for selecting them as objects of study. The very concept of 'selection' seems indeed to be missing in these presentations, even though it should provide the major thread of reasoning at this stage. When we decide to undertake an exploration of the Andean mountains, a catalogue of Carthagianian lamps, an excavation at Nijni-Novgorod, or a reinterpretation of the Persepolitan reliefs, the implication is that we give a lesser priority to other surveys, inventories, soundings, exegeses, etc. which we might have carried out in the same lapse of time, in our field of competence. The argument which we would then expect is an economic one: given the historical issues pending in a particular sector of archaeological research (Latin America, Carthage, etc.), and the means, qualitative as well as quantitative, that a given person or group can muster for undertaking work in that area, what is the most judicious project, and to which end should it be directed? (For a discussion of possible decision criteria, see Gardin 1978b.) Leaving aside the case of mandatory operations (salvage excavations, political concessions, etc.), one seldom comes upon presentations of this sort, where the objectives of the construction would be the product of an explicit and articulate argument. The logicist requirement, with respect to box 1 in our diagram, is nothing but a reminder of the need to justify the materials or problems which we choose to study by giving some thought to those which we therefore choose to ignore, even if only provisionally – which does not exclude hedonistic arguments, e.g. the maximization of pleasure, if such is the case: only, one should not confuse the interest of a research project with the interest which we take in it.

5.1.2 *Selection*

That there should exist a relationship between the nature of the objectives and the selection of materials to be studied (box 2) is a truism that we

need not labour. The rationalization of this link, however, is more difficult than one might conclude from the fact that most authors do not care
to raise the subject in archaeological publications. The more common
position indeed seems to be that the basis of the selection 'goes without
saying': if the objective is an inventory of Campanian ceramics, it goes
without saying that the catalogue should include in the long run 'all' the
known vases and sherds of this category; if our task is to publish the
Olynthus excavations, then obviously we should try to present 'most' of
the observations and data collected on the site; or again if we aim at a
reconsideration of the historical meaning of the Luristan Bronzes, we
need not mention that we shall strive to take into consideration 'as many
as possible' of the available objects, published or unpublished, etc. And
yet, nothing is less evident than such a *petitio principii*, suggested by the
terms in inverted commas. The stereotyped reference to the principle of
Exhaustiveness in any of its naïve forms ('all', 'most', 'as many as possible', etc.), tends to be perceived as a mere convention, and we no
longer regard as self-evident that even Compilations should abide by it,
as there comes a point when the costs incurred in the acquisition of new
data seem to override the marginal gain in knowledge that may accrue
(§ 3.2). As for Explanations, the very fact that they bear on specific categories of historical or anthropological information should imply that we
include in the catalogue only those materials from which the required
information can be derived. The art of data acquisition, in this case, does
not therefore consist in collecting as many of them as possible, but on
the contrary in adopting an eminently selective strategy of observation,
related to the objectives of the construction, which will reduce as much
as possible the number of objects which ought to be considered. This
reversal does not mean that the archaeologists of yesterday were to
blame when they happened to behave as naturalists or collectors of
curios, but rather that the archaeologists of today are not necessarily to
be praised when they stick to observation patterns that are more adapted
to the accumulation of taxonomic systems than to the formulation of
scientific theories. The logicist innovation, regarding box 2, lies in this
bias towards minimalist strategies, where the supreme virtue is to reduce
as much as possible the dimensions of the body of materials that will bear
out a given construction, while taking care that the latter will not easily
be disproved by a mere expansion of the data base. The interest recently
shown for 'refusal' procedures in general (non-observation, non-
conservation, rejection, etc.: Gardin 1972b), and for sampling methods
in particular (Redman 1974, Mueller 1975, Gardin 1977b) bears
witness to this new philosophy.

5.1.3 *Description*
The same remark holds for box 3 of the diagram, the *Description* of

material remains. Here again, the way we look at the latter obviously depends on the reasons for our interest in them in the first place, i.e. on the objectives of the overall construction; and the archaeologists of tomorrow may wonder how so many of their predecessors were able not only to behave as if they ignored this truism, but also to go so far as to deny it through unreasoned pleas in favour of 'complete' descriptions, or more cautiously (but not more wisely) 'as complete as possible'. We need only consider past Compilations which set up such pretensions and compare them with those which today harbour an identical dream, *à propos* of the same objects, to observe how the 'exhaustive' descriptions of either group fall short of their ambitions. Needless to say, the contrary would be surprising, in an empirical science not prone as such to stop at a unique and final vision of its materials. The acceptance of the relativity of representation systems in archaeology thus indicates a progress of scientific method, a rather humble one to be sure, but hitherto wanting in the profession. It shows itself in a variety of ways, both in Compilations and Explanations. Speaking of Compilations, we are now aware of the unrealistic character of projects aimed at the design of so-called 'universal' (i.e. all-purpose) descriptive languages, and ready to forsake the hope that data banks founded on such languages could *a priori* contain all the elements needed for the formulation of any scientific theory to come (Gardin 1975). Turning to Explanations, many archaeologists also accept the fact that typological or interpretative constructions call into play only a small fraction of the features found in the archaeological record and that this selection changes legitimately from one construction to another (Clarke 1968: 61–75), without any need for a cumulation of all the features concerned, except for purposes of retrieval in Compilations (§ 3.5). A number of us will even go so far as to condemn a recent propensity to multiply the number of descriptive variables, in an illusory attempt to foster precision and objectivity, and will advocate on the contrary minimalist strategies of description similar to those which we have just discussed in connection with processes of the selection (Speth 1972: 56–7). Finally, turning to matters of publication, we shall recommend that the descriptions which traditionally precede the interpretation of a set of objects be restricted to the features actually used in this process, *to the exclusion of all others* (Gardin & Lagrange 1975: 21–4, 62–5, 100). The convergence of these views indicates the general purport of the logicist position with respect to box 3.

5.1.4 *Ordering*

The mere accumulation of descriptions formulated in an *ad hoc* information language may be the ultimate stage of a construction C_c, when the retrieval operations are to be carried out with a computer; the *Ordering* of the data is then left to the users. Thus, a data base in which entities and their properties have been recorded in an arbitrary sequence (i.e. not prearranged) is a construction which ends at box 3, the further stages (sorting, classification, etc.) being so to speak delegated to the users, within the limits imposed by the substance of descriptions. In the case of printed compilations, on the other hand, a standard arrangement is usually necessary, though not under pretence of conveying any original meaning: the construction then includes a further stage, Ordering, subordinate to documentary or retrieval purposes only; but it does not go further, and ends at box 4.

The situation is different with constructions C_e: the Ordering of descriptive data is here understood as a preliminary to their Interpretation, the next phase in our diagram. The reason, as argued earlier (§4.3), is that interpretative constructions are as a rule suggested or supported by the observation or computation of formal structures, in the broadest sense (classes, series,), built up wtih the symbolic data chosen to represent the materials in phase 3. The process is patent in the typological constructions discussed in § 4.1 and 4.2: the quest for more or less homogeneous groups is here the basic operation, conducted in the hope that these groups will correlate with some extrinsic data (origins, associated objects, etc.) which will provide the required basis for LT inferences (or demonstrations, in the hypothetico-deductive presentation). However, there are cases when this phase seems to be lacking, as for instance in monographs bearing on single monuments or on preexisting series which are not questioned. In fact, the omission is only an illusion. In the first case, the monograph acquires explanatory power only through reasoning in which the monument under study is considered in relation to others, on the basis of this or that property: each list of 'parallels' produced in this comparative process clearly amounts to the formation of a class, from which the author draws inferences (or demonstrations) exactly in the same way as above. Identifying a monument, establishing its origin or function, restoring its original form, all such constructions, at first sight remote from classification processes, in fact imply operations of ordering in the broad sense. The same is true of our second example, namely studies of predetermined classes: these studies 'make sense', literally speaking, only in so far as they first discover phenomena of co-variation among the intrinsic or extrinsic features associated with the members of each class; the Ordering phase here again consists in observing distribution patterns from which historical inferences or demonstrations can be made.

Thus, in all circumstances, the passage from description to interpretation is strewn with combinations and arrangements of all sorts carried out on the 'data' of the former phase, Description, in order to establish 'meaning' in the latter, Interpretation. The term Ordering refers to all such operations, understood in the broadest sense: the most hazy groups of the traditional comparative method have their place here, on the same ground as the more formal orders of mathematical or computer archaeology; while the entities concerned may be of all conceivable kinds – objects and their attributes, chiefly, but also geographical areas or periods of time contrasted in terms of their archaeological 'content', trial pits or stratigraphic layers characterized by the finds made in them, etc. In all such cases, the goal of Ordering is to provide a basis for inferences (or proofs) that the description of entities or properties taken one by one would fail to support.

5.1.5 *Interpretation*

In this picture, *Interpretation* (box 5) is the quasi-inevitable complement of the preceding phase (except for Compilations, as stressed in § 5.1.3). In practice, the two operations are often blended, in so far as the choice of an ordering process is usually determined by its productiveness in terms of potential interpretations, with respect to the Objectives set in box 1. We could have expressed this interdependence by combining the two phases into one, under a single denomination x, of which the terms Ordering and Interpretation would then designate the 'formal' and the 'semantic' facets, respectively; I have chosen to uphold the distinction, however, in order to be able to account for constructions where Ordering is the final stage – for instance Compilations, as recalled above, or Taxonomies, as understood in § 4.1.1, note 5 – without any subsequent Interpretation.

The analysis of interpretative constructions in § 4.4 has shown the nature of the basic tool in that process: namely, logico-semantic organizations of knowledge (LSOs), the validity of which extends over more or less comprehensive spaces of observation and reasoning, from the broad universe which is supposed to underlie the use of 'natural' language, or the so-called natural logic – but which remains a matter of speculation – to the more 'special' or specialized fields where the elements and rules that are instrumental in building theories are paradoxically better known, but not to the point where we can yet speak of formalized constructions in any real sense (§ 4.4.3). The elucidation of the LSOs that support Explanations C_e is probably one of the most pressing tasks of theoretical archaeology in the years to come, at least in those few cases where the well-tried value of these constructions, in an empirical sense, justifies our investing some time and effort in getting to the bottom of their foundations, in a formal sense. In selecting the constructions which we regard as worthy of such 'schematizations', as we earlier proposed to call the exercise (§ 4.4.3), we should not be bound by the fluctuating prestige which some of them enjoy here and there on account of their ambitions or merely of their jargon: the obscure journey of interpretation deserves more attention in a plain typology constantly verified by empirical data than in a general theory of cultural change admirable for its scope and method, but which can never be confirmed for want of any data or reasoning that might disprove it. In other words, the logicist requirement, with respect to box 5, is the observance of a certain restraint in proclaiming that an archaeological Explanation is a 'scientific' product. The price that has to be paid in order to justify the claim goes far beyond the methods proposed by the champions of scientific archaeology, through astonishing statements such as the following, stipulating 'that they are often asking for *little more* [my italics] than that the assumptions and reasoning be made explicit' (Watson, LeBlanc & Redman 1971: 32). The example considered in §4.4.2, elementary as it is, gives an idea of what it costs to take this humble demand seriously.

A further proof may be found in the case of those highly interpretative constructs that are named 'descriptions', when we look at them through the mental template of figure 3 (§ 1.3): how do we go from the unordered array of stimuli seized by various receptors, human or mechanical, through which we 'perceive' a given object, to the ordered selection of traits by which we 'describe' this object, in terms of any representation language, natural or artificial? The process is *a priori* more straightforward than the transition from a set of objects to a statement of the historical or sociological facts which they are supposed to 'mean'; and yet, 'asking . . . that assumptions and reasoning be made explicit' in this straightforward case turns out to be an immoderate demand. Anyone can verify this assertion by reading the later reports published on the formalization of archaeological descriptions of even the most simple kind, for instance pottery shapes (see, for example, Hollerbach 1975 and his conclusion, p. 226: 'if the present thesis is an indication, coming up with good descriptions is formidable'; same conclusion in Borillo *et al.* 1973). It does not follow that we should drop altogether the idea of discovering the logico-semantic bases of archaeological Explanations: the pattern recognition analogy, and more generally all the formal analogies given out in the early pages of this book (§ 1.3), seek only to suggest that the project has inborn limitations which it would be unwise to ignore (see chapter 7).

5.1.6 *Validation*

Interpretation is in fact the last stage of Explanations: for we have found a number of reasons for locating the subsequent *Validation* process outside the scope of the construction itself, the more stringent one being that the empirical data brought into play at this stage have exactly the same epistemological status as those which have been put forward initially in support of the Explanation (see § 4.5.3). This position does not mean that we leave no room for validation processes in our diagram, but rather that we insist on placing them where their fundamental role is brought out most accurately, that is *after* the presentation of C_e: the true verification tests are not those which the author of C_e describes as such in order to broaden the empirical basis of his views, but more convincingly those which subsequent observers will carry out under that name or another when matching *new* data with C_e. Such is the reason for the situation of box 6 outside the frame of construction C^i, in an intermediate position between C^i on the one hand, and an alternative construction C^j or successive constructions C_n on the other hand, imposed by some negative aspects in the testing of C^i (fig. 25).

The virtue of this presentation is that it brings out the dynamic component in the flow of archaeological constructions, all doomed to be undone in the course of time, in such a way that no validation test *devised by their authors* can shield them from such a fate. The phenomenon is quite patent in the avatars of Compilations, and all the more readily accepted as the goals of such constructions are relatively humble (§ 3.5); but it is just as indisputable in the drift of Explanations of a higher status, notwithstanding the intelligence, rigour and learning displayed by successive commentators. No doubt, this last statement needs some qualification: an 'undone' construction does not mean an annihilated one, in the strict sense of the word, and I have no quarrel with the traditional picture of scientific progress as a dialectical process in which every explanation, every theory contributes even if negatively to the advancement of knowledge. The fact remains, however, that scientific constructions are in essence ephemeral products, and that the basic function of Validation is less to protect them against this fate than to mark the step which separates the decay of some and the growth of others, in a given field of observation.

Does it follow that the mechanisms of empirical verification play no role in the genesis of an archaeological construction? Certainly not: let us make it clear that figure 25, from box 1 to box 5, is not meant to describe the way in which a construction C^i gradually takes shape, but only its logical architecture, *once completed*. The generation process itself is usually a cyclical one, by trial and error, during which the author of C^i does indeed test a number of different answers to the questions raised here under the title of Selection, Description, Ordering and Interpretation, until he feels satisfied with a 'final' set of propositions in keeping with the Objectives of C^i. These intermediate tests might be considered as so many steps in the overall validation process; the established usage, however, is to ignore them in the presentation of C^i, or mention them only in the form of arguments in support of the proposed Explanation, which amounts to equating this process with Interpretation, *within* C^i, as I believe one should do.

Figure 26   The succession of constructions 1, 2, 3, . . . (or
stages 1, 2, 3, . . . of a given construction while it is being worked
out), each characterized by the stands taken with respect to
Objectives, Selection, Description, etc., the transition from state *n*
to state *n*+1 being determined by Validation tests of a more or
less systematic nature (fig. 25). The process stops when the
author decides that the gap between 'facts' and 'theory' –
graphically represented by segments V_1, V_2, . . . of decreasing
length – is null or minimal, according to his knowledge of both;
its metaphysical limit is the imaginary point ω already shown in
fig. 15, where a unique theory C^ω accounts for all the observable
facts.

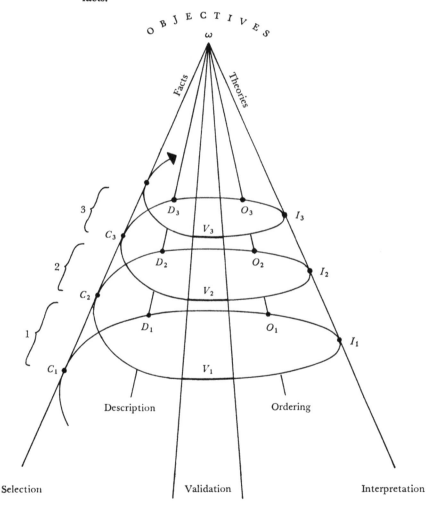

5.2 *Cyclical aspect of the process*

The preceding comments indicate the purport of the feedback circuit, in figure 25: it can be understood as referring to either of the two phenomena just discussed: (*a*) either the gestation of a given construction C^i through successive states, until it reaches its ultimate form, which can *then* be described as if it were the product of a linear process, from box 1 to box 5, according to the conventions of our diagram; or (*b*) the interrelation between competing constructions C^i, C^j, . . ., C^n, when Validation tests in the narrow sense lead to question C^i *after* it has been presented in its final form.

The cyclical nature of the process is self-evident in both cases, as illustrated by the helicoidal curve in figure 26. In case *a*, we consider C^i from within, and trace the successive steps of its formation, by trial and error, until the positions adopted with respect to the four central questions summarized above – basis of the *S*election, system of *D*escription, method of *O*rdering, logico-semantic rules of *I*nterpretation – determine a final product ω, which the author regards as consistent both with his *O*bjectives and with the empirical facts available to him (*V*alidation here being the factor of change from one state to another). In case *b*, we now consider C^i from without, and trace its replacement by (or integration with) other constructions 1, 2, 3, . . ., *n*, as the acquisition of new data (phases *S* and *D*) or the adoption of other interpretative patterns (phases *O* and *I*) – or both – leads to constant reformulations (phase *V*), towards an imaginary *O*bjective ω, symbolizing the ultimate knowledge of all things.

This is nothing more than an illustration of the so-called 'scientific

Figure 27   The conventional representation of the 'scientific cycle' (after Kemeny 1959: 86), to which I have added a diagonal division showing the respective place of the empirico-inductive approach (black half) and the hypothetico-deductive approach (white half), obviously complementary, but with their distinctive leaning for facts or theories, respectively.

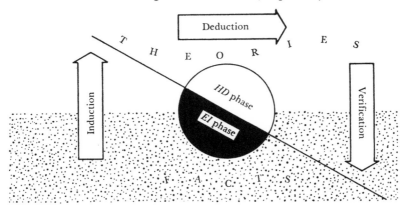

cycle', as it stands in all empirical disciplines, and of which we already had a glimpse in § 4.1.1 when observing the to-and-fro movements between intrinsic and extrinsic data, compilatory and explanatory orders, etc. (fig. 15). Figure 27 is a more conventional representation of the cycle (after Kemeny 1959: 86), which expresses the more general oscillation between the realm of material entities (lower part) and the realm of abstract concepts (upper part) – with an addition of some significance, however, namely the division of the cycle into two phases, across the diagonal. The left part, in black, corresponds to the empirico-inductive path (EI) followed in going from the observation of facts to the formulation of theories; the right part, in white, to the hypothetico-deductive path (HD) followed in going from the assertion of theoretical propositions to their verification through factual evidence. The black and white sectors formed with the horizontal line may be taken to express graphically the difference in focus or emphasis between the two approaches: in the EI approach, the breadth of factual knowledge seems to matter more than theoretical insight, whereas in the HD approach, conversely, more room appears to be given to the analysis of mental operations than to the accumulation of facts. Both paths are however conducive to the progress of theoretical constructions, in archaeology as elsewhere; and it would be an error to give an allegorical meaning to such a naïve contrast, with Black standing for the Dark age of pre-scientific archaeology and White for the Age of Enlightenment through sound science . . . This hierarchical vision of the two methods is yet defended by distinguished scholars, so that we shall have to emphasize further on the difference in the way we may look at theoretical constructions in archaeology, depending on whether we confine ourselves to the hypothetico-deductive perspective or embrace the broader view presented in this book (§ 7.1.1).

6
The form of archaeological publications

'New levels of precision in presenting data and in interpreting
them can surely lead to briefer and more interesting technical
reports as well as providing the basis for more lively literary
portrayals of what happened in history' (Isaac 1971: 128)

'Ideas about cultures deserve to be presented in the clear, crisp
language and logic of natural science devoid of unexamined
metaphor and synonymy; and to be adequately illustrated by
charts, tables and diagrams' (Cloak 1975: 940).

It may seem strange that we should turn to such a concrete matter as
the form of archaeological publications immediately after the abstract
considerations of the preceding pages. The reason is that we should
expect some kind of a relationship between form and content in this
case; the position taken in the present chapter is that this relationship
has become defective essentially because our age-worn publication
practices, unchanged to this day, are in contradiction with the logical
consequences of chapters 3 and 4 with respect to the structure and function of archaeological writings – Compilations and Explanations alike.
The matter is not purely academic: my intent is to bring out the practical evils which result from this contradiction, as well as the kind of
remedies that are likely to cure some of them in the near future.

6.1 *Rhetorical implications of the C_c/C_e dichotomy*

Let us first recall the two-fold basis of the opposition between compilatory
and explanatory publications. The former, C_c, are essentially intended
as tools for the *retrieval* of data bearing on the *physical remains* which constitute the raw materials of archaeological constructions; the latter, C_e,
aim at proposing *theories* derived from the study of these remains, on
the actions and modes of life of ancient *human groups*.

Category of constructions	Entities concerned	Major function
Compilations	Material remains, and their attributes	Retrieval
Explanations	Ancient men, their history and modes of life	Theory

The difference, summarized by the above table, is at first sight sizable enough to suggest that we should find some reflection of it in the fabric of the respective categories of publication. In a *Compilation*, the primary goal will have to be to satisfy the information requirements of a specific user group, by providing convenient ways to retrieve manifold combinations of entities and elements, in the broad sense indicated in § 4.1 (see table under Example 3: objects and their attributes, assemblages and their constituents, etc.). The emphasis will therefore be laid upon the convenience of look-up and sorting procedures, in ways which should not demand that we read the Compilation as we read a novel. Conversely, in an *Explanation*, the primary purpose will be to present the data and operations that underlie the proposed theoretical construction according to the architectural principles outlined in the preceding chapter (§ 5.1); the emphasis in this case should be on the clarity of the demonstration – for the presentation of a theory, whether typological or interpretative in the sense of chapter 4, is to be regarded as a demonstration – which implies rules of exposition of quite another sort than those of inventories or catalogues.

The archaeological literature as it stands today seems, however, to ignore this dichotomy. The common form of all publications is a *text*, written in the terms and according to the rules of a given natural language, and accompanied by *graphical documents* (photographs, drawings, charts, etc.) which are meant to illustrate or more often complement the verbal data. No doubt the style tends to be more jerky, 'telegraphic', in the case of compilatory writings; but descriptions remain even then continuous texts, which have to be read or skimmed from beginning to end whenever we are looking for occurrences of particular entities or elements mentioned in the Compilation. Moreover, indexes and tables, when they exist, do not exempt us from this drudgery, owing to the limits inherent in their printed form (number of entries, scope of combinations, etc.). In the same way, explanatory texts are normally written according to the standard rules of traditional rhetoric, without much regard for the logical articulations summarized in chapter 5, as I shall show below (§ 6.3). Thus, in both cases, the form and usage of archaeological literature are not in conformity with its function, as I see it on the basis of the analysis of the preceding chapters; and the fact that the same rhetorical principles govern the composition of both categories of constructions proves, if necessary, that not much thought has yet been given to the desirable harmony between ends and means in matters of publication. A few suggestions may therefore be welcome on the kind of steps that should be recommended, or indeed expected, on the way to more consistency if not wholesale harmony.

6.2 *Access to data in Compilations*

Regarding first Compilations, my position may be anticipated from the title of this section: their basic practical quality should be to provide users – rather than readers – with convenient channels of access to any information items singled out in the Compilation, for a broad but specified range of applications (e.g. comparative studies, storage and retrieval of excavation data, searches in museum collections, etc.). Notwithstanding stubborn opinions reviewed earlier in this book, the mere accumulation of graphic reproductions or 'iconic data' in the broad sense is not a sensible way to approach that goal, for any large-scale and open catalogue. Inevitably, *ad hoc* representation languages or more generally symbolic systems will have to be used (§ 3.3); it takes little wit to realize that data access is as broad as it can be when searches are made possible on any combination of the elements or terms defined in such systems (Gardin 1955). Printed indexes are no doubt a step in this direction, but a limited one, because only a fraction of the meaningful terms in C_c are accepted as index entries, while 'compound entries', when they exist at all, represent in turn only a small fraction of the meaningful combinations of those terms. The use of hand-sorted punched cards was an early attempt to meet the issue (Deshayes & Gardin 1956) soon replaced by electronic files, more flexible still; and the question now arises of deciding whether data bases, or data banks, as those mechanized Compilations are called, could not become the standard means of access to archaeological information, better than through printed publications.

The answer, to me, leaves no doubt: the progress of 'data networks' in the last ten or fifteen years, in many branches of the natural sciences – and more recently in the social sciences as well – will sooner or later affect the historical disciplines as well, including archaeology, leading to a revision of our present publication practices. What is a data network? Essentially, a set of interrelated research centres (rather than 'documentation' centres in the narrow sense) where data bases are brought into being in a more or less concerted fashion, either as information tools in their own right (i.e. *retrieval*-oriented Compilations), or as *theory*-oriented by-products of Explanations (see table on p. 148).

These data bases are set up on various kinds of physical support, which may be used jointly, for reasons of overall economy: i.e. not only magnetic tapes, but also microforms, card indexes, etc. The time-consuming process of searching through books and periodicals in libraries is then replaced by direct interrogations of the data, either in the research centre concerned, or at a distance, through procedures which range from simple mailing to advanced forms of teleprocessing. The major innovation does not lie here, as many believe, in the use of computers: it consists in directing towards a new form of documentation or archive centre, which should hopefully become as accessible as libraries, large bodies of factual information which were hitherto disseminated through the channels of printed publications – the goal of the transfer being to meet the logical and economical drawbacks of the latter (Gardin 1968: 106–7, figs. 1A and 1B; reproduced in Doran & Hodson 1975: 319–20).

An evolution of this sort, however, is not a matter of years: several decades will probably elapse before institutions and men prove adapted to information patterns that are still distasteful to most living archaeologists. Moreover, we still have to develop a better understanding of matters such as the boundaries of data bases (§ 3.2), the compatibility of representation languages (§ 3.3), the mechanism of updating in both cases (§ 3.5), etc., prior to embarking upon ambitious data network projects. The proposed reformation is therefore all but ripe; and the few data centres that have lately sprung up in archaeology (e.g. Chenhall 1971, Striedter 1971, Gardin 1972a, Leclant 1974, etc.) should leave us no illusions on that point. I still believe however that the trend is irreversible, on account of a kind of logico-technical rather than merely technological determinism, which I do not say is a wholly 'good' one (Gardin 1975; see below, § 7.3.3), but that we should not hope to challenge by arguments which are likely to look anachronistic to everyone in a matter of years.

6.3 *Towards a new rhetoric in Explanations*

The case of Explanations is different; for their goal is at first sight more in keeping with the function of natural discourse, the common form of argument since Aristotle. The reality, however, is more entangled. For one thing, archaeologists are not all equally happy with the form of the publications which they are supposed to read in order to keep abreast of current theories in their field; and many confess that they tend to skim this literature much in the same way as they consult Compilations. The origin of this behaviour is not to be sought only in the so-called explosion of scientific information, on the quantitative side (§ 6.3.1); the traditional practices of essay writing or composition also contribute to the adoption of look-up procedures that differ from the linear process usually associated with 'reading', as we shall see below (§ 6.3.2). We must therefore be ready to admit that even our 'natural' ways of writing should undergo some revisions, to be replaced by what I have called elsewhere a 'new rhetoric' of archaeological prose (Gardin & Lagrange 1975: 101). The expression may seem somewhat pompous; it is in keeping, however, with the extent of the proposed changes (§ 6.3.3).

6.3.1 *The inflation of Explanations*

I shall first put forward my views concerning the reading patterns which tend to prevail, in archaeology as elsewhere, as a result of the growing volume of publications. These views have no statistical basis; they merely reflect the convergent answers of a few archaeologists whom I have been able to interview on the subject, certainly not a 'representative' sample of the profession in any technical sense. The inferences derived from this narrow and informal survey are therefore mere hypotheses, as far as generality goes; they coincide, however, with observations made on a larger scale in other disciplines.

A first fact is the anxiety shared by most about the widening gap between the volume of text which everyone would wish to read, in order to keep informed of current findings in a particular field of research, and the amount of time available for this activity. Figures are sometimes produced, in order to give more weight to the phenomenon. They need not be reported here, however, since the same fact has already been established a number of times for a variety of disciplines in the last twenty years, through much more systematic methods (see for example the many studies reviewed by Lin & Garvey 1972). The avowed consequence is that instead of *reading* that much quantity of printed text, we have no other course left but to adopt cursory ways of *consulting* them – which logically leads to questioning the form of such publications, on the same ground though not in the same terms as in the case of Compilations.

Another observation concerns the inconvenience caused to readers and consultants alike by the ambivalence of most publications with respect to the C_c/C_e dichotomy, as mentioned in § 6.1. The true *raison d'être* of many articles or books is to present original objects and monuments *per se*, without having necessarily much to say about their historical or sociological import, especially when they belong to known classes or types. Yet, the outer form of such publications is often that of an Explanation C_e, with its characteristic blending of descriptive and interpretative data, even though originality lies only in the former. The reader then has to disentangle the text, in order to retrieve pieces of information that have been scattered to the winds of unnecessary 'historical comments'. Supposing there existed distinct channels of communication for new *materials* and for new *theories* – since it is a dangerous folly to pretend or require that we produce both at the same rate – the truly interpretative literature of archaeology would be reduced to quite manageable proportions, without hindering the continuous growth of Compilations in the form envisaged in the preceding section.

To sum up, the 'consuming' of archaeological publications by those for whom they are produced is made more and more troublesome as a result of the very 'conditioning' of the product, unfit for the kind of usage which their sheer number imposes on us. We now have to look more closely into the nature of our difficulties, granted that this quantitative and qualitative inflation is their source.

6.3.2 *A few shortcomings of published Explanations*
I shall only mention as a reminder the backwardness of archaeology in the way of reforms of a more general nature, such as those which have been enforced for some time in the natural sciences in order to meet the information explosion: limitations to the growth of periodicals, clearer separations between categories of publications aimed at different goals, recommendations on the 'good usage' of scientific prose, generalization of editorial practices such as author abstracts, indexation, compilation of analytical tables and indexes for serial publications, etc.[1] Few measures of this sort have yet been adopted or even seriously considered by the sponsors of archaeological research in any country or sector. But I wish to deal here with reforms of another purport, more in keeping with the internal analysis of archaeological publications which is the concern of this book.

The basis of the argument to come, on this line, is the following: the form of explanatory reports C_e, whether articles, books, or other, should be such that the reader, compelled by the factors just discussed to behave more often than not as a 'consultant', will be in a position to pick out in no time the data relevant to each of the 'boxes' defined in the preceding chapter (§ 5.1), especially the initial and terminal ones: Objectives and Selection on the one hand (i.e. the kind of archaeological materials studied and the reasons for studying them), and Interpretation on the other (i.e. the product or results of C_e). This proposition is itself the consequence of a truism: when skimming or consulting a given text in order to decide whether we should read it, we want to find out first the *raison d'être* of this text, and the nature of the *materials* concerned. The boxes Objectives and Interpretation jointly provide the answer to the former question (goals and results), the box Selection answers the latter. Then come further questions regarding the conceptual tools

---

1   A summary of the measures of this kind taken in the natural sciences since the middle of the century is given in the 'UNISIST Report' on the development of a world information system, with an emphasis on the institutional set-up which made them possible (Gardin 1971: 76–8, 105).

distinguished in our schematization: systems of representation (Description), comparative and classification methods in a broad sense (Ordering), and logico-semantic organizations (Interpretation). Clearly, we shall usually abstain from reading a text in which neither the historical product nor the archaeological materials are of interest to us, unless the 'conceptual tools' are so new and unfamiliar that the domain of application becomes indifferent.[2] Authors should therefore make a point of stating in a plain, straightforward and articulate way, first, the *raison d'être* of the text (intended purpose and conclusions reached) and the kind of archaeological materials which will be discussed; then, if such is the case, the originality of the overall reasoning process followed in going from the materials to the conclusions. The mere presence of honest and concise indications on these three points in any C_e report (of which they could or should form the author's abstract) would help in coping with the reading overloads observed.

The archaeological literature unfortunately shows no inclination for prescriptions of this kind. To begin with, we often have to read the whole text of an article or book before we discover the reason why the author thought it deserved to be published. The first lines or pages usually mention a number of sites, objects, monuments, etc., of which it is stated or postulated that they are of historical interest, as the construction itself should bear out. The latter is then exposed, usually in the order which the author is supposed to have followed, from an initial, allegedly neutral description of the raw materials to the final interpretations derived from various comparisons, classifications, correlations, etc., carried out on the raw data and others. Consequently, it is only in the course of reading that the end product of the whole effort takes shape, as well as, in a sort of retrospective way, the 'interest' of the objects or subjects mentioned in the first place. Moreover, the derivations are not all carried out at the same pace: some lead almost immediately to conclusions given in the early pages of the text, and which may not be incorporated in the final interpretation. Others, on the contrary, form extended chains of reasoning, the outcome of which is only to be found at the end of the presentation; others still proceed through successive levels of interpretation, in such a way that the reader cannot decide *a priori* whether the conclusions reached at any of the intermediate levels are not just as worthy of interest as the ultimate conclusions (examples in Gardin & Lagrange 1975: 55–83). It follows that a careful reading or even dissection of the text is here again needed in order to discover

2 I am aware of the fact that our decision whether to read or not to read a given text is often based on the name of the author or institution responsible for its publication; but it is easy to demonstrate that this procedure is the product of past experience in which we have observed that the publications of this author or institution were of interest to us on any of the three grounds mentioned: the kind of *problems* usually dealt with, the categories of *monuments* studied, or the *methods* used.

not only the goals of the construction, but the sum of its theoretical findings, disseminated throughout the argument.

These patterns of composition may no doubt pride themselves on captivating more securely the reader, by a sort of 'suspense' which hangs over the end of the tale; and there are indeed cases of enjoyable constructions in this sense, where the subtleties of thought and the refinements of language more than make up for the time spent in reading them. We cannot avoid acknowledging, however, that the present rhythms of production do not make for the exercise of such gifts, and that archaeological publications are now expected to make up for their abundance by somewhat opposite qualities, intended less to 'captivate' the reader than to free him on the contrary from the obligation to read, or at least to read thoroughly, according to a new morality of scientific prose.

Other faults of the same brand are common in the presentation of the data and operations which make up an Explanation. Speaking of the data, I have recalled the widespread usage which consists in describing the materials under study in so-called objective terms, the word 'objective' being taken in either of the two senses distinguished in an earlier section (p. 70, note 4), or both. The first acceptation is more often than not merely a formal clause: there are not too many cases where a reader can visualize the materials under consideration on the sole basis of their natural or coded description, that is, without referring to illustrations. As for the second acceptation of objectivity, epistemologically more sound, it would imply that the initial description contains all the elements called into play at the basis of the symbolic architecture of C_e, as shown on figures 20, 22, 23. This is seldom the case, for two reasons. One is that as an author comes to the establishment of parallels, he usually feels free to call on attributes and features that were not mentioned in the initial description; the other is that the same phenomenon may occur in the subsequent stages of interpretation or validation, when the author again goes back to the materials under study in order to single out new traits required for the argument presented under either of these titles (examples in § 4.4.2). The result is that when we wish to embrace the author's vision of the archaeological record that supports his construction, we cannot just consult the chapter or paragraph entitled 'Description' in the publication, because it is likely to be both irrelevant and incomplete; nor can we naïvely refer to the illustrations, since they are in this respect absolutely mute. We are well and truly forced to run through the whole text in order to bring together the scattered pieces of the architecture, and reconstruct in the author's place the set of descriptive elements really present in the foundations of C_e. Anyone who has tried his skill at this exercise knows the time and irritation that it costs (Borillo 1970, Lagrange 1973, Gardin & Lagrange 1975).

When we come finally to the mechanism of explanation proper – that is, the search for patterns (Ordering) to which we attach some meaning (Interpretation), according to the schematization of chapter 5 – the major deficiency of archaeological publications is not so much the dispersal of the author's clues as the fact that they are most of the time extraordinarily thin and scanty. We are all aware for instance that parallels (comparisons), taxonomic or typological groups (classifications) or even chronologies (seriations) have long been presented as if they were natural orders, 'imprinted on the soul by the dictates of Nature itself'.[3] It is only recently that archaeology has discovered both the utility and the difficulties of eliciting the formal basis of such orders, by mathematical or logical ways (§ 5.4) which, besides, have not ousted, for many good reasons, the traditional ways of intuition. The weakness of current presentations is not that they go by the dictates of Nature, but only that they display so little curiosity for their own formal roots, once experience has shown that they may contain a parcel of 'truth', in empirical terms (see below § 7.2). The same observations apply to the interpretation of the formal orders, the final stage of Explanations: most authors seem satisfied with a mere statement of the successive inferences that lead to the final conclusions of C_e, without showing much concern for the highly controversial logico-semantic organizations that underlie the whole structure (§ 4.4), and constitute the ultimate 'justification' of the proposed explanation according to Scriven's analysis (1959: 445–51).

It is therefore incumbent on the reader, once more, to elucidate the underlying assumptions in order to see through the inner logic of any given Explanation, beyond what little is said about it by the author himself. The delegation of so many responsibilities to the consumer obviously does not make for an easy assimilation of the product; other forms of 'conditioning' are therefore required, in the industrial (and probably also in the psychological) acceptation of the term. I shall suggest a few of them right now.

6.3.3 *Normative suggestions*

The innovations to be considered follow from the arguments developed in § 6.3.1 and 6.3.2, and I shall present them in the same order, in the form of six principles relating to the composition of explanatory texts C_e.

Principle 1. In order first to cope with the qualitative aspect of the inflation earlier discussed (§ 6.3.1), a new publication policy is required, based on a clearer distinction between the two major functions recalled at the beginning of this chapter: the dissemination of new materials on the one hand, or new arrangements of known materials, primarily for

3 Herbert of Sherbury, *De Veritate* (1624), trans. by M. H. Carré, University of Bristol Studies no. 6 (1937), cited from N. Chomsky, *Cartesian Linguistics*, p. 60, Harper and Row, New York, 1966.

documentation purposes (C_c), and the dissemination of new ideas or theories on the other hand, based on the study of published or unpublished materials (C_e). A two-fold polarity is here at stake: not only 'materials' *vs.* 'ideas', but also 'new' (or unpublished) *vs.* 'already known' (or published); the table below summarizes the resulting combinations.

Distinctive contents of publications C_c and C_e

Materials \ Ideas	known	new
known	— 1	C_e 3
new	C_c 2	$C_c + C_e$ 4

Case 1 is in principle excluded; we may, however, relate it to a perfectly legitimate category of publications, the so-called popularization of knowledge. The only reason for leaving it aside here is that it is foreign to the field of theoretical archaeology, as understood in this book; I would otherwise have been in favour of its inclusion in the realm of archaeological publications, even though it is by no means self-evident that archaeologists are the most talented persons for the job (§ 7.3.3).

Case 2 corresponds to Compilations in the strict sense, a category of works for which we have advocated a gradual reorientation towards new forms of 'publication' in the etymological sense, through data centres and data networks, in order to reduce accordingly both the volume of printed materials and the time spent in exploring them (§ 6.2).

Case 3 covers Explanations, again in the strict sense, that is, works meant to disseminate new ideas about published materials, rather than to present hitherto unknown archaeological data. The printed literature remains here the most convenient means of exposition.

Case 4, lastly, designates the category of construction which archaeologists are most eager to produce, containing both original materials and new historical views. The two functions C_c and C_e are here blended or at least coexistent in the same work; there is a good case for dissociating them to a degree, however, in providing for *two* parallel publications of a different nature, consisting one (C_c) in recording the original materials in public data files, as recommended in § 6.2, the other (C_e) in printing the historical views in the usual way, but with only the amount of descriptions and illustrations needed to support them (see below, Principle 5). Divisions of this sort have become common in a number of natural sciences where the data to be stored for retrieval currently amount to millions (Gardin 1971: 103–4). I fail to see how archaeology could escape the same fate, however contrary to the time-honoured habits of past and present scholars.

Principle 2. A provocative way to present these views would be to lay down that the use of the printing press is not a natural right tied to archaeological discovery, but rather a privilege reserved to the more gifted in the way of historical constructions, even if these have to be based on original materials excavated by others. Without going to such extremes, we should nevertheless retain the idea that adding more pages to the congested stores of scientific writings is a bold decision: we must be convinced not only that our new thoughts on any given materials are worthy of such a costly step (not merely in financial terms), but also that a reasonable number of readers will share the same conviction. In other words, the first step in the argument should be, so to say, a *defence of the text* against potential charges regarding its value for the advancement of historical or anthropological knowledge. I can hear the protests: are not all archaeological writings secure from such charges as they stand already? And how can we safely predict that anyone of them will not contribute in some way – let alone negatively – to the progress of knowledge? My answer to such objections, all perfectly sound, is that I am not here discussing slippery criteria of value judgments, but only the forms and norms of argument in current publications: a host of texts could be cited which hardly contain a sentence on their *raison d'être* or which only touch upon the subject through a laconic and stereotyped preamble on the 'interest' or 'importance' of the entities which are about to be discussed – sites, monuments, inscriptions, etc. I am not hinting that silence or discretion is necessarily of evil import, or that it inevitably betrays poverty of ideas; my only point is, in keeping with the analysis of the preceding section, that the reader should be spared the pains of having to rediscover through a careful scrutiny of the whole text the nature of the task (historical, anthropological, methodological) which the author has set about, and the reasons why he gave it precedence over alternative research activities in his field of competence. The gist of the matter, ultimately, is a call for plain and articulate preambles on the author's goals, which will enable the reader to decide without further exegesis the time that he will spend on this or that publication – how much, when, and how – according to his interests or leisure of the moment.

Principle 3. This elementary prescription implies another one, concerning the presentation of the state-of-the-art relevant to the subject of the publication. The reader should here again be given a way to apprehend at a glance the various sources in which the author has found the substance of his speculations: these indications are of much help in assessing the nature of the problem under study, and they should be cited at the same time as the objectives are being exposed, rather than distilled as the argument proceeds, in connection with particular steps such as comparison, seriation, interpretation, etc. The reader will thus be spared the trouble of having to run through the whole text in search of the references which constitute the basic literature on the subject, in contrast with works that are related to it only indirectly or marginally according to the author's argument.

Principle 4. The explanatory constructions of archaeology are based on various sets of attributes associated with material remains, from which interpretative propositions are built according to the process indicated in § 4.4. It is important that this 'base' be presented as clearly as possible, since the whole theoretical construction depends on it. Only three categories of constituents need to be considered in its definition: (*a*) the material entities selected as units of description, from the more extensive (e.g. geographical regions, survey or excavation areas, etc.), to the more minute (e.g. 'Kleinfunde'), through as many intermediate categories as may be needed (sites, districts, structures, etc.); (*b*) the relations observed or postulated between these entities (inclusion, neighbourhood, association, etc.); (*c*) lastly, the attributes selected for the characterization of entities, both intrinsic and extrinsic, as contrasted above (§ 4.1.1). A convenient way to present the data bases that lie at the bottom of constructions C_e consists in distributing these categories of information into the two 'parts of speech' defined in chapter 5 as Selection and Description, one including the *a* and *b* data (Selection, § 5.1.2); the other the *c* data (Description, § 5.1.3). The rhetorical innovation, however, will not lie in the observation of this simple dichotomy, but in the obligation to collect *all* the data relevant to each part in a *unique* section or chapter of C_e, clearly distinguished from the others, instead of keeping on with the damaging dispersion observed in most archaeological writings, including the most carefully composed ones, as recalled in the preceding section.

Thus, in the part entitled Selection, the reader will have to be provided with systematic indications concerning the *space of entities* in a physical as well as in a logical sense: (*a*) geography, topography; (*b*) natural and cultural entities taken as recording units; (*c*) systems of localization (i.e. spatial relations between *a* and *b*); (*d*) logical relations implied by the definition of entities (e.g. hierarchical inclusion, for instance between a 'house' and a 'room' in that house; functional dependency, for instance between a category of fixed structures designated as 'potter's kiln' and a category of movable structures entitled 'misfired sherds', etc.); (*e*) spatial relations between the *b* units, according to the system of localization selected in *c*; (*f*) lastly, if applicable, the selection or sampling procedures used in order to reduce the number of entities in the data base. This may seem to be a long-winded list; yet, all this information has to be brought together if the reader is to be able to grasp swiftly the author's 'topology', instead of having to search the whole text in order to reconstruct it from scattered bits and pieces. The consequence, therefore, is not necessarily an expansion of the text, but rather a rallying of dispersed data, together with explanations which may well take the form of graphic materials (diagrams, charts, tables), more compact and often clearer than written discourse in this connection.

In the same way, the part entitled Description will have to give a systematic account of the *space of attributes* associated with the foregoing entities, that is, for each category of entities (e.g. environment, sites, structures, ceramics, etc.), the complete list of attributes (or categories, variables, etc.) used in the construction, together with the definition of the individual attribute states (or features, values, traits, etc.) differentiated in each category. It is indeed essential that the reader should apprehend at a glance the system of representation which underlies an Explanation: the reasonable course, then, is to present it as such, which can be done in the form of 'codes' as described in § 3.3.1, i.e. lists of descriptive terms, accompanied by verbal or pictorial definitions, irrespective of their place or role in the overall architecture of C_e. The obligation to make these codes explicit in archaeological publications is not an immoderate requirement, especially since a few compact tables would here again be sufficient in most cases; but it would be enough to precipitate innovations of a more radical order in the very substance of interpretative constructions. We would first discover that the latter often rest on perceptual data that do not compel immediate and universal recognition (for instance in palaeography, stylistic analysis, etc.), and which no one has yet tried to define in truly operational terms. We would also have to acknowledge the part of idiosyncratic choices in the substance of descriptions, that is, in the way we 'see' the physical entities under study, the same ones giving rise to different representations according to what we want them to 'mean' in the subsequent stages of the construction. Finally, we might be led to recognize at last that there is no such thing as a good or a bad description *per se*, its value lying exclusively in the quality of the inferences that are derived from it: a descriptive feature that remains unused throughout a given construction C_e may no doubt be a perfectly 'objective' fact of perception, one that we are entitled to declare useful for *recognition* purposes (i.e. retrieval), but not for *cognition*, at least in the terms of this particular construction.

An additional advantage of systematic presentations of the underlying codes in constructions C_e is that they would also help in the design or updating of Compilations themselves. The attributes and features singled out in the design of Explanations that we come to regard as established – until we have proof to the contrary – should indeed be incorporated sooner or later into the fabric of constructions C_c, failing which the latter are doomed to go astray in the sterile sands of 'objective' observations for which we have no use (see § 3.5, and § 4.1.1, note 4). It is therefore essential that every author make a strict rule of drawing complete lists of the traits inherent in his theoretical constructions, for the benefit of future compilers, rather than force the latter to recapture those traits through a time-consuming process of textual criticism which borders on absurdity.

Principle 5. The entities, their mutual relations, and their attributes thus form the raw material of Explanations; the operations by which we are led from this point to the final interpretations are usually rather monotonous, notwithstanding our more or less conscious efforts to disguise this fact under a wealth of rhetorical variations. This is true, first and foremost, of the presentation of comparative data, where we strain our ingenuity to find a dozen different ways of expressing the similarities (or dissimilarities) perceived between objects or traits x, y, z: 'This trait is also found at . . ., on . . .', 'a parallel can be drawn between this type and objects originating from . . .', 'this monument shows interesting links with . . .', 'the excavations of . . . have produced comparable objects', etc.[4] Synoptic tables would serve the purpose just as well: the reader would find in them the plain *correlanda*, without circumlocutions, and for each group of them the few observations which the author thinks fit to justify the parallel or indicate its limitations, without any pretence of giving in this way a formal basis to the proposed series.

Should this formal basis exist, however, in the form of a well-defined ordering procedure in the broad sense of § 5.1.4, the method followed would certainly deserve a mention; but the essential element, at this stage, remains the *product* of ordering (not only comparative series, but also taxonomic classes, types, seriations, etc.) rather than the *method* of production, for the same pragmatic reason as above: the 'value' of the proposed orders will ultimately be determined by the empirical validity of the inferences derived from them, much more than by the formality of the ordering process. Consequently, intuitive series or classes deserve the same interest as the computed ones, formalization being merely a welcome addition to the process, which does not carry the same weight, epistemologically speaking, as the observation of meaningful configurations *per se*.

Comparisons, classifications, seriations, etc., the ways of ordering archaeological data are fundamentally monotonous, and there is no reason to hide this fact through endless stylistic variation. Monotony is also present in the interpretation of such configurations, at least as we have analysed it in § 4.2 and 4.4: our conclusion then was that the mental processes followed, in going from the products of ordering to the

---

4 Most archaeologists seem to indulge in naïve exercises of this sort; my own writings are no exception, as stressed by the above enumeration borrowed from the self-criticism of one of them under an assumed name (Chevrier 1959: 313).

final explanatory propositions, were not highly diversified, so that it was easy to expose them in schematic forms, less prolix but just as substantial as traditional discourse. The example considered in § 4.4 will probably be regarded as a rather narrow basis for such a sweeping statement; I am therefore ready to concede that my conclusion is more in the nature of a guess, and that the two further rhetorical innovations which I wish to submit should be regarded at this stage as predictions rather than prescriptions. The first one concerns the exposition of the logical operations which connect the propositions brought forth in the Description and Ordering phases to the terminal statements of Interpretation: inasmuch as the intermediate steps can be represented as a process of successive derivations, in the sense of § 4.4.1, the most appropriate presentation would seem to be in the form of tables and diagrams of the same vein as those which have been illustrated above (figs. 20 to 23; and also Gardin & Lagrange 1975: 49–53), though certainly different as we move from one construction to another. The logical articulations of the interpretative process stand out more clearly in graphic displays of this sort than in the linear flow of discourse, where they tend in fact to be blurred by a wealth of rhetorical expedients. Secondly, the justifications needed for *some* derivations could be included in the same tables and diagrams, in the form of short notes associated in one way or another to the corresponding inferences. The only information required in these notes would be a mention of the facts that are put forward in support of the transition from a proposition or set of propositions formulated at any level n of the inference process, to a proposition of level $n+1$, in the inductive or deductive direction (Gardin & Lagrange, *loc. cit.*, tables 7 and 8, column 'Foundations').

The supporting facts in question belong to a continuum which goes from tautologies, truisms, or allegedly universal truths, to the more local, culture-bound assumptions or postulates. The founding of the derivation from a 'large bird held on a gloved hand' to 'hawk', in our past example, is of the former sort (fig. 22); while the transition from 'a man touching the belt of a seated figure' to the 'submission of the one to the other' illustrates the latter (fig. 23). In the first case, no reference is usually given in support of the derivation; while in the second, the presence of bibliographic or other references indicate on the contrary the need felt by the author to justify the inference or deduction. This usage is not a bad one: it would indeed be absurd to make it binding upon authors, for the sake of an 'explicitly scientific archaeology', to state all the systems of definitions, hypotheses or observations which underlie the most commonly accepted derivations. Yet we would have to be sure that the absence of an explicit justification, for any derivation $\{P_i, \ldots, P_n\} \rightarrow P_{n+1}$, always means that the author regards the latter as a tautology or a self-evident truth. We have many reasons to doubt it: as an example, suffice it to recall, in Roux's study (§ 4.4), the relation between the 'identical clothes' of the two figures and the derived assumption that the latter belong to the 'same lineage' – a relation which the author merely states, without justifying it, but which he would certainly not go as far as calling a necessary truth, if the question was put to him in those terms. This is why it might be wise to require, at least from the constructions which claim formal virtues, that *all* derivations be accompanied by a short note indicating in an explicit way either the postulate or the 'dictate of Nature' which is supposed to justify the lack of any further justification . . . (with or without the empirical or logical basis of that postulate itself in each particular case, according to the author's enthusiasm for analyticity), or the culture-bound facts which are called on to ground the inference, following in this case the established usage.[5] The virtue of this safeguard against the dangerous facilities of arguments by common sense would be that it would bring into relief the predominance of 'natural' derivations of the first kind, and hence the tendency of historical explanations to partake all of the same vague *plausibility*, as already suggested by their proliferation and well-accepted heterogeneity (§ 4.4.3). As a corollary, we might come closer to an understanding of the limitations of formal exercises that bear only on the initial phases of the construction (Selection, Description, Ordination), to the exclusion of Interpretation itself (as demonstrated from another angle by Cowgill 1977). On the other hand, the foundations of derivations of the second kind, those which are acknowledged as culture-bound and relative, could here again take the form of additional tables and diagrams, in the vein of those which we have proposed elsewhere for the expression of the logico-semantic organizations (LSOs) involved in that process (Gardin & Lagrange 1975: 40–8, 69–83), in preference to the necessarily more tortuous ways of ordinary discourse, ill-suited to the purpose. The reader would thus immediately grasp the logical and semantic presuppositions of archaeological Explanations, without having to reconstruct the text to that end. Moreover, the relative uniformity of such diagrams would make it easier to compare them, from one author or from one construction to another, in order to reach a more systematic understanding of their epistemological relations (convergence, contradiction, compatibility, etc.), failing which it is difficult to perceive in the flow of transient Explanations the cumulative character inherent in scientific constructions.[6]

5 See for instance in Gardin & Lagrange (1975, *loc. cit.*) the use of the symbol 'Sém. U' ('sémantique universelle') in the first case, *without further indications,* in contrast with symbol 'Sém. L' ('sémantique locale') which is always followed by a reference to the sources from which the author draws the founding data. On the limited value of eliciting the logical or empirical basis of the 'truisms' found by the hundred in historical explanations, see Scriven (1959: 472), and the discussion below, § 7.1.1.
6 A tentative systematization of this sort, bearing on the formal relations between the various interpretations given of the same monument prior

Principle 6. I have indicated above our reasons for considering that Interpretation is the final phase of constructions C_e, and that any concluding argument presented as a 'validation' of C_e can, and therefore should, be considered as an inherent part of that phase (§ 5.1.6). The sixth rhetorical principle is nothing but the statement of this obligation, as formulated in an earlier work: 'it will be found profitable to consider Validation as a mere broadening of the empirical basis which supports the Interpretation, on account of the equivalence observed between the formal mechanisms of both [as recalled in this book: § 4.5] . . . The deductive part of the construction should be restricted to drawing from the hypothesis a number of implications which still call for empirical verification, rather than those which establish its validity according to the author, and which may for this reason be transferred back to the inductive basis' (*ibid.*, p. 101). The 'implications of the hypothesis', in this formulation, are the propositions which the author believes he can deduce from his final interpretative statements C_e, and which should indeed be regarded as so many hypotheses calling for further empirical verification, but through facts *unavailable to the author* according to this argument. It follows that the drawing of these deductions, or 'predictions', as they are called in the hypothetico-deductive model, may as well be left to others, that is to subsequent authors responsible for the discovery of *new* facts in which they find a confirmation or disproof of C_e. Such was the purport of my proposal, in chapter 5, regarding the positioning of Validation outside the field of any individual construction C^i, in a kind of interspace between two consecutive constructions C^i, C^j, of which the latter verifies, or not, all or part of the former (fig. 26). The author of an Explanation is however free to take a step in this direction by deriving himself some predictions of his theory, for others to verify; it is only in this restricted sense that Validation can constitute the ultimate part of speech, in our 'new rhetoric' of archaeological constructions.

The six principles just discussed all proceed from the same assumption: archaeological publications, even those which deal with Explanations rather than Compilations, are more often skimmed or consulted rather than truly read; it is therefore essential to see that their form is adapted to this twentieth-century usage of scientific texts. The traditional rules of composition do not seem to be particularly well-suited to meet the reader's major requirements, namely an easy access to each of the basic components of any construction, as summarized in chapter 5. Hence the idea of resorting to new modes of presentation, which all rest on a common principle: the rearrangement of information into homogeneous sets

to Roux's, will be found in Gardin & Lagrange (1975: 32–48). It shows how a logico-semantic 'calculus' is conceivable, once the corresponding LSOs have been elicited, which actually generates Roux's interpretation as a kind of formal consequence or synthesis of the former ones.

which hard-pressed 'consumers' should be able to locate and to consult independently, while immediately understanding through their articulation better than through the traditional 'thread of discourse' the logical place of each in the overall construction (Grimes 1975). The articulation of discourse into distinct parts is a first step in that direction: objectives of the construction (Principles 1 and 2), selection and symbolization of the data (Principles 3 and 4), operations carried out on the data in order to reach the final explanatory propositions and their implications (Principles 5 and 6). The condensation, or in the modern jargon, 'compaction' of information in each part, through synoptic tables and diagrams instead of linear discourse, is the second step. Neither measure should however be understood as the beginning of a formalization of archaeological writings, to the detriment of literary qualities; I have stressed more than once that our schematizations or systematizations had little to do with formalization in any serious sense.[7] As for the literary qualities of our writings, I must confess that I fail to see them, as publications stand today. If they have to be re-invented – which I firmly believe – it will be first through a reassessment of scientific discourse which, far from proscribing literature in the more ambitious sense, assigns to it a privileged function in the progress of archaeological knowledge, on the strength of arguments altogether different from those of the present book, though by no means in conflict with them,[8] as I hope to show in the next chapter (§ 7.3).

7 See § 1.3.5 and 4.4.3. As might be expected, the same view is shared by most of the logicians who have studied the modes of reasoning that underlie the handling of natural language in daily life: see for instance Perelman (1971), who recommends in this case 'a non formal approach', also associated with the definition of a 'New Rhetoric', the constituents of both showing however little analogy with their respective counterparts in this book because of an obvious difference in purpose.

8 Some readers may wonder why I have not taken the trouble to apply the principles advocated in this chapter to my own archaeological writings . . . The reasons for this avowed inconsistency are basically institutional, and therefore irrelevant to the subject of this book. They do not, however, carry the same weight today as they did ten or twenty years ago; I shall therefore try the path of consistency in future publications, for the good or evil of archaeologists interested in the history of Central Asia.

7
The limitations of theoretical archaeology

Theoretical archaeology, finally, comes out as the science of symbolic constructions produced by archaeologists as they write about material remains. The archaeological literature is the realm where those constructions can be examined *in vitro*, as we have done first from the point of view of substance (chapters 2 to 5), and then form (chapter 6) – an essentially descriptive investigation, in keeping with the above definition, but which has led us to a few normative views as well (chapters 5 and 6). I would not reject these views outside the scope of theoretical archaeology, however, but rather suggest that the word 'science' in our definition be understood in the ambivalent sense which some dictionaries ascribe to it: the *science* of symbolic constructions in archaeology is also the *art* of producing good ones, from a logicist viewpoint.

This vision of things admittedly raises a few problems. First, ideas differ as to what a 'good' construction is in archaeology, so that we shall have to look more closely into the relations between theoretical archaeology as we see it and other schools of thought known for their normative zeal in promoting a 'new archaeology' (§ 7.1). Secondly, the movement which I have called 'logicist' for want of a better term is obviously not such as to concern archaeology alone; and the moment has come to consider another set of relations, more illuminating than the former, between theoretical archaeology and other disciplines exposed to the same trend (§ 7.2). The interest of this excursion into foreign territory is first that it should remove all doubts on our objectives, which are at the same time commonplace and yet more radical than those of the new archaeology; but above all it will give us an understanding of the *limitations* of the movement – practical, theoretical, philosophical – which will lead us to recommend, by way of conclusion, yet another kind of archaeological discourse, far removed from the ascetic schemes of logicism (§ 7.3).

7.1 *Is theoretical archaeology new?*

This interrogative title covers in fact two questions: one in which we refer to the particular school or schools with which the adjective 'new' has come to be associated in the last fifteen years, in order to bring out analogies and differences with our subject (§ 7.1.1), the other in which we consider archaeology as a whole, irrespective of distinction between schools, areas, periods, etc., in order to assess the attention that the problems raised in this book may have already received, under any title (§ 7.1.2).

7.1.1 *In relation to the new archaeology*

Speaking of the *new archaeology*, it would be both tedious and vain to reopen a debate now fortunately closed on what it is, or is not; I shall only take up the two major themes which seem to run through the writings of archaeologists generally associated with that movement, and compare them with the positions adopted in this book.

(*A*) One such theme is the stand taken in favour of research objectives that go beyond the acquisition and study of archaeological remains *per se*, in order to merge ultimately with the goals of cultural or historical anthropology. More specifically, we are invited to cultivate the more systematic forms of anthropological or historical reconstitutions, in the hope of reaching 'laws' of human behaviour of a less primitive kind than traditional explanations through influences, inheritance, or cultural norms (§ 4.3). For some, this trend is nothing less than a 'revolution', a radical change in the 'paradigms' of archaeological explanation – the usual reference being the book by Kuhn (1970) from which these concepts are borrowed – under the terms of which 'all our existing textbooks have to be scrapped and completely rewritten' (Renfrew 1973a: 11). For others, the break with the past is not so clear-cut, and a number of standard works published in the 1950s are cited in witness of a comparable trend (e.g. Watson 1972: 210–12, with references to Walter Taylor, Sol Tax, Leslie White, etc., advocates of the same orientation twenty years earlier). It doesn't matter much whether we take sides with one group or the other for our present purpose: *all* explanatory constructions are amenable to the kind of analysis presented in this book, whatever their respective 'paradigms' may be. An interpretation of the variability of a given set of archaeological materials in terms of movements of peoples or ideas (invasions, commercial expansion, religious proselytism, etc.), however old-fashioned it may seem, is no less worthy of logicist investigation than an explanation of the same phenomenon through 'developments in subsistence, in technology and in social organization which lead to the local and spontaneous evolution of these things' (Renfrew, *loc. cit.*). Furthermore, the two categories of explanations may share in the same 'truth', if one of them accounts for an aspect of the phenomenon which does not exclude the other, while facts are available as 'verifications' of both. Last but not least, the formulation problems which have been our major concern arise in the same terms in both cases, and more generally in all forms of discursive explanations, old or new; this was our reason for considering at once the full range of interpretative patterns, without regard for their present standing (§ 4.3), in order to bring out the unity of their formal structure (§ 4.4). The question of the relative value of a paradigm or another for the interpretation of archaeological data is thus irrelevant on the level of abstraction adopted in the present investigation.

(*B*) A likely objection to this argument is that the novelty does not consist so much in the selection of any particular paradigm of explanation as in the formulation of the corresponding laws of human behaviour, seen from the standpoint of synchrony (anthropology) or diachrony (history); whereupon one will contend that the major trait of the new archaeology is its adhesion to the 'covering law model of scientific explanation, with an emphasis on the hypothetico-deductive method for the testing of conclusions derived from archaeological data' (Watson 1972: 212). Clearly, my analysis of archaeological constructions has taken quite a different course. In the first place, the relation between scientific explanation and the concept of *law*, to me, is not the quasi-tautology which the champions of both seem to have in mind, in archaeology as elsewhere. The fact that certain phenomena are amenable to the formulation of a law does not mean that the statement of the latter constitutes an explanation of the former: a number of logicians have already laboured this point, and one of them has even taken the pains to restate it for the benefit of archaeologists alone (Morgan 1973: 264–5). Conversely, many phenomena can be explained without referring to laws, even in the harder sciences; more precisely, the expression of certain regularities in the form of laws is often nothing more than a trick of presentation, which may result in concealments or even distortions of the observed data. This point has been brilliantly taken up by Michael Scriven (1959), *à propos* of historical explanations in general: it is always possible, with regard to a particular event (for example the fact that 'Cortes sent out a third expedition to Baja California after the failure of the first two': p. 447) to formulate a law from which this event can be deduced, in keeping with the covering-law model (for example this one: 'All confident wealth-seeking people undertake any venture which offers wealth', by which we shall explain that Cortes, 'a confident and wealth-seeking man' decided to send out a new, hopefully profitable expedition, despite the failure of the first two: p. 454). The mechanism no doubt recalls our own use of *ad hoc* logico-semantic organizations in the rationalization of interpretative propositions (§ 4.4.2, 4.4.3). The difference – a major one – is that our LSOs are not meant to express general laws, but only particular relational patterns called forth in support of various inferences in a given construction C_e. Scriven has rightly expatiated on the place of such 'justifications' in historical explanations (1959: 445–50), and on the absurdities that spring from our insistence in giving them the form of laws (*ibid.*, pp. 454–8); they should be regarded at most as 'normic statements', or 'truisms', put forward as the basis of the successive derivations from which most historical explanations are evolved (*ibid.*, pp. 464–7).

The limits of deduction in the genesis of our constructions follow from the same observations: for it is through the same tricks of presentation that theories appear to be the product of hypothetico-deductive processes.[1] I have already presented elsewhere this challenge of the HD model in archaeology (Gardin 1974c: 343), which Scriven had done before me for history in a most effective way: 'the explanation *when dressed in its deductive robes* becomes a proof or a justification of an explanation' (1959: 450, italics mine). In other words, an explanation is necessarily pre-existent to its proof in the hypothetico-deductive sense, so that the problem remains of eliciting the mechanisms by which explanatory constructions are built in the first place, at the end of a cyclical process in which deduction does not play the most prominent part (§ 5.2).

To sum up, I would say of hypothetico-deductive archaeology what Lakatos (1976) recently wrote of the 'formalist' or 'deductivist' excesses of mathematics itself, and which his reviewer P. Thuillier ably summarizes as follows: 'any undertaking which sets as a major and quasi-exclusive goal the reconstruction of mathematics in an axiomatico-deductive way is an authoritarian and mystical travesty. Authoritarian, because it seeks to impose on research work a rigid framework which may curb imagination. Mystical, because it reinforces beliefs in the 'divine' character of mathematical certainty and dissimulates, willy nilly, the heuristic approaches which underly the activity of mathematicians' (Thuillier 1977: 74). To be sure, our heuristic approaches themselves are no less amenable to rationalization, as others have emphasized (Doran & Hodson 1975: 343); theoretical archaeology, as understood in this book, has no other goal than to clarify the logico-semantic operations that underly *both* inductive and deductive constructions in archaeology.

(*C*) The preceding argument, under paragraphs *A* and *B*, shows that we have to give a negative answer to the first of the two questions raised at the beginning of this section: theoretical archaeology is *not* another avatar of the new archaeology, nor even a branch or a facet of the latter. The only point in common would be an equal concern for the elicitation of mental processes in archaeological constructions, but in ways which are so radically different that the analogy cannot be

---

1 An example of such a trick has been given above, at the end of § 4.4.2, in connection with Roux's presentation of the data that were supposed to *validate* his hypothesis, deductively, in contrast with the data previously used by him to *generate* it, inductively.

carried very far. A converse relation, however, might not be improper, that is, a vision of the new archaeology as a branch, or rather a truncated form of theoretical archaeology . . . (*a*) Truncated first as regards the variety of constructions on which the new archaeologists tend to concentrate, namely Explanations built on anthropological or ecological paradigms, in contrast with the wider range considered in this book, which includes constructions currently regarded as trivial (Compilations) or old-fashioned (Typologies); and (*b*) truncated also with respect to the mechanisms of reasoning themselves, since the new archaeology honours *only* those of deduction and proof, whereas theoretical archaeology covers *also* those of induction and invention.

This inclusion of one perspective into the other accounts for the asymmetry of their relation: while new archaeology and theoretical archaeology readily converge in the criticism of many traditional ways of reasoning, it may also happen that 'new' constructions be taken as the object of 'theoretical' reconstructions, by virtue of the same epistemological concern carried to a higher point.[2] In such circumstances, any amalgamation of the two approaches would be a logical error.

7.1.2 *In the history of archaeology*

Let us now turn to the second question: does our concern for rationality indicate a turning-point in the history of archaeology, traditional or modern? The answer is essentially a matter of appreciation. If what is meant is that no archaeologist has ever touched upon the theoretical problems raised in this book, I certainly have to resist any such claim. Long before the methodological debates of the last decades, similar ideas were expressed on the need to promote an archaeology which would not be just 'an empirical practice but a theory, logically constructed',

2 This is not the place to sketch out the usual outcome of such interesting exercises; I may, however, give a few examples of methodological issues raised by the analysis of 'new' constructions, in the logicist perspective. (*a*) In all cases, the presuppositions or hypotheses explicitly stated as foundations of the successive steps of *Interpretation* (e.g. Hill 1968) are themselves in need of some sort of systematization, either in the form of 'justifications' in Scriven's sense, or LSOs in our terminology, failing which it is difficult to come to a clear vision of the epistemological relations between different Explanations (convergence, contradiction, compatibility, etc.), as argued under Principle 5 of § 6.3.3. (*b*) The method of *Ordering* used is sometimes in contradiction with the goal of the work: thus in Whallon (1972), where the chi-square computation is hardly consonant with the initial idea of reconstructing the logical steps followed by a human brain in evolving a typology. (*c*) In other cases, the formal procedure suggested for the *Selection* of the materials rests on postulates that are at best unverified, at the worst unverifiable (e.g. Redman & Watson 1970), etc. Anyone familiar with the substance of these three standard examples of the 'new' approach will understand the purport of my reservations, even if he disagrees with them.

an archaeology which not only 'establishes facts but also tries to explain their reality by causes and by laws', etc. (Deonna, *L'archéologie, son domaine et son but*, Paris, 1912, p. 38, cited from the translation by Borillo 1971: 10). And we would have no difficulty in finding scholarly works of an admittedly 'traditional' brand, in their subject and style, where the concern for rationality is highly tangible, if only for certain aspects or phases of the construction (e.g. Vallois 1944 and 1966). It is nevertheless probably true that theoretical or methodological trends are more pervasive to-day than ever before, and that the younger archaeologists are less reluctant to follow them. But this is not enough to justify current claims that a 'revolution' is on its way in archaeology, leading to a hitherto unknown science, through the alternative or complementary paths of explication, formalization, and, why not, logicization . . . Before we take any final stand on this point, it is only prudent to acknowledge that a comparable movement is in progress in several fields of anthropological research other than archaeology; we run the risk of overrating its significance if we fail to appreciate, through the lessons of those analogous efforts, a number of limitations which should urge us to be more cautious in our prophecies. Such is the aim of the two following sections.

7.2 *Logicist perspectives in the sciences of man*
I have stressed on several occasions the banality of the schematizations presented in this book, all derived from an analysis of the 'scientific cycle' more or less applicable to any discipline (§ 5.2). It is therefore no wonder that we should find signs of similar theoretical concerns in a number of human sciences which had hitherto escaped or resisted epistemological doubts: psychology, literary studies, musicology, etc. Among such signs, I shall first mention a growing awareness of the flimsiness of most constructions produced in these domains, even when they display a strong bias for scientific method, and use the jargon or the tools of 'established' disciplines such as mathematics or linguistics. Feelings of this sort are not yet readily formulated in writing; but they are voiced nowadays quite freely in scientific assemblies, so much so that a standard list can already be drawn up of the more common objections, among which most readers will probably recognize two or three overheard in public or private debates. (*a*) First, the 're-tooling' of the human sciences which is given as a sign of the alleged revolution, in Kuhn's terminology (1970), is often nothing more than a metaphorical use of concepts and procedures forged in other contexts, which is not enough to confer a scientific status on the resulting constructions. (*b*) Second, the selection and formulation of what authors call the 'data' in those constructions usually do not follow any clear rule; such an extensive freedom of perception and language does not make for a speedy convergence of

theoretical efforts. (*c*) In the same way, the 'operations' carried out in the construction process remain largely unexplored, and it is not enough to claim that they are governed by a discursive or natural logic, yet unborn, to transform them into articulations of a well-formed scientific construction. (*d*) This generalized licence in the selection of elements and relations that go into the making of our constructions is certainly not foreign to the amazing abundance of 'scientific papers' published in our disciplines. (*e*) Such verbal excesses can only persist in fields of research (or discourse) where it is not yet required that published constructions bear some verifiable relation with the empirical world to which they are supposed to refer, 'verification' being here understood in the operational sense discussed in § 4.5.3. (*f*) In such circumstances, it is difficult to define criteria by which we could demonstrate that a given interpretation or theory marks 'progress' in comparison with another, in any area of research; as a result, our constructions often seem to follow one another in an erratic fashion, inasmuch as we are allowed to produce them without taking into account their relations with past or present competing theories.[3]

Etc.: this list, though incomplete, is enough to raise some anxiety (for more ample developments on this topic, see Gardin 1974a, 1977b); the measures generally suggested in order to dispel anxiety are not very different from those discussed in this book. The most radical one consists in advocating an overall reformulation of constructions according to the principles of *systems analysis*, presented as the most appropriate method-ological framework for bringing order into the confused world of human sciences – assuming we really want to take the word 'science' seriously (e.g. Laszlo 1972a, b; Sutherland 1973; Mattessich 1978; and for archaeology in particular, Flannery 1973). To be sure, the essence of systems analysis is not everywhere understood in the same way; but the general course is akin to the philosophy of logicism, as stressed in the opening chapter of this book (§ 1.3.5), while for practical purposes both approaches end up with comparable normative proposals.

Analogies are closer still when we come to the specific tools of analysis,

---

3 This is at least suggested by the study of 'chains of citations', in fields such as sociology, literary studies, etc.: an author who has been abundantly cited in his lifetime often vanishes from subsequent bibliographies in a matter of years, while no written account is to be found of the scientific reasons for this unexpected fate. Further, if we make the fair assumption that anyone interested can guess what those reasons are, in *all* such cases, then an additional subject of wonder is that still no steps should be taken to avoid the repetition of the phenomenon, once it has been acknowledged. Yet further, authors living at the same time seem entitled to discourse upon the same subject without showing any concern for the total heterogeneity of their respective views: an excellent demonstration of this point has been given by Johanna Natali (1976) *à propos* of the *thirty-two* articles published by reputed scholars between 1962 and 1976, on Baudelaire's poem 'Les Chats' (fourteen lines).

as envisaged in a number of projects different from ours. One such tool is the *language of representation* which is gaining widespread recognition as a basic component of scientific constructions: the fundamental distinctions made in § 3.3 between natural language (NL), information language (IL), and scientific or specialized language (SL) are finding their way into a growing number of books, with a clear grasp of their respective functions in the progress of the human sciences from observation to theory (e.g. Miller & Johnson-Laird 1976: 109–31, 164–7, etc.). Then, the *logico-semantic organizations* instrumental in interpretation processes (§ 4.4) are also being gradually acknowledged, under a variety of designations which all express the same quest for a higher rationality in scientific explanations, half-way between the loose and ill-defined rules of natural logic and the much too restrictive theorems of formal logic (cf. the 'procedural semantics' of Miller & Johnson-Laird, a suggestive name for the interpretative apparatus which they have in mind, applicable to the analysis of both NL and SL constructions in the same way as our LSOs: *op. cit.*, pp. 167, 210–11, 290). Lastly, the *quasi-algorithmic forms* given to logicist reconstructions (§ 1.3, 4.4.3, etc.) are now to be found in a growing number of essays dealing in their own way with the rationalization of existing constructions, in fields such as the analysis of myths (Klein *et al.* 1974), musicology (Nattiez 1975: 253 *et seq.*), literary criticism (Molino 1974, Natali 1976), etc. The reasons for this convergence are easy to guess: in giving an algorithmic structure to the reasoning which leads to a given theory, we can verify step by step the basis of the proposed schematization. Advocates of systems analysis, in particular, tend to identify with this kind of formulation, to the point of writing actual programs that simulate the generation of theories (Weinberg 1972); let us emphasize however that we have not carried our own requirements that far (§ 1.3.5), for fear of the possible negative returns of this additional intellectual effort.[4]

We are thus entitled to conclude that our concern for a better understanding of the foundations of archaeological constructions is only a particular manifestation of a broader movement which today affects the human sciences in general, and which can be defined as an extension to them of the epistemological requirements of natural sciences. Does this mean that we are on the eve of a Copernican revolution in the study of human phenomena in general, and those which concern past societies

4 'There is a popular illusion that confronting a computer with one's ideas enforces rigor and discipline, thereby encouraging the researcher to reject or clarify fuzzy ideas. In the very narrow sense that the human must behave exactly like a machine in order to communicate with it, this is true. But in a more useful sense, the effect is the opposite: it is all too easy to become immersed in the trivial details of working with a problem on the computer rather than think it through rationally. The effort of making the computer understand is then mistaken for intellectual activity and creative problem solving' (Lee, cited in Clark & Cole 1975: 50).

in particular? The absurdity of this prophecy is unmistakable if we only bear in mind the fumbling ways of all the endeavours mentioned above, including the present book itself. The major purport of such efforts, it seems to me, is to bring out the fact that the business of science is not as straightforward as the frequency of our allusions to science would seem to indicate, and that it imposes in particular two obligations which observers of nature have been struggling to combine for over three centuries: *efficacy* on the one hand, understood as the power of a construction to effect the aim intended, and *rationality* on the other, by which I mean the search for continuous and consistent chains of operations linking observation and theory. Let us assume, in a deliberately naïve way, that we are able to decide whether a construction is 'good' or 'bad' under each of the two conditions taken separately; by combining our marks, we obtain four broad classes of constructions, as shown in the following table: (*a*) the constructions of *Science*, in the more binding sense of the word, which satisfy both requirements; (*b*) the constructions of *Practical lore*, that is constructions which 'work', in so far as we can verify that their effects meet their purpose, but for reasons which are unexplained, illusory, or ill-formulated; (*c*) the constructions of *Alchemy*, which are conversely based on a perfectly well-defined generative procedure, but unable to achieve their ultimate purpose; (*d*) finally, a fourth category for which it is natually difficult to find a name – since its two-fold negativity would lead us to believe that constructions of that sort just do not exist in our disciplines – but which I have made a point of individualizing under a newly-coined designation, because of its conspicuous weight in the sciences of man: *Feuilleton*.[5]

Categories of constructions	according to their merits (+) or demerits (−)	
	practical : Efficacy	theoretical : Rationality
a Science	+	+
b Practical lore	+	−
c Alchemy	−	+
d Feuilleton	−	−

The progress of scientific thought throughout the ages can be schematically described as a kind of to-and-fro movement between the observation of the effective power of mental constructs that we regard as ill-formed

5 Literal translation of the German word by which Herman Hesse designates the 'pleasant tattle' produced in inordinate quantity by many learned men of our times, with no concern for scientific quality in any of the two above senses, nor for literary pungency, and which consequently leaves absolutely no trace (see note 3): references in Gardin (1974a: 57–8).

(as in *b*), and the design of supposedly more rational models that fail to produce the object intended (as in *c*). From time to time, felicitous conjunctions of the practical and theoretical virtues are acknowledged as 'scientific' constructions in the full sense, to be eventually replaced by others of the same brand as new observations and speculations change our appreciation of felicity. Meanwhile, a current stream of constructions easily disqualified on both grounds flows on, also under the banner of Science, but which I propose to single out, after Herman Hesse, as Feuilleton.

The strength of this crude systematization is that it makes it possible to indicate clearly where the borderline lies between constructions that are worthy of interest, in a scientific perspective, and those which are not: this line is to be traced under *c*, rather than under *a*. In other words, coming back to our limited subject, logicism does not urge us in any way to reject from the field of theoretical archaeology the 'imperfect' constructions of categories *b* and *c*. On the contrary, we need to embrace both in order to reach constructions of category *a*, with the help of logicism . . . by which I mean the following. (*a*) The so-called traditional archaeology has provided and is still providing us with explanations unworthy of the name, with regard to our formal requirements, but which do give us some durable control of the empirical data, in cognitive terms (predictions, diagnoses, etc.). In considering them as Practical lore, I do not mean to debase them, far from it, but rather to designate them as mental constructs that are most worthy of the attention of 'archaeological theorists' (see §§ 4.2.3, 4.4.3). (*b*) Conversely, the so-called modern archaeology is distinguished by the use of 'objective' procedures for acquiring archaeological data (through measuring instruments, cameras connected to a computer, etc.), for quantifying them in the logical sense (e.g. pattern recognition programs), and then ordering them in many different ways (e.g. numerical taxonomy, automatic classification and seriation, etc.). The interpretation of the products of these procedures, however, remains 'subjective', and usually takes the form of a rationalization, in either of two senses: the author may choose to evolve formal configurations first, and then look for their possible meaning (heuristic rationalization), or on the contrary begin with established Explanations and try to give then a formal basis, retrospectively (axiomatic rationalization). The adjective 'alchemical' given to constructions of this sort is again devoid of any disparaging intent; it simply expresses the fact that their higher virtue usually lies more in the systematic approach than in the cognitive product. (*c*) Suppose now that Practical lore and Alchemy cooperate instead of altercate with each other; from the reciprocal fertilization of their respective knowledge, the 'Janus-faced constructs' advocated by Sutherland (1973: 5, 23, 30, 55, etc.) will be born, 'with one face turned towards the empirical justifications, and the other towards the higher-level conceptual framework with which it must articulate' (*op. cit.*, p. 12), that is, the constructions of Science under the terms of our definition.[6]

These precisions should dispel any remaining doubts on our goals. Theoretical archaeology is not, to put it bluntly, a new New archaeology, pitted against all the others. It is harsh and radical only in its aversion for constructions of the 'Feuilleton' sort, and perhaps in its readiness to include in that category a number of works which could after all be granted for a while the higher status of Practical lore or Alchemy, pending a more widely accepted confirmation of their inanity from both standpoints. Barring that, *all* constructions are *a priori* regarded as equally worthy of interest, and the only demand of the theoretical archaeologist is that he should not be blamed for his concern to make them more worthy still, in the sense and through the ways which have been discussed in this book.

Should we be more apologetic, and stress the fact that our scheme fits into the general pattern of well-known philosophical movements? I would first mention the analytical philosophy of Moore and Russell, set on a theory of knowledge which is likewise based on a logical analysis of the semantic and syntactical properties of discourse, more specifically the discourse of science; then logical empiricism, an offshoot of this philosophy (Carnap, Neurath, etc.), in search of a calculus which would generate the conclusions of a verified theory from a set of initial descriptive propositions; or again, the operational school of Bridgman, according to whom the meaning of propositions has to be linked to the methods used in their generation or verification; or the semiotics of Peirce and Morris, when this term still designated the study of symbolic systems (natural language, scientific languages), rather than the strange 'pantology' which it has come to cover in the human sciences (Gardin 1974a: 48–55), etc. The reference to these illustrious names should not be misunderstood: as their number and diversity witness, I do not claim affiliation to any one of them in particular, but only to a broader movement of ideas which, seen in a proper time perspective, seems to embrace them all – namely, a kind of logical positivism now so widespread, in the modern philosophy of sciences, that it 'ceases to exist in our eyes as a distinct *school*' (Kolakowski 1976: 225). The term 'logicism', in the loose sense which we have given it, is enough to hint at this vague paternity; it would have been as pedantic as pointless to specify further the roots of the name or the thing.

6 There are naturally other ways to formulate this dual requirement of
  scientific constructions, in disciplines where it still is an issue (i.e. in
  the human sciences, principally); but the substance of the formulation
  is always the same, namely the obligation to show an equal concern
  for 'norms of internal consistency (systemicity) and norms of external
  correspondence with observation (testability)', according to one of the
  current phraseologies (Colby 1975: 99), or again 'ritualistic judgment'
  and 'performance judgment', in Dunnell's recent formulation (1978: 193).

7.3   *The limitations of logicism*

Despite so many precautions, the real intentions of this book will probably be misjudged, especially as regards what might be called the future of logicism. It is therefore appropriate to conclude with an analysis of the *limitations* of the scheme, hitherto masked by the apologetic character of our presentation. Limitations are manifest, to me, on three levels: theoretical, practical, and philosophical. I shall discuss them in this order.

7.3.1   *Theoretical limitations*

The less serious ones are the theoretical limitations, because they are the easiest to uncover. I have stressed on several occasions that the formalization of archaeological reasoning, in actual applications, concerned only the initial phases of our constructions, from the acquisition of the data to their arrangement into various 'orders' – e.g. systematic procedures of data collecting (Selection), measurement techniques, pattern recognition methods (Description), algorithms of Comparison, seriation, classification (Ordering). The interpretation of such orders, however, is usually left to the 'subjective' sagacity of the archaeologist. It is easy to understand that a construction obtained in this way, 'formalized' as it may be, has *a priori* no firmer basis than one in which the initial operations are themselves subjective: the rigour of the former phases cannot be transferred *de jure* to the latter (for a lucid argument of this point, see Cowgill 1977).

Suppose now that interpretation itself has been the object of a systematization, in the form of a logico-semantic calculus of the kind described in § 4.4. We then come up against the obstacle discussed in § 7.1.1, *B*, which is merely a manifestation of the limitations of artificial intelligence in general (§ 4.4.3): the tentative laws formulated so as to give an axiomatic turn to the calculus are for the most part truisms or *ad hoc* propositions directly inspired by the empirical interpretation itself, and we ignore the extent to which they are applicable to other constructions (for a similar criticism of the 'systems approach to explanation', see Salmon 1978: 181–2).

These reservations are not meant to dissuade us from investigating the mathematical, logical and semantic foundations of our constructions; they have to be kept in mind, however, as a curb to startling prophecies on the progress of an 'explicitly scientific approach' in archaeology.

7.3.2   *Practical limitations*

The game of explicitation is not only tricky in principle: it is also a costly one, in many different ways, which takes us to the practical limitations of the logicist scheme. Let me first indicate what I mean here by costs. Needless to say, I am not essentially referring to financial costs: logicist studies may require the use of computation facilities (e.g. Lagrange 1973) which are still regarded by some as costly, but this is certainly not the major practical barrier. A more real one, to me, is the time required for shaping a construction in conformity with logicist principles. The essays summarized in § 4.4 already gave a hint of this; and anyone can guess that the application of the rhetorical recommendations stated in § 6.3.3 is not easy, in so far as it takes more effort to present the same construction in ten pages than in a hundred. In other words, the logicist scheme entails investments of an intellectual sort, and one may legitimately wonder whether they are justified by the returns gained or expected from them.

Secondly, it stands to reason that studies of this sort are not accessible to everyone, not because they are basically 'difficult', but only in that they require a turn of mind which is not, thank goodness, equally distributed. Hence the fear, here again legitimate, that a split may form between theoretical archaeologists and others, with the risk that an unpleasant hierarchy may develop between them. In the same way, the expansion of data banks or data networks, recommended in the name or the rationalization of documentation activities (§ 6.2), is likely to precipitate a *de facto* specialization of the archaeologists least gifted for interpretative constructions into the unalluring tasks of compilation, ending up with other forms of hierarchy as disgraceful as the former. Further, access to archaeological data may then become restricted to individuals connected in some way or other with the institutions responsible for the management of those banks or networks, as in a number of natural sciences doomed earlier than archaeology to centralized or bureaucratic forms of research organization.

Atomistic division of labour, pervasive hierarchies, administrative subjection, etc., these evils are well known; they tend to permeate the whole world of scientific research, in the train of a silent revolution whose name we keep updating: industrial, technological, cybernetic, bureaucratic, etc. The hard sciences, or 'Big Science', are surely in a bad position to resist the trend, for obvious reasons; but what about archaeology? What happens in this discipline being of little consequence – thanks to our blessed inability to formulate historical laws serviceable for 'social control' (Popper 1957), or to impart to everyone a vision of 'archaeology serving Humanity' (Ford 1973) – couldn't we dream of a special fate, away from the constraints of production? And if it is true that the logicist scheme is likely to be attended by so many evils, would it not be wiser to forsake it, on the strength of the argument, after all pleadable, that the elevation of archaeology to the dignity of Science is not worth this price?

The question makes sense only inasmuch as we believe that our individual inclinations or decisions are enough to alter the course of evolution, even on such minor matters as the way to do or not to do things in archaeology. Being unsettled on this point, I have no answer to offer; but it is unrealistic to plead the cause of theoretical archaeology without giving some consideration to problems of that sort as well.

7.3.3 *Philosophical limitations*

'Logical empiricism', according to Kolakowski (1976: 229), 'is the product of a culture in which technocratic efficiency is considered as the supreme value, a culture which we have grown into the habit of calling technocratic. Logical empiricism is the ideology of technocracy, disguised in the form of an anti-ideological view of science cleared of value judgements'. The observations just made suggest that we are not far removed from endorsing that statement, which broadens the scope of the questions just raised. For how could we fail to see that the logicist way of going about archaeological constructions is likely to be extended to the very object of the latter, that is to the human events and behaviour which we propose to 'explain' through the study of material remains? And how could we deny that we shall then be contributing, if only in proportion to the significance of our field, both to an unhealthy organization of labour, reflecting the order of technocracy, and to an abstract, cold vision of human history in which it is not sure that our descendants or ourselves will take a lasting interest?

Questions of this sort cannot be dismissed in a few lines by mere declarations of faith, some in favour of the rationality of the natural sciences extended to all things human, others in favour of the specificity of a human order irreducible to the reason of science. It is all too easy to demonstrate the outrageous aberrations to which *both* religions have led societies throughout history, down to the present time. But it is nonetheless necessary to choose between the two systems at any given moment, in order not so much to exclude one in the name of the other, but rather to defend whichever of the two is most threatened, *here and now*. I am well aware of the implications of this relativist position: it is the adhesion given to any kind of dualistic philosophy asserting the necessity of contraries, at the cost of an unending conflict between two 'forces' or 'principles' equally indispensable to the movement of life, and which cannot therefore be contrasted in terms of Good or Evil. Yin and Yang, Apollo and Dionysus, Animus and Anima . . . one has only to speak this language, under any of its many historical forms, to incur the condescension, if not condemnation, of those who 'know' on which side stands the unique Virtue. Having no such certitude, I can only refuse the dilemma, *sub specie aeternitatis*, while still professing to have an answer to the alternative, *hic et nunc*.

At the risk of being taxed with inconsistency, I shall contend bluntly that the dangers of the Rational ideology are today the greatest. This is not the place to vindicate the case: it has been presented a number of times in the last years by more enlightened persons, who can hardly be denied the quality of scientists even by those who take the opposite view, both in the East and in the West, or North and South.[7] Therefore, while the position taken in the preceding pages is that the human sciences are exposed to a criticism apparently rooted in the scientist ideology, as Kolakowski calls it (*op. cit.*), it does not follow that I adhere to the latter as regards the conduct of the more consequential affairs of the world, or even the minor concerns of archaeology. I should reaffirm at this stage that the exploration carried through in the present book is by no means a disguised campaign against the innumerable writings which speak of men and things of the past in other ways than those of logicism. God forbid: I feel no embarrassment in confessing that the historical works which I prize most are those which bear the mark of a strong personal relation between the author and his subject, a relation expressed and communicated through a kind of discourse which has little to do, needless to say, with the logicist rhetoric. The narratives which travellers produced until the turn of this century are treasures of 'subjective' observations on past and present societies, compared with which our 'scientific' publications often have an air of signal poverty (mine included). I find in Gibbon or Yourcenar[8] pressing reasons for reading again handbooks of Roman history which had provided me with stores of information in school years, but little clues as to the value of this information – by which I do not mean the exchange-value, amply established by the very special economy of academic life (examinations, diplomas, careers), but the value-in-use, in other grades of life. Et cetera.

'Pressing reasons for reading' . . . From Marguerite Yourcenar to the handbooks which she too must have found useful, and from the handbooks to the 'Mémoires d'Hadrien' which I need just as much, I am claiming nothing more than the complementarity of the two ways, as inseparable from each other, over a span of time, as life and death on the larger scale of natural history. The analogy is a cliché; but the choice of the cliché is not indifferent. What it means to convey is that the two ways

---

7 A 'bibliography' would here be ridiculous: one has only to read the newspapers, or any of the several books written on the counter-cultures which are developing in many parts of the world – including in places of learning – to understand the origin and nature of the dangers to which I am referring. To those who would still wonder how the same person can develop an interest in the ways of logicism and at the same time take a stand 'Against the imperialism of instrumental reason', I would recommend the chapter which bears this title in the beautiful book recently written by Joseph Weizenbaum, Professor of Computer Science at the Massachusetts Institute of Technology (1976: 258–80).

8 Gibbon's *Decline and Fall of the Roman Empire* (first published in 1776–88), ed. J. B. Bury, 7 vol., 1896–1900; and Marguerite Yourcenar's *Mémoires d'Hadrien*, Plon, Paris, 1951.

are doomed to coexist, even though they are largely antithetical to the point of trying now and then to exclude each other through violent acts. The 'life experience' of the proper order of things, as we perceive it or as we learn it from our society, may stamp out for a while the disturbing reason of a Socrates, or the impossible truths of a Galileo; to-day, conversely, the rational order of things borne out by science is trying hard to stamp out the life experience of unsatisfied citizens, through exactly the same processes – prison, abjuration, death. Luckily, the counter-movement is already taking shape, but again with the same excesses: we are invited to come back to a tradition 'that calls radically into question the validity of the scientific world view, the supremacy of cerebral cognition, the value of technological prowess . . . *Analysis and debate must finally yield to the claims of ineffable experience*' (Roszak 1969: 82, italics mine). Thus spoke the Judges of Athens and Rome . . . Will there be no end to the cycle? This is what modern reformulations of the ancient dualistic intuitions would seem to imply: the Principle of Pleasure is set against the Principle of Reality (Freud), as Eros to Thanatos (Marcuse), or Experience to Theory (Laing), in such a way that angels and demons are continually changing sides, making it nonsensical to look for Good or Evil only in one camp. Their antagonism indeed never ends, except for occasional truces, during the blessed periods of Enlightenment where an equilibrium sets in for a time between the two parts.

Having no taste for the other periods, it is only consistent that I should end my excursion into the ways of Science by a defence of Literature: the two forms of mental activity are for me alternative ways by which we give free rein to the same impulse, ignorant of its origin or destination, but aware at least of the aberrations that inevitably occur whenever one form of knowledge wants to impose the condemnation of the other. I therefore do not consider tolerance in this case as a matter of ethics, but rather, in an evolutionary perspective, as a matter of survival. It was in the name of this forced liberalism that I proposed earlier not to exclude from Science the efficacious practices of Practical lore, nor the procedural explorations of Alchemy; it is in the name of the same disposition that I now acknowledge the no lesser though different efficiency of Literature in eliciting the meaning of human phenomena.

There is one way to knowledge, however, which I regard as wholly ineffectual, notwithstanding its pretence to scientific virtues: it is the track leading to what I called, after Hermann Hesse, the Feuilleton. The significance of this restriction will be apparent only to those who feel as I do that the writings produced in the human sciences in general, or archaeology in particular, belong for a large part to that category.

Synopsis

The following diagram provides a restrospective justification of the order adopted in the presentation of this book, and more specifically of the underlying relations between the seven chapters. It may be regarded as a jocular exercise in logicist analysis, since any reader should be able to effect it himself on our table of contents after having read the book.

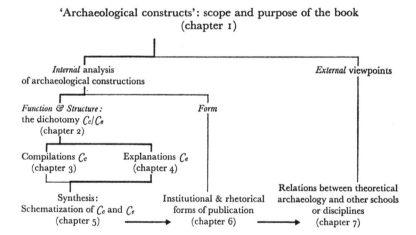

'Archaeological constructs': scope and purpose of the book
(chapter 1)

Internal analysis
of archaeological constructions

External viewpoints

Function & Structure:
the dichotomy C_c/C_e
(chapter 2)

Form

Compilations C_c
(chapter 3)

Explanations C_e
(chapter 4)

Synthesis:
Schematization of C_c and C_e
(chapter 5)

Institutional & rhetorical
forms of publication
(chapter 6)

Relations between theoretical
archaeology and other schools
or disciplines
(chapter 7)

Glossary and abbreviations

The following definitions are those of the more *basic notions*, recapitulated in the hopefully logical order of their discussion in this book.

Archaeology The sum of studies bearing on material objects which may help to reconstitute, in conjunction with other data, the history and ways of life of ancient peoples (specific events, daily activities, institutions, beliefs, etc., § 1.1.4).

Constructions Any written text presented as a distinct unit in the archaeological literature – article, book, printed lecture, with the appended illustrations – for the purpose of exposing the results of a survey or excavation, the content of a collection, the interpretation of an object or group of objects, or the lessons that may be drawn from any such data with respect to the history and ways of life of ancient peoples (§ 1.3.5).

Logicism, logicist analysis Expressing in the form of chains of explicitly defined operations the reasonings that underlie the constructions of archaeology (§ 1.3.5).

Compilations Sets of propositions interrelated in various ways, describing material remains that have been brought together in a systematic whole so as to facilitate the study of ancient peoples (§ 2.3).

Explanations Ordered sets of propositions meant to provide a reconstitution of past events or ways of life related to particular individuals or groups, on the basis of the properties exhibited by a given body of material remains, together with other possible information sources (§ 2.4).

Typologies (*a*) In the broadest sense: any classification of material remains used as the basis of inferences relating to facts that are not included in the initial representation of those materials (§ 4.1). (*b*) In an operational sense: the systematic matching of intrinsic properties with extrinsic attributes, through constant to-and-fro motions between the two sets, so as to ground the largest number of attributions L, T, F on the smallest number of properties P, G, S (§ 4.1.2, beginning).

(*c*) In a more restrictive sense: any ordering of material remains based on a systematic matching of intrinsic and extrinsic attributes, out of which the author seeks to derive information concerning in the first place the situation of those remains in space and time (§ 4.1.2, end).

Theoretical archaeology (*a*) The study of the abstract or formal aspects of constructions produced by archaeologists (§ 4.4.3).

(*b*) The science of symbolic constructions in archaeology, as well as the art of producing good ones, from a logicist viewpoint (beginning of chapter 7).

The following list sums up the special symbols used in the book, and their broad meaning:

C Constructions (§ 1.3.5)

C_e Compilations (§ 2.3)

C_e Explanations (§ 2.4)

EI   The empirico-inductive approach (method, school), in contrast with HD, the hypothetico-deductive approach (§ 5.2)

F Functional attributes of archaeological materials, in a utilitarian or in a sociological sense (part of the L, T, F trilogy: § 4.1.1)

G Geometrical properties of archaeological materials (part of the P, G, S trilogy: § 4.1.1)

H Human groups mentioned in defining the scope of a given field or piece of archaeological research (part of the L, T, H trilogy: § 1.1)

HD   The hypothetico-deductive approach (method, school), in contrast with EI, the empirico-inductive approach (§ 5.2)

IL   Information language, the family of metalinguistic systems used for the storage and retrieval of archaeological data (part of the IL, NL, SL trilogy: § 3.3)

L (*a*) Locational attributes of archaeological materials (part of the L, T, F trilogy: § 4.1.1)

(*b*) Geographical or local units mentioned in defining the scope of a given field or piece of archaeological research (part of the L, T, H trilogy: § 1.1)

LSO   Logico-semantic organizations used as the basis of inferences in archaeological constructions or reconstructions (§ 4.4.2)

NL   Natural language, the family of languages used in the archaeological literature for describing and interpreting material remains (part of the IL, NL, SL trilogy: § 3.3)

OI, OX   Orderings of archaeological materials based on intrinsic features alone (*OI*) or on a combination of intrinsic and extrinsic features (*OX*) (§ 4.1.1)

P Physical properties of archaeological materials (part of the P, G, S trilogy: § 4.1.1)

P_i, P_0, P_n Intermediate propositions (P_i) derived from archaeological descriptions (P_0) or hypotheses (P_n) in the rationalization of Explanations, inductive or deductive (§ 4.4.1)

S Semiotic properties of archaeological materials (part of the P, G, S trilogy: § 4.1.1)

SL Scientific language, from *special* or *scholarly* terminologies closely associated with NL, to the more autonomous *symbolic* systems used in building up archaeological theories (part of the IL, NL, SL trilogy: § 3.3)

T (*a*) Temporal attributes of archaeological materials (part of the L, T, F trilogy: § 4.1.1)
(*b*) Time units mentioned in defining the scope of a given field or piece of archaeological research (part of the L, T, H trilogy: § 1.1)

Bibliography

Allard, M., Elzière, May, Gardin, J.-C., and Hours, F. 1963 *L'analyse conceptuelle du Coran, sur cartes perforées*. Mouton, The Hague & Paris. For a reappraisal of the problems of representation raised by this work (in the sense of § 3.3), see Gardin, J.-C. 1977a.

Alouche, F., Bely, N., Cros, R.-C., Gardin, J.-C., Levy, F., and Perriault, J. 1967 *Economie générale d'une chaîne documentaire mécanisée*, Gauthier-Villars, Paris.

Ankel, C. 1969 'Zur maschinellen Auswertung vorgeschichtlicher Keramik', *Archäographie*, **1**, 25–8.

Ascher, R. 1968 'Time's arrow and the archaeology of a contemporary community', in K. C. Chang (ed.), *Settlement archaeology*, pp. 43–52, National Press, Palo Alto, Calif.

Ascher, R. and Ascher, M. 1965 'Recognizing the emergence of man', *Science*, **147**, no. 3655, 243–50.

Bar-Hillel, Y. 1960 'The present status of automatic translation of languages', in Alt, F. L. (ed.), *Advances in Computers*, vol. 1, Appendix III. Academic Press, New York. Reprinted in Bar-Hillel 1970, chapter 12.

– 1970 *Aspects of language. Essays and lectures on philosophy of language, linguistic philosophy, and methodology of linguistics*. North Holland, Amsterdam.

– 1975 'The impact of the essentially pragmatic character of natural language on linguistic information processing', in Debons, A. and Cameron, W. J. (eds.), *Perspectives in Information Science*, pp. 297–305, NATO Advanced Study Institute, Aberystwyth, Wales, UK, 13–24 August 1973. Noordhoff, Leyden.

Bely, N., Borillo, A., Siot-Decauville, N. and Virbel, J. 1970 *Procédures d'analyse sémantique appliquées à la documentation scientifique*, Gauthier-Villars, Paris.

Benzecri, J.-P. (ed.) 1973 *L'Analyse des données*, 2 vol. (1, *La Taxinomie*; 2, *L'analyse des correspondances*), Dunod, Paris.

Binford, L.-R. 1962 'Archaeology as anthropology', *American Antiquity*, **28**, 217–25. Reprinted in Binford 1972: 20–32.

– 1965 'Archaeological systematics and the study of cultural process', *American Antiquity*, **31**, 203–10. Reprinted in Binford 1972: 195–207.

– 1968a 'Some comments on historical versus processual archaeology', *Southwestern Journal of Anthropology*, **24**, 267–75. Reprinted in Binford 1972: 114–21.

– 1968b 'Archaeological perspectives', in Binford, S. R. and Binford, L. R. (eds.), *New Perspectives in Archaeology*, pp. 1–32, Aldine Publishing Co. Chicago.

Binford, L. R. 1972   *An Archaeological Perspective.* Aldine Publishing Co., Chicago.
Binford, S. R. and Binford, L. R. 1968   *New Perspectives in Archaeology.* Aldine Publishing Co., Chicago.
Bobrow, D. G. and Collins, A. (eds.) 1975   *Representation and Understanding.* Academic Press, New York.
Bonichsen, R. 1973   'Millie's Camp: an experiment in archaeology', *World Archaeology*, 4, 277–91.
Bordes, F. 1961   *Typologie du Paléolithique supérieur et moyen.* Institut de Préhistoire, Université de Bordeaux, France.
Borillo, A. *et al.* 1973   'Description des outils (mathématiques, linguistiques et informatiques) impliqués par la construction d'une chaîne automatique intégrée de traitement de l'information textuelle et graphique', *Information Storage and Retrieval*, 9, 527–60, Pergamon Press.
Borillo, M. 1970   'La vérification des hypothèses en archéologie: deux pas vers une méthode', in Gardin, J.-C. (ed.), *Archéologie et calculateurs*, pp. 71–90, Editions du CNRS, Paris.
– 1971   'Formal procedures and the use of computers in archaeology', *Norwegian Archaeological Review*, 4, 2–27.
Brend, R. M. 1972   *Selected Writings. To Commemorate the 60th Birthday of K. L. Pike.* Mouton, The Hague.
Brézillon, M. 1968   'La dénomination des objets de pierre taillée', *Gallia-Préhistoire*, ive supplément, Editions du CNRS, Paris.
Bromlej, Ju. V. 1977   *Otcherki istorii etnosa* (Features of the history of the concept of 'ethnos'). Nauka, Moscow.
Burling, R. 1964   'Cognition and componential analysis: God's truth or hocus-pocus?' *American Anthropologist*, 66, 20–8. With discussions by Dell Hymes and Charles Frake, and a rejoinder by Burling, pp. 116–22.
Burnham, P. 1973   'The explanatory value of the concept of adaptation in studies of culture change', in Renfrew, C. (ed.), *The Explanation of Culture Change: Models in Prehistory*, 93–102, Duckworth, London.
Carroll, J. B. 1964   *Language and Thought.* Prentice Hall, Englewood Cliffs, NJ.
Cattenat, Annette and Gardin, J.-C. 1978   'Diffusion comparée de quelques genres de poterie caractéristiques de l'époque achéménide sur le Plateau iranien et en Asie centrale', in Deshayes, J. (ed.), *Le Plateau iranien et l'Asie centrale, des origines à la conquête islamique*, 225–48, Editions du CNRS, Paris.
Chang, K. C. 1967a   *Rethinking Archaeology.* Random House, New York.
– 1967b   'Major aspects of the interrelationship of archaeology and ethnology', *Current Anthropology*, 8, 227–34.
– (ed.) 1968   *Settlement Archaeology.* National Press, Palo Alto, Calif.
Chen, C. H. (ed.) 1976   *Conference Record: 1976 Joint Workshop on Pattern Recognition and Artificial Intelligence*, held at Hyannis, Mass., 1–3 June 1976. Institute of Electrical and Electronics Engineers (IEEE) Computer Society, Long Beach, California.
Chenhall, R. G. 1968   'The logic of models used for processing archaeological data on computers', in Jaulin, B. (ed.), *Calcul et formalisation dans les sciences de l'homme*, 95–105. Editions du CNRS, Paris. Amplified under the same title in *Archäographie*, 1 (1969), 29–57.
– 1971   'The archaeological data bank: a progress report', *Computers and the Humanities*, 5, 159–69.
– 1975   *Museum Cataloguing in the Computer Age.* American Association for State and Local History, Nashville, Tennessee.
Chevrier, P. 1959   Review of J.-C. Gardin, 'Céramiques de Bactres' (Klincksieck, Paris 1957), in *Syria*, 36, 307–14.

Childe, V. G. 1956 *Piecing Together the Past. The Interpretation of Archaeological Data*. Routledge and Kegan Paul, London.

Christophe, J. and Deshayes, J. 1964 *Index de l'outillage, sur cartes perforées: outils de l'âge du bronze, des Balkans à l'Indus*. Editions du CNRS, Paris.

Clark, J. and Cole, S. 1975 *Global Simulation Models*. Wiley, London and New York.

Clarke, D. L. 1968 *Analytical Archaeology*. Methuen, London.

– (ed.) 1972 *Models in Archaeology*. Methuen, London.

– 1973 'Archaeology: the loss of innocence', *Antiquity*, **47**, 6–18.

Cloak, F. T., Jr 1975 Review of Tom McFeat, 'Small-group culture' (Pergamon Press, New York, 1974). In *American Anthropologist*, **77**, 938–40.

Colby, K. M. 1975 *Artificial Paranoia: A Computer Simulation of Paranoid Process*. Pergamon Press, New York.

Collier, S. and White, J. P. 1976 'Get them young? Age and sex inference on animal domestication in archaeology', *American Antiquity*, **41**, 96–102.

Conklin, H. C. 1955 'Hanunóo color categories', *Southwestern Journal of Archaeology*, **11**, 339–44. Reprinted in Hymes 1972: 189–92.

– 1972 *Folk Classification*. Department of Anthropology, Yale University, New Haven, Connecticut.

Cowgill, G. L. 1975 'On causes and consequences of ancient and modern population changes', *American Anthropologist*, **77**, 505–25.

– 1977 'The trouble with significance tests and what we can do about it', *American Antiquity*, **42**, 350–68.

Coyaud, M. 1966 *Introduction à l'étude des langages documentaires*. Klincksieck, Paris.

Cros, R.-C., Gardin, J.-C. and Lévy, F. 1964 *L'automatisation des recherches documentaires*. Gauthier-Villars, Paris, 2nd edn., 1968.

Damerau, F. J. 1976 'Automated language processing', in Williams, M. E. (ed.), *Annual Review of Information Science and Technology*, **11**, 107–61. American Society for Information Science, Washington.

De Prospo, E. R., Altman, E. and Beasley, K. E. 1973 *Performance Measures for Public Libraries*. American Library Association, Chicago, Illinois.

Deetz, J. F. 1965 *The Dynamics of Stylistic Change in Arikara Ceramics*. University of Illinois Press, Urbana.

– 1967 *Invitation to Archaeology*. The Natural History Press, Garden City, New York.

Deshayes, J. 1973 'La date des tumuli de Sé Girdan', *Iran*, **11**, 176–8.

Deshayes, J. and Gardin, J.-C. 1956 *Le fichier mécanographique de l'outillage: outils du bronze, des Balkans à l'Indus*. Institut français d'archéologie, Beirut.

Digard, F. *et al.* 1975 *Répertoire analytique des cylindres orientaux, établi sur ordinateur*. Editions du CNRS, Paris.

Dixon, J. E., Cann, J. R. and Renfrew, C. 1968 'Obsidian and the origin of trade', *Scientific American*, March 1968. Reprinted in Fagan, B. M. (ed.), *Avenues to Antiquity*, Readings from *Scientific American*, 133–40, W. H. Freeman & Co., San Francisco.

Doran, J. E. and Hodson, F. R. 1975 *Mathematics and Computers in Archaeology*. Edinburgh University Press, Edinburgh.

Dundes, A. 1962 'From etic to emic units in the structural study of folktales', *Journal of American Folklore*, **75**, 95–105.

Dunnell, R. C. 1978 'Style and function: a fundamental dichotomy', *American Antiquity*, **43**, 192–202.

Ericson, J. E. and Stickel, G. 1973 'A proposed classification system for ceramics', *World Archaeology*, **4**, 357–67.

Fagan, B. M. (ed.) 1975   *Avenues to Antiquity*, Readings from *Scientific American*, W. H. Freeman, San Francisco.
Farradane, J. 1974   'The evaluation of information retrieval systems', *Journal of Documentation*, **30**, 195–209.
Feyerabend, P. 1978   *Against Method*. Verso, London.
Flannery, K. V. 1967   'Culture history versus cultural process: a debate in American Archaeology', *Scientific American*, **217**, 119–22.
– 1973   'Archeology with a capital S', in Redman, C. (ed.), *Research and Theory in Current Archeology*, 47–53, John Wiley, New York.
Ford, R. I. 1973   'Archeology serving humanity', in Redman, C. (ed.), *Research and Theory in Current Archeology*, 83–93, Wiley, New York.
Fritz, J. M. and Plog, F. T. 1970   'The nature of archaeological explanation', *American Antiquity*, **35**, 405–12.
Gardin, J.-C. 1955   'Problèmes de la documentation', *Diogène*, **11**, 107–24 (also in English, same issue).
– 1958a   'On the coding of geometrical shapes and other representations, with reference to archaeological documents', *Papers of the International Conference on Scientific Information* (ICSI), Washington, DC, 75–87.
– 1958b   'Four codes for the description of artifacts: an essay in archaeological technique and theory', *American Anthropologist*, **60**, 335–57.
– 1962a   'Documentation sur cartes perforées et travaux sur ordinateur dans les sciences humaines', *Revue Internationale de la Documentation*, **29**, 83–92.
– 1962b   'La syntaxe dans les langages documentaires', in *Information Retrieval*, IBM European Education Center, Blaricum (Holland), 1–7.
– 1963   'Problèmes d'analyse descriptive en archéologie', in Courbin, P. (ed.), *Etudes archéologiques*, 133–50. Service d'édition et de vente des publications de l'Education Nationale (SEVPEN), Paris.
– (ed.) 1964a   *Le Syntol, étude d'un système général de documentation automatique*, 4 vols. Presses Académiques Européennes, Bruxelles. Volume 1 expanded in Cros, R.-C., Gardin, J.-C. and Lévy, F., *L'automatisation des recherches documentaires*, Gauthier-Villars, Paris, 1964; 2nd edn. 1968. On the underlying philosophy of SYNTOL (*Syn*tagmatic *O*rganization *L*anguage), see also Gardin, J.-C. 1965a and 1973.
– 1964b   'A research program in document retrieval for the behavioral sciences', *The American Behavioral Scientist*, **7**, 12–17.
– 1965a   *Syntol*. Rutgers Series on Systems for the Intellectual Organization of Information, Rutgers University, New Brunswick, NJ.
– 1965b   'On a possible interpretation of componential analysis in archaeology', in Hammel, E. (ed.), 'Formal Semantic Analysis', *American Anthropologist*, vol. 67, no. 5, Part 2, 9–22.
– 1965c   'Free classifications and faceted classifications: their exploitation with computers', in Atherton, P. (ed.), *Classification Research*, Elsinore, 14–18 Sept. 1964, 161–8, Munksgaard, Copenhagen.
– 1966   'Eléments d'un modèle pour la description des lexiques documentaires', *Bulletin des Bibliothèques de France*, **11**, 171–82.
– 1967a   'Methods for the descriptive analysis of archaeological materials', *American Antiquity*, **32**, 13–30.
– 1967b   'Recherches sur l'indexation automatique des documents scientifiques', *Revue d'Informatique et de Recherche Opérationnelle*, **1**, no. 6, 27–46.
– 1968   'On some reciprocal requirements of scholars and computers in the Fine Arts and Archaeology', in Metropolitan Museum of Art (ed.), *Computers and Their Potential Applications in Museums*, 103–24, Arno Press, New York.

Gardin, J.-C. 1969 'Semantic analysis procedures in the sciences of man', *Social Science Information*, **8**, 17–42. Published in French in Pouillon, J. and Maranda, P. (eds.), *Echanges et Communications: Mélange offerts à Claude Lévi-Strauss à l'occasion de son 60e anniversaire*, 628–57, Mouton, The Hague and Paris 1970; also in Gardin, J.-C. (1974a: 76–119).

  – 1971 *UNISIST, Study Report on the Feasibility of a World Science Information System*. Unesco, Paris. (Translations in French, Russian, Spanish, and other languages.)

  – (ed.) 1972a *L'Informatique et l'Inventaire Général*. L'informatique appliquée à la réalisation de l'Inventaire Général des Monuments et des Richesses Artistiques de la France (avec la collaboration de M.-T. Baudry, E. Chouraqui, and others). Ministère des Affaires Culturelles, Paris.

  – 1972b 'The rejection of archaeological data', Paper read to a conference on computer archaeology held at Waterloo Lutheran University, Canada, April 1972; revised version in Gardin (1978b).

  – 1973 'Document analysis and linguistic theory', *Journal of Documentation*, **29**, 137–68 (French translation in Gardin, J.-C. 1974a: 120–76).

  – 1974a *Les analyses de discours*. Collection Zethos, Delachaux et Niestlé, Neuchâtel and Paris.

  – 1974b 'Les projets de banques de données archéologiques: problèmes méthodologiques, technologiques et institutionnels', in Borillo, M. and Gardin, J.-C. (eds.), *Les Banques de données archéologiques*, 15–26. Editions du CNRS, Paris.

  – 1974c 'A propos des modèles en archéologie' (review of Clarke, D. L. (ed.), *Models in Archaeology*, Methuen, London 1972). *Revue Archéologique*, 1974, fasc. 2, 341–8.

  – 1975 'Effets logiques des bases de données sur les disciplines d'érudition', *Revue internationale des Sciences Sociales*, **27**, 815–30; English version in the same periodical, *International Social Sciences Journal* ('Logical effects of data bases on the study of historical sources'), 761–76.

  – 1976 *Code pour l'analyse des formes de poteries*, established in 1956, revised in 1974. Editions du CNRS, Paris.

  – 1977a 'L'Analyse conceptuelle du Coran (1963) et l'état présent des sciences du discours', *Cahiers du Centre de Recherches et d'Etudes Linguistiques* (à la mémoire de Michel Allard), Aix-en-Provence.

  – 1977b 'Archéologie et calcul: à propos de deux ouvrages récents (review of Doran & Hodson 1975 and Mueller 1975). *Revue Archéologique*, 1977, fasc. 2, 307–20.

  – 1978a *Code pour l'analyse des Ornements*, established in 1956, revised in 1973. Editions du CNRS, Paris.

  – 1978b 'Les stratégies de recherche en archéologie', in B. Groslier (ed.), *Coûts et profits en archéologie*, Editions du CNRS, Paris.

  – 1979 'A propos de 200 projets de recherche en informatique et sciences humaines', *Informatique et sciences humaines*, **40–41**, 393–406.

Gardin, J.-C. and Garelli, P. 1961 'Etude des établissements assyriens en Cappadoce, par ordinateur', *Annales*, Sept.–Oct. 1961, 837–76. Presented in English by Gardin, J.-C., 'Reconstructing an economic network in the Ancient East with the aid of a computer', in Hymes, D. (ed.), *The Use of Computers in Anthropology*, 377–91, Mouton, The Hague, 1965.

Gardin, J.-C. and Gentelle, P. 1976 'Irrigation et peuplement dans la plaine d'Aï Khanoum de l'époque achéménide à l'époque musulmane', *Bulletin de l'Ecole Française d'Extrême Orient*, **68**, 59–99.

  – 1979 L'exploitation du sol en Bactriane antique', *Bulletin de l'Ecole Française d'Extrême Orient* (in print).

Gardin, J.-C. and Lagrange, Marie-Salomé 1975   *Essais d'analyse du discours archéologique.* Notes et monographies techniques, no. 7, Centre de Recherches Archéologiques, CNRS (Sophia Antipolis, Valbonne 06560, France). For another essay of the same sort, see Lagrange and Bonnet (1978).

Ginouvès, R. 1971   'Archéographie, archéométrie, archéologie: pour une informatique de l'archéologie gréco-romaine', *Revue Archéologique*, 1971, fasc. 1, 93–126.

Gochet, P. 1978   *Quine en perspective.* Flammarion, Paris.

Goodenough, W. H. 1970   *Description and Comparison in Cultural Anthropology.* Aldine Publishing Co., Chicago.

Grimes, J. F. 1975   *The Thread of Discourse.* Mouton, The Hague, Paris.

Grize, J.-B. 1974   'Logique mathématique, logique naturelle et modèles', *Jahresbericht der Schweizerischen Geisteswissenschaftlichen Gesellschaft*, 1974, 201–7.

Guénoche, A. and Tchernia, A. 1977   'Essai de construction d'un modèle descriptif des amphores Dressel 20', in Vallet, G. (ed.), Colloque international du CNRS sur les *Méthodes classiques et méthodes formelles dans l'étude typologique des amphores*, 241–59, Ecole française de Rome.

Gundlach, R. 1969   'ARDOC – Ein System zur maschinellen Verarbeitung und Auswertung archäologischer Daten', *Archäographie*, **1**, 58–72.

Hammel, E. A. (ed.) 1965   'Formal semantic analysis', *American Anthropologist*, **67**, no. 5, Part 2, Special Publication.

Harris, M. 1976   'History and significance of the emic/etic distinction', *Annual Review of Anthropology*, **5**, 329–50.

Hester, T. R. and Heizer, R. F. 1973   *Bibliography of Archaeology I: Experiments in Lithic Technology and Petrography.* Addison-Wesley Module in Anthropology, no. 29, Reading, Mass.

Higham, C. F. 1972   'Initial model formulation in *terra incognita*', in Clarke, D. L. (ed.), *Models in Archaeology*, 453–76, Methuen, London.

Hill, J. N. 1968   'Broken K Pueblo: patterns of form and function', in Binford, S. R. and Binford, L. R., *New Perspectives in Archaeology*, 103–42, Aldine Publishing Co., Chicago.

– 1972   'The methodological debate in contemporary archaeology: a model', in Clarke, D. L. (ed.), *Models in Archaeology*, 61–107, Methuen, London.

Hill, J. N. and Evans, R. K. 1972   'A model for classification and typology', in Clarke, D. L. (ed.), *Models in Archaeology*, 231–73, Methuen, London.

Hiż, H. 1967   'Grammar logicism', *The Monist*, **51**, 110–27.

Hodson, F. R., Kendall, D. G. and Tăutu, P. (eds.) 1971   *Mathematics in the Archaeological and Historical Sciences.* Proceedings of the Anglo-Romanian Conference, Mamaia, 1970. University Press, Edinburgh.

Hollerbach, J. M. 1975   *Hierarchical Shape Description of Objects by Selection and Modification of Prototypes.* Report AI-TR-346, Artificial Intelligence Laboratory, MIT, Cambridge, Mass.

Hutchins, J. 1975   *Languages of Indexing and Classification.* Peter Peregrinus, Stevenage (Herts.).

Hymes, D. (ed.) 1964   *Language in Culture and Society: A Reader in Linguistics and Anthropology*, Harper and Row, New York.

– 1970   'Linguistic models in archeology', in Gardin, J.-C. (ed.), *Archéologie et calculateurs*, 91–118. Editions du CNRS, Paris.

Institute of Archaeology, Leningrad 1970   *Teoretitcheskie osnovy sovetskoj arkheologii* (Theoretical foundations of Soviet archaeology). Working papers for the seminar organized by the Leningrad section of the Institute of Archaeology, Academy of Sciences of the Soviet Union, 1970.

Isaac, G. L. 1971   'Whither archaeology?' *Antiquity*, **15**, 123–9.

Kamenetskij, I. S. 1970 'Arkheologitcheskaja Kul'tura – eë opredelenie i interpretatsja (Archaeological culture: its definition and interpretation), *Sovetskaja Arkheologija*, 1970, no. 1, 18–36.

Kamenetskij, I. S., Marshak, B. I. and Sher, Ja. A. 1975 *Analiz arkheologitcheskikh istotchnikov (Vozmozhnosti formalizovannogo podkhoda)* [The analysis of archaeological materials (The potentialities of a formal process)]. Nauka, Moscow.

Kemeny, J. G. 1959 *A Philosopher Looks at Science.* Van Nostrand, New York.

Klein, S. *et al.* 1974 *Modelling Propp and Lévi-Strauss in a Metasymbolic Simulation System.* UWCS Tech. report 226. Also in press in *Patterns in Oral Oral Literature*, edited by Jason, H. and Segal, D., as a retroactive contribution to this volume of the 1973 World Conference of Anthropological and Ethnological Sciences, Chicago. French version in *Informatique et Sciences Humaines*, no. 28 (1976), 63–133.

Klejn, L. S. 1970 'Problema opredelenija arkheologitcheskoj kul'tury' (Problems in the definition of an archaeological culture), *Sovetskaja Arkheologija* 1970, no. 2, 37–51.

– 1971 'Was ist eine archäologische Kultur?' *Ethnographisch-archäologische Zeitschrift*, **12**, 321–45. Additional comments on the same topic in vol. 13 of the same journal, 367–8.

– 1977 'A panorama of theoretical archaeology', *Current Anthropology*, **18**, 1–42.

Klejn, L. S. *et al.* 1970 'Diskussija o ponjatii "Arkheologitcheskaja kul'tura" v problemnom arkheologitcheskom seminare Leningradskogo Universiteta' (Discussions of the concept 'archaeological culture' in the archaeological seminar of the Leningrad University, 1968), *Sovetskaja Arkheologija*, 1970, no. 2, 298–302.

Kluckhohn, C. 1951 'Values and value-orientations in the theory of action', in Parsons, T. and Shils, E. A. (eds.), *Toward a Theory of Action*, 388–433. Harvard University Press, Cambridge, Mass.

Kolakowski, L. 1976 *La philosophie positiviste*, translated from Polish (*Filozofia Pozytywistyczna*, Geisenheyner and Crone, Stuttgart, 1966). Denoël, Paris.

Krieger, A. D. 1944 'The typological concept', *American Antiquity*, **9**, 217–88.

Kroeber, A. L. 1952 *The Nature of Culture.* University of Chicago, Chicago.

Kuhn, T. 1970 *The Structure of Scientific Revolutions.* Revised edition. University of Chicago Press, Chicago.

Lagrange, Marie-Salomé 1973 *Analyse sémiologique et histoire de l'art. Examen critique d'une classification.* Klincksieck, Paris.

– 1975 *Code pour l'analyse des monuments civils*, established in 1965, revised in 1969. Editions du CNRS, Paris.

Lagrange, Marie-Salomé and Bonnet, C. 1978 *Les chemins de la memoria: nouvel essai d'analyse du discours archéologique.* Editions du CNRS, Paris.

Lakatos, I. 1976 *Proofs and Refutations.* Cambridge University Press.

Lakoff, G. 1970 'Linguistics and natural logic', *Synthese*, **22**, 151–271. French translation: *Linguistique et logique naturelle*, Klincksieck, Paris, 1976.

Lakoff, G. and Thompson, H. 1975 'Introducing cognitive grammar', in Cogen, C., *et al.* (eds.), *Proceedings of the 1st Annual Meeting of the Berkeley Linguistic Society*, **1**, 295–309, University of California, Berkeley.

Laming-Emperaire, Annette 1969 *Guide pour l'étude des industries lithiques d'Amérique du Sud.* Ecole Pratique des Hautes Etudes, Paris.

Laszlo, E. 1972a *The Systems View of the World.* G. Braziller, New York.

– (ed.) 1972b *The Relevance of General Systems Theory.* G. Braziller, New York.

Le Maître, J. 1978 *La rationalisation des systèmes documentaires en archéologie.*

Centre de Recherches Archéologiques, Sophia Antipolis, Valbonne, 06560, France.

Le Rider, G. 1975   *Code pour l'analyse des Monnaies*, established in 1956, revised in 1973. Editions du CNRS, Paris.

Leclant, J. 1974   'Mise en place d'un inventaire systématique de la documentation concernant la civilisation méroïtique', in Borillo, M. and Gardin, J.-C. (eds.), *Les Banques de données archéologiques*, 267–75. Editions du CNRS, Paris.

Leroi-Gourhan, A. 1964   *Les religions de la préhistoire*. Presses Universitaires de France, Paris.

Leroi-Gourhan, A. *et al.* 1966   *La Préhistoire*. Collection Nouvelle Clio, Presses Universitaires de France, Paris.

Lévi-Strauss, C. 1958   *Anthropologie structurale*. Plon, Paris.

Lighthill, Sir J. 1973   'Artificial intelligence: a general survey', in *Artificial Intelligence: A Paper Symposium*, 1–21, Science Research Council, London.

Lin, N. and Garvey, W. D. 1972   'Information needs and uses', in Cuadra, C. A. (ed.), *Annual Review of Information Science and Technology*, **7**, 5–37. American Society for Information Science, Washington.

Longacre, W. A. 1970   *Archaeology as Anthropology: A Case Study*. Anthropological Papers of the University of Arizona, no. 17, University of Arizona Press, Tucson.

Lyonnet, Bertille 1977   'Découverte de sites de l'âge du bronze dans le N.E. de l'Afghanistan: leurs rapports avec la civilisation de l'Indus', *Annali dell' Istituto Orientale di Napoli*, **37** (n.s. 27), 19–35.

MacEwen, W. J. 1963   'Forms and problems of validation in social anthropology', *Current Anthropology*, **4**, 155–69.

Malina, J. 1975   *Archeologie: jak a proč?* (Archaeology: how and why?), Regional Museum, Mikulov, and Socialist Academy ČSR, Břeclav, 1975.

Masson, V. M. 1976   *Ekonomika i social'nyj stroj drevnikh obshtshestv*. Nauka, Leningrad.

Mattessich, R. 1978   *Instrumental Reasoning and Systems Methodology – An Epistemology of the Applied and Social Sciences*. D. Riedel Publishing Co., Dordrecht and Boston.

Meadow, Ch. T. 1973   *The Analysis of Information Systems*. 2nd edn., Melville Publishing Co., Los Angeles, California.

Meggers, Betty J. (ed.) 1968   *Anthropological Archaeology in the Americas*. Anthropological Society, Washington.

Mel'čuk, A. and Žolkovskij, A. K. 1970   'Towards a functioning "meaning text" model of language', *Linguistics*, **57**, 10–47.

Miller, G. A. and Johnson-Laird, P. N. 1976   *Language and Perception*. Cambridge University Press, Cambridge.

Moberg, C.-A. 1969   *Introduktion till Arkeologi*. Carl-Axel Moberg and Bokforlaget Natur och kultur, Stockholm. French translation: *Introduction à l'archéologie*, Maspero, Paris, 1976.

– 1975   'Concepts of prehistoric change, and methods for its study: on some recent attempts', mimeographed document, University of Göteborg, Department of Archaeology, Gothenburg.

– 1976   'Structureville', mimeographed document, University of Göteborg, Department of Archaeology, Gothenburg, 1 Nov. 1976.

Molino, J. 1974   'Sur les titres des romans de Jean Bruce', *Langages*, **35**, 86–94.

Montgomery, Christine 1972   'Linguistics and information science', *Journal of the American Society for Information Science*, **23**, 195–219.

Morgan, C. 1973   'Archaeology and explanation', *World Archaeology*, **4**, 259–76.

Mueller, J. W. (ed.) 1975 *Sampling in Archaeology*. The University of Arizona Press, Tucson.

Muscarella, O. W. 1973 'The date of the tumuli at Sé Girdan', *Iran*, **11**, 178–80.

Nasatir, D. 1973 *Data Archives for the Social Sciences: Purpose, Operation and Problems*, Unesco, Paris.

Natali, Johanna 1976 *De l'analyse documentaire à l'analyse poétique: à propos des critiques des 'Chats' de Baudelaire*. Thèse de 3e cycle présentée à l'Université de Paris I, miméogr.

Nattiez, J. 1975 *Fondements d'une sémiologie de la musique*. Union générale d'éditions, Paris.

Nelken-Terner, A. and MacNeish, R. S. 1971 'La Vallée de Tehuacan (Mexique): 12,000 ans de préhistoire', *Annales* (Librairie Armand Colin, Paris), no. 6, Nov.-Dec. 1971, 1141–78.

Nivelle, Nicole 1975 *Code pour l'analyse des monuments religieux*, established in 1965, revised in 1973. Editions du CNRS, Paris.

Noël, J. 1973 'Vers une linguistique du discours', *Cahiers internationaux de symbolisme*, **26**, 49–65.

Norman, D. A., Rumelhart, D. E. and LNR Research Group 1975 *Explorations in Cognition*. Freeman, San Francisco.

Paris, S. G. 1975 *Propositional Logical Thinking and Comprehension of Language Connectives*. Mouton, The Hague and Paris.

Perelman, C. 1971 'The new rhetoric', in Bar-Hillel, Y. (ed.), *Pragmatics of Natural Languages*, Humanities Press, New York.

Petöfi, J. S. and Rieser, H. (eds.) 1973 *Studies in Text Grammar*. D. Reidel Publishing Co., Dordrecht (Holland) and Boston (USA).

Pike, K. L. 1967 *Language in Relation to a Unified Theory of the Structure of Human Behavior*. Mouton, The Hague and Paris.

Pimenov, V. V. 1977 *Udmurty. Opyt Komponentnogo analiza etnosa*, Nauka, Moscow.

Plog, F. T. 1973 'Diachronic anthropology', in Redman, C. (ed.), *Research and Theory in Current Archeology*, 181–98, John Wiley, New York.

Popper, K. 1957 *The Poverty of Historicism*. Routledge and Kegan Paul, London.

Redman, C. L. (ed.) 1973 *Research and Theory in Current Archeology*. John Wiley, New York.

– 1974 *Archaeological Sampling Techniques*. Addison-Wesley Module in Anthropology, no. 55, Reading, Mass.

Redman, C. L. and Watson, P. J. 1970 'Systematic, intensive surface collection', *American Antiquity*, **35**, 279–91.

Renfrew, J. M. 1969 'The archaeological evidence for the domestication of plants: methods and problems', in Ucko, P. J. and Dimbleby, G. W. (eds.), *The Domestication of Plants and Animals*, 149–72, Duckworth, London.

Renfrew, C. 1973a *Social Archaeology*. An inaugural lecture delivered at the University, 20 March 1973. University of Southampton.

– (ed.) 1973b *The Explanation of Culture Change: Models in Prehistory*. Duckworth, London.

Reynolds, W. E. 1975 'The use of roof beams for defining social groups: an application of cluster analysis', *Newsletter of Computer Archaeology*, **10**, no. 4, 1–19.

Robin, R. 1973 *Histoire et linguistique*. Armand Colin, Paris.

Roszak, T. 1969 *The Making of a Counter Culture*. Doubleday and Co., New York.

Roulet, E. 1974   *Linguistique et comportement humain: l'analyse tagmémique de Pike*. Delachaux et Niestlé, Neuchâtel.
Rouse, I. 1960   'The classification of artifacts in archaeology', *American Antiquity*, **25**, 313–23.
– 1972   *Introduction to Prehistory. A Systematic Approach*. McGraw Hill, New York.
– 1973   'Analytic, synthetic and comparative archaeology', in Redman, C. (ed.), *Research and Theory in Current Archeology*, 21–31, John Wiley, New York.
– 1977   'Pattern and process in West Indian archaeology', *World Archaeology*, **29**, 1–11.
Roux, J.-P. 1971   'Essai d'interprétation d'un relief figuratif seldjoukide', *Arts Asiatiques*, **23**, 41–9.
Sahlins, M. 1976   *The Use and Abuse of Biology: An Anthropological Critique of Sociobiology*. The University of Michigan Press, Ann Arbor.
Salmon, M. H. 1975   'Confirmation and explanation in archaeology', *American Antiquity*, **40**, 459–70.
– 1976   ' "Deductive" versus "inductive" archaeology', *American Antiquity*, **41**, 376–80.
– 1978   'What can systems theory do for archaeology?' *American Antiquity*, **43**, 174–83.
Salomé, Marie-Rose 1978   *Code pour l'analyse des textes orientaux*, established in 1958, revised in 1977. Editions du CNRS, Paris.
– 1979   *Code pour l'analyse des représentations figurées sur les vases grecs*, established in 1960, revised in 1965. Editions du CNRS, Paris.
Schank, R. C., Goldman, N. M., Rieger, J. III and Riesbeck, C. K. 1975   *Conceptual Information Processing*. American Elsevier, New York.
Schank, R. C. and Rieger, C. J. 1974   'Inference and the computer understanding of natural language', *Artificial Intelligence*, **5**, 373–412.
Schiffer, M. B. 1972   'Archaeological context and systemic context', *American Antiquity*, **37**, 156–65.
– 1976   *Behavioral Archeology*. Academic Press, New York.
Schiffer, M. B. and Rathje, W. L. 1973   'Efficient exploitation of the archeological record: penetrating problems', in Redman, C. (ed.), *Research and Theory in Current Archeology*, 169–79, John Wiley, New York.
Scholtz, S. and Chenhall, R. G. 1976   'Archaeological data banks in theory and practice', *American Antiquity*, **41**, 89–96.
Scott, C. T. 1965   *Persian and Arabic Riddles*. Mouton, The Hague.
Scriven, M. 1959   'Truisms as the grounds for historical explanations', in Gardiner, P. (ed.), *Theories of History*, 443–75, Free Press, New York.
Seyrig, H. 1934–1966   *Antiquités syriennes*, 6 vols., Geuthner, Paris. The main studies on the religion of Palmyra mentioned in § 4.4 are in volumes I (1934), 27–32, 87–131; II (1938), 9–39, 73–106; IV (1953), 1–44, 208–14; V (1958), 99–116; VI (1966), 31–3, 72–8.
Sher, Ja. A. 1976   'Metodologitcheskie voprosy arkheologii' (Methodological issues in archaeology), *Voprosy Filosofii*, no. 10, 67–79.
Smith, B. D. 1977   'Archaeological inference and inductive confirmation', *American Anthropologist*, **79**, 598–615.
Soudsky, B. 1966   *Bylany*, Pamatniky nasi minulostii 4, Academia, Prague.
South, S. 1977   *Method and Theory in Historical Archaeology*. Academic Press, New York and London.
Speth, J. D. 1972   'Mechanical basis of percussion flaking', *American Antiquity*, **37**, 34–60.
Steward, J. 1955   *Theory of Culture Change: The Methodology of Multilinear Evolution*. University of Illinois Press, Urbana.

Striedter, K. H. 1971 'Der "Atlas Africanus" des Frobenius Institutes. Konzeption und Perspektiven', *Paideuma*, **17**, 206–15.

Sutherland, J. W. 1973 *A General Systems Philosophy for the Social and Behavioral Sciences*. G. Braziller, New York.

Swanson, D. R. 1960 'Searching natural language text by computer', *Science*, Oct. 1960, 1099–1104.

Swanson, Rowena W. 1975 'Design and evaluation of information systems', in Cuadra, C. (ed.), *Annual Review of Information Science and Technology*, **10**, 43–101; American Society for Information Science, Washington DC.

Swartz, B. K., Jr 1967 'A logical sequence of archaeological objectives', *American Antiquity*, **32**, 487–97.

Thomas, D. H. 1972a 'A computer simulation model of Great Basin Shoshonean subsistence and settlement patterns', in Clarke, D. L. (ed.), *Models in Archaeology*, 671–704, Methuen, London.

– 1972b 'The use and abuse of numerical taxonomy in archaeology', *Archaeology and Physical Anthropology in Oceania*, **7**, 31–49.

Thuillier, P. 1976 'Goethe l'Hérésiarque', *La Recherche*, no. 64, 147–55.

– 1977 'Les mathématiques: science divine ou science humaine?', *La Recherche*, no. 74, 71–4.

Trigger, B. 1974 'The archaeology of government', *World Archaeology*, **6**, 95–106.

Tringham, R. and Dimbleby, G. W. (eds.) 1972 *Man, Settlement and Urbanism*. Duckworth, London.

Tyler, S. A. (ed.) 1969 *Cognitive Anthropology*. Holt, Rinehart & Winston, New York.

Ucko, P. J. and Dimbleby, G. W. (eds.) 1969 *The Domestication and Exploitation of Plants and Animals*. Duckworth, London.

Vallet, G. (ed.) 1977 *Méthodes classiques et méthodes formelles dans l'étude typologique des amphores*. Ecole Française de Rome, Rome.

Vallois, R. 1944 and 1946 *L'architecture hellénique et hellénistique à Délos jusqu'à l'éviction des Déliens*. De Boccard, Paris. I, *Les Monuments*, 1944; II, *Grammaire historique de l'architecture délienne*, 1966.

Vickery, B. C. 1973 *Information Systems*. Butterworths, London.

Vignaux, G. 1976 *L'argumentation. Essai d'une logique discursive*. Librairie Droz, Genève.

Waterhouse, Viola G. 1974 *The History and Developments of Tagmemics*. Mouton, The Hague and Paris.

Watson, R. 1972 'The "new archeology" of the 1960s', *Antiquity*, **46**, 210–15.

– 1976 'Inference in archaeology', *American Antiquity*, **41**, 59–66.

Watson, P. J., LeBlanc, S. A. and Redman, C. L. 1971 *Explanation in Archaeology: An Explicitly Scientific Approach*. Columbia University Press, New York.

Weinberg, G. M. 1972. 'A computer approach to general system theory', in Klir, G. (ed.), *Trends in General System Theories*, 98–141, Wiley Interscience, New York.

Weizenbaum, J. 1976 *Computer Power and Human Reason*. Freeman, San Francisco.

Whallon, R. 1972 'A new approach to pottery typology', *American Antiquity*, **37**, 13–33.

White, L. A. 1959 *The Evolution of Culture*. McGraw Hill, New York.

Whorf, B. L. 1956 *Language, Thought and Reality: Selected Papers*, ed. J. B. Carroll, Wiley, New York.

Willey, G. R. 1953 *Prehistoric Settlement Patterns in the Viru Valley, Peru*.

Bulletin 155, Bureau of American Ethnology, Smithsonian Institution, Washington DC.

Willey, G. R. (ed.) 1956   *Prehistoric Settlement Patterns in the New World.* Viking Fund Publications in Anthropology, no. 23, Wenner-Gren Foundation for Anthropological Research, New York.

– 1968   'Settlement archaeology: an appraisal', in Chang, K. C. (ed.), *Settlement Archaeology*, 208–26, National Press Books, Palo Alto, California.

Winograd, T. 1972   *Understanding Natural Language.* Edinburgh University Press, Edinburgh.

Ziegler, A. C. 1973   *Inference from Prehistoric Faunal Remains.* An Addison-Wesley Module in Anthropology, no. 43.

Index

Propositions, in archaeological constructions, 5–7, 13–15, 78 n., 104–7, 161
Publications, their form and function in archaeology, 147–64

Rathje, W. L., 104, 106
Rationalization of pre-established constructions, 12, 14, 74–5, 86–90, 102–4, 168, 174; see Laws, Reality
'Reality' of archaeological constructions or reconstructions, 12, 14, 30 n., 98 n., 119, 121–2, 124
Reconstruction of typologies or explanations, see Rationalization
Redman, C., 1, 99, 102, 131, 138, 142, 169
Renfrew, C., 78, 100, 104, 166
Representation of archaeological materials, see Description, Drawings and photographs, Symbolic systems
Reynolds, W. E., 103
Rhetorical considerations about archaeological writings, see Literary, Publications
Rieger, J., 123
Rieser, H., 122
Robin, R., 122
Roszak, T., 180
Roulet, E., 30 n.
Rouse, I., 29, 70 n., 79, 80, 102 n.
Roux, J.-P., 108, 109, 110–20, 125, 131, 132, 161, 163 n., 168
Russell, B., 175

Sahlins, M., 104
Salmon, M. H., 118, 176
Salomé, M.-R., 41 n., 55 n.
Sampling, 138, 158, 169 n.; see Selection
Sapir, E., 40 n.
Saussure, F. de, 40
Schank, R. C., 123
Schematization *vs.* formalization, 125, 164; the schematization of archaeological constructions, 135–46
Schiffer, M. B., 1, 104, 106
Scholtz, S., 33
'Science', as a mode of knowledge among others, 173–4; the scientific ideology, 178–80; science and language, see Symbolic systems
Scientific or scholarly language (SL), 40–2; its relation with information language (IL), 45–6, 50–4
Scott, C. T., 30 n.
Scriven, M., 117 n., 155, 162 n., 167, 168, 169 n.
Selection of materials in archaeological constructions, 5–7, 36–8, 81, 137–8, 158–9, 169 n.
Semantics, semantic elements in formal

systems, 116 n., 124; in the schematization of reasoning processes, see Logico-semantic organizations; in information systems, see Paradigmatic organization. 'Natural semantics', 'Universal semantics', 116–18, 121, 161–2
Semiology, see Symbolic systems
'Semiotics' (*S*), iconic and graphical elements recorded as intrinsic attributes or properties of archaeological materials, 68, 78; semiotics as defined by logicians, see Symbolic systems
Seyrig, H., 104
Shaumian, S. K., 53 n.
Sher, Ja. A., 126 n.
Similarities, see Comparison, Dissimilarities
Simulation, of behavioural systems, 99–100; of reasoning processes, 14–15, 122; see 'Reality', Systems analysis. Simulation tests, see Validation
Smith, B. D., 117 n., 118
Socrates, 180
Soudsky, B., 78
South, S., 1
Speth, J. D., 83, 139
Statistics, see Mathematics, Sampling
Steward, J., 99, 101
Stickel, G., 41 n.
Strategies of data collecting, 6–7, 137–9; see Selection
Striedter, K. H., 150
Sutherland, J. W., 171, 174
Stylistic analysis, stylistic groups, 64, 68, 114–15, 129 n.
Swanson, D., 49
Swanson, R., 61 n.
Swartz, B. K., 79, 80
Symbolic systems for the representation and handling of scientific data, 32–4, 41–3, 175; see Information language, Scientific language
Syntagmatic organization, syntagmatic relations, 45–6, 51 n., 120; see Logico-semantic organizations
Systems, see Information systems, Symbolic systems. Systems analysis, 14–16, 171–2. Behavioural systems, 99–101

Tăutu, P., 82
Tax, S., 167
Taxonomies, 70 n., 82; see Classification, Typologies
Taylor, W., 166
Tchernia, A., 88
Tests, see Validation
Thomas, D. H., 84, 99, 100
Thompson, H., 124
Thuillier, P., 128, 168

For EU product safety concerns, contact us at Calle de José Abascal, 56–1°,
28003 Madrid, Spain or eugpsr@cambridge.org.

www.ingramcontent.com/pod-product-compliance
Ingram Content Group UK Ltd.
Pitfield, Milton Keynes, MK11 3LW, UK
UKHW010045140625
459647UK00012BB/1612